STORIES FROM ELSEWHERE

BY JIM CURTISS

Published by Gallivant Multimedia

ISBN-13: 978-0-6152-1274-6

For Jarmila

Dear Reader,

This collection of stories was borne of an abiding interest in the places that – by design or by accident – I happened to have found myself.

I do not claim to be an anthropologist carrying out a series of deep investigations of my adopted cultures. Indeed, as a writer and editor who works at home, I've realized that my wife and I carry around a bubble of our amalgamated cultures wherever we go. Nevertheless, while living abroad I have done all the things, as well as many others, that I would normally have done in my homeland and the surprises I've stumbled upon have been remarkable.

For example, I often bought bags of cherries from the roadside stands in Poland, and after washing them would eat them straightaway. This continued until one day I offered a friend some of the cherries – she took a handful and began to dissect them, and to a one, they were *filled* with worms. They don't use pesticides here, she explained as she picked out the worms and *then* ate the cherries. I couldn't help but think about the buckets full of cherries I'd already eaten and enjoyed and wondered how many worms I'd also enjoyed.

Which is a pretty good analogy for living abroad, actually. So often what you see is not what you get, and while hardly ever hazardous per se, such situations can nonetheless be disquieting.

It's difficult to keep one's bearings in foreign environments, and without having my lovely wife there to help me through the more challenging bits, I doubt I would have gotten as much out of them – or have enjoyed them as much.

Jim Curtiss   Seville, 2008

Table of Contents

Non-fiction

Kde domov můj 2
The glorious tradition, I and II 2,4
That look 6
Windsurfing for beginners 8
Segway into Seville 9
Mañana in Seville 11
The person I want to be 12
Just take it 15
A sort of homecoming 17
Foreigner mojo 29
But what if... 30
Paranoid? Who, me? 31
You don't need it 33
Let's have a ball 34
Football 36
Weekend adventure 38
Notes on a trip to America 39
The mob 40
A trip to Naples and Amalfi 41
State College for a month 45
Urine trouble 46
Expatriatism 49
Bearly related 51
A time for making friends 52
The friendly skies 53
Yeah, I'm the tax man 54
Don't wave for me, Saxon-Anhalt... 56
The laser pointer 57
Power distance 58
Semana Santa 60
A force to be reckoned with 61
Googled 63
Batminton 64
Easter Monday in Zdeslav 66
The Mad Russian 69
Boundary conditions 70
The best offense is a good defense 74
The shocking true story of why socialism really failed 77
Here and now 79
The resume 82
(Don't) Trust your government 84
No pride in prejudice 87
How Nice 90
Eyes of blue 95

Fiction

Report this 97
Węgierska Górka 99
Democracy 103
Just enough to be dangerous 105
Soon enough 106
Change me 108
Bad Trip, 2001 112
In Misery 117
Sheboygan, Poland 125
Excerpt I from Every Thing Counts (The Akashic Reader) 139
Excerpt II from Every Thing Counts (The Akashic Reader) 151

Kde domov můj
Spain, 2006

The Czech National Anthem, *Kde Domov Můj*, holds a special place in my heart. Perhaps this is because I'm married to a Czech, but *kde domov můj*, which translates to *"Where is my home",* also captures the essence of our *Wanderlustful* lifestyle.

We've moved house again, you see. And not just across the state. No, what we've managed is to move *from* a country where we spoke the language, had work and a circle of friends, and *to* a country where we don't speak the language, only one of us is employed, and we know just a handful of people.

And as we schlepped our most valuable possessions through foreign airports, train stations and cobbled streets, we again exposed ourselves to the world in a way that never ceases to unsettle. Indeed, soon after moving into our hotel room in Seville, the bad dreams commenced. Every night hence we were intimidated by macho border guards, chased by stomping flamenco dancers, or were forced to fight *el toro* with our constricting blankets.

The bad dreams only stopped when we rented our own *apartamento.* Homeless no more, we are now settled enough to dream of the sunny skies, full-bodied Rioja, and yummy tapas that lured us away from Central Europe in the first place.

Which reminds me of our last visit to my wife's home village. After drinking enough Pilsner Urquell to transform the language barrier into a fence that we could lean upon and converse over, my Czech brother-in-law again questioned our lifestyle. "Jim," he asked, "where is your home, really?"

"Wherever your sister is," I answered, half in jest.

But the question is actually no joke to a pair of Global Village Gypsies like my wife and I, and the answer to *kde domov můj* continues to be *nevíme* – Czech for "we don't know."

The glorious tradition I
Spain, 2007

It was torturously hot standing in the June Andalusian sun, but we had arrived late and the shady spots were already occupied. Hundreds of people were gathered outside the square and eventually a flatbed truck with an attached hydraulic arm came along. Strapped to the flatbed was a crate, higher than a man, filled with a ton of disoriented bull.

The hydraulic arm maneuvered the container into place against the 8-foot-high metal posts; these were placed at the end of strategic streets of the village to keep the bull contained, and were spaced so that a person, but not a bull, could slip through them. We were standing above a wide cul-de-sac at the foot of the village with hundreds of people milling around inside and outside of the posts. The people inside looked far more nervous than those outside.

Two men lifted the crate's sliding door and an enormous black bull erupted out of it. He charged at the nearest man but his hooves slipped on the smooth rocks of the village street and he couldn't gain any momentum. Men climbed the sides of buildings, holding on to the iron grating over windows to get out of the bull's way as he strode after the scattering crowd. A man darted out to taunt the bull, which jerked hard to the right, slipped badly on the smooth surface, and thudded to the ground. The woman next to us laughed, and my irritation with her made me realize I was rooting for the bull.

The bull had a thick rope, perhaps 100 meters long, tied around his head. It was under the horns but above his eyes and was carried by dozens of men who had stretched it far into the village. Naturally the bull hated this – he tried again and again to wrest it off by bucking his head. Sometimes the bull would charge directly at those who were holding the rope, and they would drop it and run like hell until the bull got distracted. Then they'd gather up the rope and try to keep it taut, sometimes trying to guide the bull this way or that.

The bull and the crowds were mostly out of sight within the village, but when they were nearby there were very dramatic events. Once, an overweight man wearing a dirty white shirt strayed too close and the bull started after him. Unfortunately for the man, the bull had a length of slack rope, and a downhill as well, and was just ON HIS ASS for about 30 meters before the rope became taut and the bull's head was violently jerked around. During his sprint, the man's face had the sheerest look of terror that I have ever seen. He was literally running for his life, and never once did it occur to him to drop his beer.

The same scenario was later repeated with a man in his 20s. Good thing he was so young, because halfway through his sprint he lost a shoe and the bull actually put the base of its horns on his back and gave a shove. This pushed the man forward just enough to keep him out of reach until the rope became taut and the bull was again jerked to the ground. More laughter from the woman next to us.

There were hundreds of people running with (but mostly from) the bull. Despite my general distaste for the spectacle, it *was* amusing to see a mass of humanity scatter any time the bull would even think about running their way. Several times the older men played with the younger boys by yelling "Here he comes, here he comes," and the boys would take off running before realizing they were being toyed with.

The crowd reacts
Villaluenga del Rosario, Spain

The action went on for more than an hour and the last time the bull came into view, it was exhausted. Tongue hanging out, he would huddle in a corner and refuse the village matador's cape for long periods of time. The matador was dressed in jeans and a t-shirt, not the fancy-boy traditional suit. The matador wanted to draw him nearer to the crate, but the bull would refuse until suddenly making a furious charge and getting his neck twisted in return. Finally the men succeeded in pulling the bull back into the container with the rope, sometimes having to yank his tail and maneuver his rear end. The bull was completely spent. Though capable of giving a scare to anyone who strayed too close, he mostly stood there, probably wondering how his day had turned to such shit. I'm absolutely certain that when it was finally put back into the container and the cheer went up, the bull was relieved to have that mess behind him.

A bit unnerved by the whole scene – especially by the seeming lack of sportsmanship with the rope around the bull's head – we were nonetheless happy to see they weren't going to kill the thing on the street.

As we walked away from the square, the local man who had befriended us again tried to earnestly convey the glorious tradition that is bullfighting. He lost us, however, when he mentioned that the town's restaurants would later pay a premium to serve that particular bull's meat.

The glorious tradition II
Spain, 2008

Bullfighting is a savage cultural relic that should be abolished.

At least, that was my unvoiced opinion, one which allowed me to go for almost two years of living in Seville without having to witness the spectacle in person. Several discussions with fellow expats who had gone to the *corrida*, had come away shaken by it, and had vowed never to return helped cement this opinion.

Another reason for my aversion is that I happened to see a televised bullfight during the first month of living here (funny how it's televised in Spain the same way spectator sports are in other countries.) What especially bothered me during that broadcast was the *sound* of the bull dying. Apparently the *toreador* had not killed the bull cleanly, and there were some tragic moments of coughed up blood and death screams that the microphones happened to pick up. My revulsion at this led me to promise that I'd never spend money to help perpetuate such a practice.

And by no means am I alone in my distaste for the sport. A Gallup poll conducted in 2006 showed that 72% of Spaniards said they had no interest in bullfighting. Joan Herrera, a former Catalan Green Party deputy, even said in the February 11th, 2008 English Edition of El Pais that "Bullfights are part of an outdated tradition with sadistic overtones."

Of course to every argument there is another side, such as this one from bullfighter Luis Francisco Esplá, from the same edition of El Pais, "The bullfight has its order, it is a ritual and it teaches children a series of values and guidelines that no longer exist in the wider society."

What those values and guidelines may be is open for debate, which is likely why Catalonia now restricts children under 16 from attending bullfighting events.

At any rate, my anti-*corrida* vow held strong for a good year, until my wife's colleague told us about of a different sort of bullfighting, called *corrida de rejones*, which is done from atop horses. The colleague had seen it, had been terribly impressed, and was colorful enough in her description that my wife, a person who is brought to tears by the merest hint of injustice or brutality, decided that she was attending the *rejoneo* when it came to town. Was I *sure* I didn't want to come, she asked. Wouldn't I regret the missed opportunity?

Which is how I came to be seated in the nosebleed section of the Plaza de Toros de la Real Maestranza de Caballería de Sevilla during the recent Feria de Abril.

The lineup of six *rejoneadores* that included Diego Ventura, Leanardo Hernandez and Andy Cartegena, who are some of the more important *rejoneadores* in the sport, had sold out weeks in advance.

For those readers who are unfamiliar with the *corrida de rejones*, it breaks down like this: Also known as a *rejoneo,* the *corrida de rejones* begins when the *rejoneador* meets the bull after it enters the ring. The *rejoneador*, atop his horse, then provokes the bull to charge and evades the attack, often by a very close margin. This is where most of the tension of the *corrida de rejones* comes from – the less space there is between the bull and the horse, the more dangerous it is. By and by, the *rejoneador* begins to thrust the *rejones de castigo* or "lances of punishment" into the bull's haunches. This naturally angers the bull into charging further, which causes the bull to bleed a lot, which tires the bull, which allows the *rejoneador* to do his fancy badass riding stuff until the bull is sufficiently tired, at which point the *rejoneador* kills the bull with the *rejón de muerte,* or "lance of death".

If I sounded dismissive just now, forgive me, but putting the whole spectacle into words just makes it seem a touch ridiculous. I mean, what sport requires instruments that sound like a Tarantino film?

All that aside, I didn't know any of this at the beginning of the *rejoneo.* The only thing I knew was that there were horses involved. Involved how, I wasn't sure.

The show began with much pageantry and parading with the trained, handsome horses. Then there were some impressive tricks of horsemanship before the ring was emptied of all but one rider who stood in the center of the ring. After a pause, the bull was released into the ring. He was enormous and black and immediately charged at a *toreador* who was playing peek-a-boo behind a wall just inside the ring's fence. Then the bull, who was just unbelievably fast, went after the horse.

The rider stood his ground at first, then pulled to the side, presenting the bull with the profile of the horse before urging it out of the way at the very last second. The bull's horns barely missed the horse's rear, and the bull followed in a tight circle after the horse, which skittered away just out of reach.

This sort of taunting and chasing went on for awhile and then the rider disappeared into a tunnel. The *toreadors* ran out to keep the bull's attention, and soon the rider returned on a different horse. Collecting a long *rejone de castigo* from one of his handlers outside of the ring, the rider faced the bull and charged head on. The bull charged as well, and it looked as if they would collide until the very last moment, when the rider veered left, forcing the tip of the *rejone de castigo* into the bull's shoulder. As if by magic, a flag appeared at the end of the lance, which captured the bull's attention as the rider circled, keeping the distance between the horse and the bull as minute as possible.

The chest-tightening tension that this proximity created was intense. The intricate dealings between the rider, who was handling the horse as if it were an extension of his legs, and the bull, who was determined to return the punishment that he himself was receiving, was also mesmerizing. Indeed, every time the bull came close to the horse, a strange feeling welled up inside me. I was concerned for the horse because it was an innocent part of the show, but this concern was mixed with a very real desire for the bull to get back at the man for those confounded lances.

> I wanted and I didn't want the bull to deliver a horn, and so I gasped when the bull got near the horse and rider, and cheered with relief when they escaped.

It was an altogether confusing feeling; I wanted and I didn't want the bull to deliver a horn, and so I gasped with anticipation when the bull got near the horse and rider, and I cheered with relief when they escaped.

With each switch of horses, the lances that the rider employed became shorter, and as the bull grew tired, the space that the rider could risk between the bull and his horse became smaller. This resulted in a heightened tension because the horse seemed to be in greater danger and the rider had to lean further and further over to insert the lances. By the fourth change of horses, the bull's shoulders were covered in blood and he was less given to charge, so the rider approached the side of the ring and was given the *rejón de muerte*.

Man, horse and bull faced off before their final charge. The bull was again tricked into thinking he could get a horn into the horse and instead found himself with a long sword through his midsection. The crowd cheered because the bull had been killed cleanly, meaning with one thrust, and just then I made the mistake of looking over at my wife, who was in desperate need of some tissues.

Seeing her cry over the bull's death made me suddenly realize that I had been cheering with the crowd, and a fleeting sense of shame came over me. I had been swept up in the emotion of the *corrida de rejones* myself. I stopped cheering then, and comforted my wife as the bull was hitched to a team of mules and dragged from the ring. It left a trail of blood in the sand, which was swept over by a team of custodians.

There were five more riders on the program that day, and though I'm not comfortable admitting it, I was completely and utterly engrossed with each of them. It was awe-inspiring. It was tension-filled and strange and tragic and violent and so many other things that I am unable to express, and in the end, right or wrong, I'm certain that April day at the *corrida de rejones* will remain one of my most vivid and evocative memories of Spain.

That being said, I am also certain that I will not go again.

That look
This article first appeared in the March – April 2008 issue of InSeville Magazine

Replenishing yourself is an important part of the Turkish bath experience; dizziness and fainting can result if one is not properly hydrated. Or so cautioned the receptionist at Aire de Sevilla Arabian Baths here in Seville, Spain.

"Drink plenty of the complimentary tea to be found in the Relaxation Room," he advised.

So later, as I made my dry-mouthed way from the thermal baths over to the Room of 1,000 Bubbles, I tried to pour myself some of the tea. Bad luck; the pot was empty. I brought this to the attention of a nearby attendant, and instead of a willing nod of compliance, she gave me *that look* and shuffled off.

You may know the look I'm talking about; it generally originates from people who have never tread the minefield of foreign language usage and therefore just don't grasp the complex mixture of apprehension and embarrassment that manifests itself when one is a beginning speaker. I mean, *ok*, perhaps I mis-conjugated the verb and asked *them* to fill the pot or something. But what I said to the attendant certainly had to do with tea and the empty pot I was holding up, so why not just intuit that the tiny thing is empty again, spare me the sourpuss, and bring some more tea, *por favor,* before I frickin' pass out?

Which the *chica* eventually did, but not without shooting me another one of those sideways glances.

I suppose I should be used to such looks. I've now lived in five European countries without having known much of their respective languages beforehand, so I've suffered through years of the bloody things. Nevertheless, as I pondered the tea episode during the meditatively buoyant salt bath, it occurred to me that I'm kinda getting fed up with them.

I mean sure, living abroad is great: I'm a freelance writer, I'm married to a beautiful Czech woman and we live in southern Spain. I speak varying degrees of four languages, I've traveled all over, and I have friends on every continent save Antarctica.

But still, I'm marginalized wherever I go; I'm a foreigner where we live, a foreigner where my wife is from, and an expatriate oddball out of touch with my culture when I visit home.

Which reminds me: the other day we were talking to our local barman – himself an Argentinean – and we were discussing how the longer one stays out of one's native country, the less one feels comfortable with one's countrymen. The barman has been away from Argentina for 3 years and already feels a stranger there. Myself, I've been an expat for going on ten years now, and it's gotten so bad that I actually find myself passing judgment on my baseball-hat-, white-socks-, Bermuda-shorts-wearing countrymen who I can spot a mile away because it's like looking in the frickin' mirror.

But back to the Turkish baths. I sat there in my American stockiness and looked around at the other bathers. Most of the men were skinny, no shoulders at all, and as macho custom dictates, I sized them up and reckoned I could bonk them into the ground should it come to that. But the thing is, in all the time I've lived abroad, it's *never* come to that. It's peaceful here. True, I've seen some arguments, and I've seen a shouting match that would have ended in at least a stabbing in the States. But here, the angry parties vented and then went on their way (probably back home to stew about what they *would* have done).

The point is, my size is misplaced here. For example, though I admire some of the current clothing styles, more often than not when I try on a spiffy new shirt, it turns out to be so tight that I have to double-check to make sure I'm not in the children's section. And when I play soccer, my opponents run circles around me unless I'm able to get in an "accidental" shoulder or hip check. Heck, the other day our goalie even said to me, "Jim, your strengths are of no use here."

Ok, it's likely he didn't mean "here" as in "all of Europe". Nevertheless, as I sat in the steam bath sweating like a Capitalist Pig, my mind got to work and for the gazillionth time I thought about moving back home.

But then it occurred to me that my strengths seem to have put me right where I am: self-confident enough that I don't mind being a minority; flexible enough to repeatedly adapt to foreign locales; curious enough to actually want to learn about people and their confounding languages.

I carried these fuzzy thoughts with me as I exited the baths and walked home, where I discovered that my downstairs neighbor was making gazpacho. At midnight. You know how to make gazpacho? You have to use a blender for the tomatoes.

Hard-working blenders are not conducive to sleep, so I put in my earplugs and lay down, hoping that the gazpacho-making would finish. It eventually did, but the heavy garlic odor lingered, perhaps prompting the frustrating dreams I had of my mother's pork roast and how, even though I had a place at the table, I was treated as if I wasn't there.

In the morning when I woke up, my head was just *pounding*.

I apparently hadn't rehydrated myself properly.

Windsurfing for beginners

This article first appeared in the 2007 September - October issue of InSeville Magazine

My friend's dream of becoming a professional windsurfing instructor at Tarifa was brought up often enough over beers that we eventually decided to join him in the adventure. It's likely that I had more enthusiasm for the endeavor than his wife did; I've surfed, skated and snowboarded for years, while she was only coming along as payback for making him take that Sevillana dance course. Pedro and Federica rounded out our group of 5 would-be instructors.

An internet search brought up dozens of schools in Tarifa, but we learned that the high winds there would likely be a bit too much for us to handle straightaway. We eventually settled on a school in Islantilla, where a beginner's course of ten hours runs €110, and the moderate wind and small waves are ideal for novices.

On our first day we arrived at 10 a.m. to discover our instructor blearily shuffling around in the sand. He was in his early 20s and had obviously had a good time the previous night. Perhaps this is why our instruction was a bit patchy, or it could just be that in windsurfing, only the barest amount of instruction is really necessary. Sure, you need to know a couple of technical things about the board and the wind, but other than that it's a remarkably intuitive sport. As Federica related, "It's really a learning-by-doing activity. You become more and more sensitive every time and this is something that people cannot explain to you."

Once we actually got in the water, our instructor buzzed around in a motor boat, yelling out sporadic directions and hauling us to and fro. The hauling was especially welcome, as we were all struggling mightily with the waves. Pedro characterized our first day like this, "It's not rocket science, but it

does need a lot of perseverance and patience."

Indeed, patience and perseverance are the key elements for the beginner, because there are roughly eight main challenges to overcome in order to windsurf.

1. You need to stand on the board. Luckily the school provides beginners with the windsurfing equivalent of a cargo ship, so this step comes relatively quickly.

2. You need to squat down and grab the uptake rope. Balance is key here, but this stage is also achieved relatively quickly.

3. You need to uphaul the sail from the water. This is perhaps the hardest part of learning the sport. It's possible you will spend your entire first day learning only this. And it's demanding – it takes a lot of strength and balance just to get the sail out of the water. Waves also conspire to knock you down. Personally, this was my most difficult time, because I discovered that an unforeseen fear of the ocean would overcome me every time I fell in, leading me to scramble back onto the board like a frickin' cat.

4. You need to overcome your fear of the ocean. Perhaps you don't believe you are or will be afraid of the water, but once you are alone out in the middle of it, a kilometer or more from the shore, fear will come. You will think the worst and will likely talk to yourself and your God. This is normal. But don't despair – you overcome this phase when you begin spending more time on the board than in the water.

5. You need to bring the sail to an upright position. Again, harder than it sounds. During the many opportunities you have to lose your purchase, it is essential to keep the sail out of the wind by holding onto the handle properly, that is, on or nearby the mast. If you hold it *improperly*, the wind will either push the sail into you and send you over backwards, or the wind will push the sail away from you and invite you into the water with it.

6. You need to catch, or "sheet into" the wind. Depending on how you get up, the wind can either be with you or against you. If you're lucky, you will be standing on the proper side of the sail and can sheet into the direction you are pointing. If you're unlucky, the wind will want you to go in the opposite direction. This results in the board kind of automatically changing its direction and twisting under your feet. With equal portions luck and balance, you may be able to maneuver the board around and then sheet in, but more than likely you will not. Instead, you'll have to jump into the water to reposition the sail.

7. You need to steer. To go to one side, you tilt the sail backwards, toward the tail of the board. To go to the other side, you lean the sail forward, towards its nose. The resulting direction depends on which side of the sail you're facing; if you have your left foot forward, leaning the sail to the rear means you'll go left; leaning the sail forward will take you to the right.

8. You need to use your weight as a counter-balance for the wind. You've seen those guys leaning far out over the water and basically just hanging onto their sails for balance? Well forget that. Instead, beginners will awkwardly stick their ass out while trying to keep their balance for a good long while. And they'll still fall in.

Naturally, we didn't get anywhere close to number eight on the first day. Instead, two of us bailed out early, two of us barely got the sail out of the water, and only one was able to actually sail. The second day was far better – all of us got up, but differences between the sexes began to emerge. As Fede said, "Learning the correct technique is really important. For men this is also important, but they can always compensate for imbalance with their strength, whilst for us (women) this is more difficult."

Still, by the third session, some of us had even managed to turn the board and maneu-ver it in the direction we wanted it to go. And according to a beginner's criteria, this is like saying that one _can_ windsurf.

The crowning moment of our course came during the very last lesson, some two months after our first time on the board. The wind was blowing strongly, and at one point Pedro and I both caught it and headed straight out to sea. And then it happened: we both completely attuned ourselves with the speed and balance and brilliance that is windsurfing. During that three minute stretch of time, the world became only the water, the wind and us, acting in symphony with our boards. It was simply perfect.

In the end, it will be those three minutes of bliss – not the struggles needed to get there – that I will take away from learning to windsurf in Islantilla. And as for becoming an instructor at Tarifa... I'm afraid that's gonna take awhile.

Segway into Seville

This article appeared in the 2007 September - October issue of InSeville Magazine

If you happen to pass Lope de Rueda 14 after hours, the dark street, coupled with the building's crumbling façade might lead you to wonder what kind of shady business they operate at blobject, Seville's authorized Segway dealership and tour operator. But visit during opening hours and you're treated to one of those _ciudad antigua_ epiphanies: once past the airy reception desk, the premises spread out into a bright courtyard where the company's fleet of Segways are parked. Wide and spacious, the courtyard has been fashioned into a sort of rumpus room for the Segways – this is where the practice sessions, which precede any tour, take place.

As I walked in, a family of four were reluctantly finishing up their allotted time. After they left, with much heel-dragging by the 10 year-old boy, Ruben Garcia Lopez, a guide and trainer with blobject, showed me what the family had written in the register book – needless to say it was glowing. And it wasn't the only entry with such accolades. Apparently, riding a Segway is such a departure from the norm that one can't help but step off the thing wearing a silly grin.

Invented by Dean Kamen in 2001, the Segway – widely known as the Segway PT (personal transporter) – is a kind of self-balancing, two-wheeled scooter that employs on-board computers, gyroscopic sensors and an electric motor to propel it. Without going too far into the science, the Segway's sensors detect whether it's leaning forwards or backwards, and the motor's attempt to bring the thing back into balance results in forward or backward motion. To go right or left, one twists a control on the handlebar.

Ruben demonstrated this for me and it looked like fun, if not a touch dangerous, so I asked him about the possibilities of crashing. "In the two years I've been doing this, I haven't seen anyone crash," he responded.

Nevertheless, the last couple of years haven't been without challenges for Segway. In 2006, the company voluntarily recalled approximately 23,500, that is, ALL of its personal transporters. According to a report on the U.S. Consumer Product Safety Commission website dated September 14, 2006, "The personal transporter can unexpectedly apply reverse torque to the wheels, which can cause a rider to fall."

The problem has since been rectified with a software upgrade, and if sales results are any indicator, the company is doing better all the time. According to an email interview with Segway spokeswoman Carla Vallone, despite the recall, Segway sales have grown 50 percent annually since being introduced in 2002.

My own introduction to a Segway came when Ruben invited me to hop aboard. "Riding a Segway is really intuitive," he had commented earlier, and this assessment proved to be spot-on. I was leaning and scooting all over the place within two minutes. Did I pull a Bushie and go over the handlebars? No way – Segways have three settings which determine the maximum allowable speed, and since blobject sets theirs at the beginners level, there isn't much to worry about.

Indeed, when Jeran Richardson, Caron Lewis and Emma Bates, all from the U.K., recently signed up for a Segway tour, they were up and rolling around the courtyard in a matter of minutes, even if Emma – whose birthday was a big reason for the Segway tour – seemed a bit nervous.

When asked why they were taking a Segway tour instead of, say, a horse and carriage ride, Jeran replied, "We saw these people riding through town on what looked like a giant Hoover, and we thought it might be fun, so here we are."

It is precisely this sort of novelty that convinces people to take a Segway tour. Because in addition to covering more distance than you can on foot, on a Segway you also have a better view. And perhaps most importantly, you learn a unique skill on what is arguably one of the coolest gadgets around.

Mañana in Seville

This article first appeared in the 2007 September - October issue of InSeville Magazine

Perhaps we were silly not to keep looking for an apartment with a guest room. And perhaps we naïvely accepted the "Everything is new" pitch of Mila, our soon-to-be landlady. But the fact of the matter is we were just plain tired of living out of our suitcases and were ready to have a home again.

So we took the fifth apartment we were shown by Don Juan Pedro, our English-speaking real estate agent here in Seville. The first four apartments suffered from various drawbacks: too far from the city center, too expensive, too dowdy, too unfurnished. But the fifth place, the one we ultimately took, seemed juuuuust right. It had a huge living room with a wall of built-in bookshelves, and another wall of fancy colored glass. Two little balconies opened up just a step away from my future workspace. Marble floors lay sumptuously throughout. The capper? A huge roof terrace with a view of the cathedral.

In truth, I had been prepared to refuse the place if our condition of a remodeled kitchen was not met. But upon second inspection, Jarmila declared it fit and decided that a new kitchen was no longer necessary. She could deal with the gashes in the countertop as long as they straightened the ancient stove ventilator. "No problem," said Mila, "I'll take care of it."

Signing the contract and all the other details were made simple by Don Juan and Mila, and we walked away from the signing with a set of keys and a lot of optimism.

So naturally, complications immediately arose.

On the day I trundled our four giant suitcases to the new flat, the workers came by to fix the kitchen exhaust fan. I left them alone to do this, which is probably why I did not hear the breaking glass. Apparently, while moving the exposed exhaust pipe they punched the end of it through a window pane.

"No problem," they said cheerily, "we'll fix it Mañana," the Spanish word for "tomorrow" or "morning".

"Great," I thought. "These guys are really on the ball."

Which brings us to our first cultural lesson. In addition to its other meanings, Mañana is also widely used to mean, "some indistinct time in the future, hopefully after someone else does the job, or after the situation sorts itself out."

So we had a pane missing from our kitchen window for a week. Luckily it doesn't rain much here. In the meantime, we realized that the marble floors were unpolished and in their rough state would be impossible to keep clean. "No problem," said Mila. "I'll send a cleaning lady over Mañana."

"Wait... do you mean Mañana as in tomorrow morning?"

"Oh... uh... yes," she replied, "She can come tomorrow if you like."

"Fine. Tomorrow, then."

So the next morning, the cleaning lady and I moved all the furniture, then she flooded the place with foul-smelling chemicals and got down to scrubbing. I left and returned after she had finished and let herself out. The floors were obviously still rough, so Mila reluctantly agreed to send over a floor polishing crew... Mañana.

Problem is, before Mañana arrived, the movers delivered our 45 moving boxes. These boxes, along with all the furniture, then had to be shifted around the apartment to facilitate the floor polishing, which added at least four hours to the work.

Then came the electrical issues: there were exposed wires in the closet that I was afraid to go near, and another outlet actually exploded when I plugged a lamp into it.

"Mila, we need some electricians," I told her. She sent some over Mañana, and while they were there, I asked them to also install a light fixture in the bedroom. "No problem," they said, and in the process smashed a big hole in the ceiling.

When they were showing me this, they cheerily said, "We spoke to the other guy and he'll fix it Mañana."

> ## "Great," I thought. "These guys are really on the ball."

Which brings us to our second cultural lesson. For a beginner in the Spanish language, it's almost impossible to get a Spaniard – in Spanish – to provide a concrete time for Mañana.

"What time Mañana," you might ask. But you might just as well ask why flamenco dancers wear those dresses for the look you'll receive.

The point is we had a hole in our ceiling for two weeks.

And then one Sunday morning I walked into the kitchen for a cup of coffee and instead stepped into a flood – the washing machine had spewed its dirty water onto the floor somehow.

I called Mila and she promised they would check it out... Mañana.

I didn't pin her down to a specific day because I naturally assumed that a problem as serious as flooded floors would merit a next-day Mañana. The handyman eventually showed up at 5 p.m. – Wednesday – and his bright idea was to extend the washer's drainage pipe upwards – as if water from a clogged pipe wouldn't crawl up those extra 6 inches. I shook my head and told him the pipe was clogged, so he went to the store for

some liquid Drano. He came back three hours later with a substance that guaranteed to dissolve all clogs, natural or man made. Opening the bottle, he sniffed it, made a face, and poured it down the drain. Smoke billowed upwards from the chemical reaction, we both jumped backwards, and in no time the water was flowing again. Unfortunately, it was flowing out of the now-dissolved plastic pipes, and was eating a hole through the wooden cabinet underneath the sink.

The man scratched his head and declared that he would come back, you guessed it, Mañana.

As of this writing, he has yet to return. Which isn't so bad, really. Because now when my wife asks when I'm going to wash the clothes, I just smile nicely and say, "Mañana."

The person I want to be
Spain, 2008

A sunny September day in the Alhambra castle complex, Granada, Spain. We had just completed our tour of the magnificent royal palace, and were wandering through the urbane, terraced garden filled with palm trees and tropical flowers. Streams of water calmly flowed between glassy pools that endlessly fill themselves. As for wildlife, the pools brimmed with fish and the air was a cacophony of birdsong, so it was no surprise to see dozens of cats strolling around as if they owned the place.

My wife, mother-in-law and I had been on our feet for the previous three hours, our curiosity and moods somewhat benumbed by the over-the-top sublimity of the Alhambra. I guess this is why none of us were certain we'd really heard the calls for help. We cocked our heads until we were sure, then fanned out and attempted to find the source of the cries.

We were at the exit of the gardens near the Charles V Palace when we finally pinpointed it: a kitten had wandered into the drainage system, and was now trapped under a narrow metal grating. It was hiding in a pipe just out of sight, mewing its poor head off.

"It is just a cat," he said. "There are hundreds here."

I tried to lift up the grating, but it wouldn't budge; it was cemented in place. I then tried to lure the kitten out with some lunchmeat, but she would show nothing more than her little pink nose. I let the meat drop and she darted out to snatch it – she was pure white, sullied by the pipes.

Momentarily at a loss, we discussed what to do and couldn't think of a thing. Then two American ladies happened by. Even without the matching outfits – t-shirts, shorts and hiking boots – one could tell they were mother/daughter. They had also heard and were alarmed by the kitten's meowing and joined us in brainstorming how to help the little thing get out.

Just then a guard who had been sitting on a nearby bench slouched over to us. He asked if anyone spoke Spanish and I told him I spoke a little.

Lightly touching my elbow, he took me aside and said, "Man, it's just a cat. There's hundreds of them here."

I looked at him blankly. "So what – we just leave it?"

He shrugged and gave me an uncaring look. The American ladies apparently didn't speak Spanish and there was no reason to get my wife angry, so I did not yet translate.

Instead, I asked the guard if there was a way to get the grating out of the ground.

"No, I don't think so."

"You don't think so, or you are certain?"

He straightened up and said, "I am certain," though he looked anything but. At this affront, he turned and went back to his bench.

I told the ladies that the guard didn't want to be bothered, that he said there was nothing to do about it. My wife and mother-in-law, Czechs who are not surprised when the authorities are of no use, kind of shrugged in resignation, but the Americans were indignant. They couldn't believe that the guard was going to let the poor kitten die. They encouraged me to get him to do something – to call someone, maybe. But having lived in Spain for the previous year, I told them I wasn't surprised by the guard's reaction; that in my experience, a laid-back, borderline uncaring attitude was fairly common. Still, they couldn't believe, simply could not believe, that someone would let a kitten die just out of laziness. It was completely beyond them.

My mother-in-law speaks neither English nor Spanish, so the whole situation was a bit distant to her. She understood the cat was stuck and also felt bad about it, but being 68 and having been on her feet for the past three hours, she was also looking for a place to sit down – preferably a place with air-conditioning and caffeinated beverages. But in truth, it wasn't only my mother-in-law. I was tired as well, and so was my wife. Worse, we were deflated by the carelessness of the guard's reaction. So more out of avoidance than anything else, we said good-bye to the American ladies and let the kitten situation fade away.

Confession: by the time we were drinking Cokes in the shade, I had pretty much forgotten about the kitten. Instead, we chatted about the marvels we had seen that day – of which there had been scores. After we had our feet back under us, I told the ladies that they should start towards the exit without me – I was going to visit the Charles V Palace (which they had already done) and then catch up with them.

After parting ways, I walked back through the crowd towards the palace and noticed that a scrum had formed where we'd first heard the kitten. Drawing closer, I saw that the group were standing near an open pit in the sidewalk, the American ladies directing things.

And you know, I immediately felt ashamed. I realized I'd done the same thing that the lazy guard had done: just shrugged my shoulders at the unfairness of the situation and then promptly forgotten about it. But not those two American ladies, boy. They had apparently caused enough of a fuss that the guard had called in someone to pry up a huge cement access panel, and had then enlisted a gang of do-gooders to help them out.

I felt my shame morph into a sort of inspired resolve, and before I knew it I had thrust myself back into the fray. The situation was this: the three-foot sewer access hole that had been uncovered was crisscrossed by pipes, making it difficult to get at the kitten, even though it was now visible in an adjoining drainage pipe. A Spanish kid in his early 20s was laying on the ground, trying to grab at the kitten, but thus far he'd only managed to scare the poor thing further.

Someone produced a piece of wood that we lowered into the opening of the kitten's pipe, but it still only led about halfway to the surface. The plan was, we would lure her onto the wooden plank and then grab her. But how? I had a sandwich in my backpack, so I fished it out and lay myself on the ground. I put three pieces of lunchmeat on the plank – one at the opening, one a bit further out, and finally one that was far enough out that, should she take it, the kit-

ten would be exposed, affording me a chance to grab her. The kitten cooperated with the plan, darting out for the first piece right away. A few moments later she gingerly stepped onto the plank to snatch the second bit with her paw. The third piece she didn't want to risk, but eventually she stuck her head completely out and as she was making for it, I lunged. For a fleeting second, I had a good hold of her neck, but she managed to twist free of my grasp and pull back into her hole.

"Ya wussed out," barked the older American in my ear. She had been watching over my shoulder.

"He blew it," she announced to the crowd. "He wussed out."

The crowd's mood palpably deflated. I stood up, feeling like I really had blown it – like I'd actually managed to kill the kitten when all I'd wanted was to save her. She'd never come out now. People began drifting away, and the Americans huddled with another woman, no doubt discussing how I'd screwed everything up.

The guard began speaking about covering up the hole; he said we'd done what we could and the hole couldn't be left open for someone to fall into.

In the middle of this dour shuffling around, a woman suddenly yelled out, "*La madre!*" (The mother!).

Those of us remaining looked around. About 20 yards away, an adult cat – white herself – was looking intently in the direction of the hole. The guard motioned us back and we cleared out to give her some room. Right on cue, the kitten mewed. At this, the mother pricked up her ears and with obvious concern trotted over to the hole.

She peered over the edge and meowed, and suddenly the kitten began mewing its head off. The wooden plank was still in place, so the mother crawled down, got the kitten by the scruff of the neck and hauled her up to safety.

And I tell you, when she emerged with that kitten in her mouth, I didn't know whether to laugh or cry, so I did both. I mean, I was a complete mess. And I wasn't the only one, either. A round of applause broke out and there was all sorts of back-slapping and hand-shaking. Heck, the American ladies even hugged the guard! It was a regular love-fest.

In the milling about that followed, I gravitated over to the Americans and through our small-talk was again impressed with their can-do attitude.

They related how they had pushed forward when others (including me) had given up, and in the end had accomplished what they'd set out to do. And in this case, it was something hugely worthwhile – the saving of another being's life.

We eventually parted ways – hugging, actually – and as I walked off it occurred to me that I used to be just like those ladies. There had been a time – a long time, actually – when I had been prepared to do the right thing despite what anyone else had to say on the matter. I had the self-confidence, the moxy, to set a course and follow it through to completion despite the obstacles.

And I'm not suggesting that such traits are necessarily American and not Spanish, but here in Andalusia, there's a prevailing tendency to put things off, to let things go, to reckon that things will sort themselves out. Which is exactly how I'd treated the kitten situation: I'd acted like it would sort itself out. And yes, in the end it did, but only because other, more caring people had stepped up and done the right thing.

Lost in thought but still walking, I realized that in fact I do belong to that group of people who want to help when things go wrong, but I hadn't done so with the kitten because I was just being lazy.

Fair enough, I told myself: laziness can be overcome.

Feeling somewhat... lighter now, and content with how things had turned out, I hurried to catch up to my wife and mother-in-law.

The best part of the story? When I told my wife how I'd returned and helped save the kitten, I saw something that I hadn't seen in awhile, something that I hadn't known was missing but that was immediately recognizable: reflected in her eyes once again was the person I want to be.

Just take it
Sevilla, 2008

The baggage carousel at Madrid's Barajas airport was crowded, and as I maneuvered the luggage trolley through the mostly dark-haired crowd, a tall blonde woman walked up to me and addressed me in English. Jarmila was off waiting for our luggage.

"Pardon me," said the woman in an indistinct European accent. "We've just flown in from Cuba and we forgot about this bottle of liqueur we are carrying. They're going to take it when we go through security again, so do you want it?"

I blinked at her. "What?"

She repeated the story.

After listening again, I said, "But you're not supposed to take things from strangers, are you?"

"I suppose not, but either we give it away to someone, or the security guards will take it and throw it in the rubbish."

I nodded. "Why not drink it before you get on the plane?"

She observed, correctly, that it was just 10 in the morning.

I nodded again. "But... you know, I'm not really sure what to do here."

"Just take it," she said, holding it out to me. "It would be a pity if it went to waste."

Hesitantly, I took the bottle from her hands and examined it. The liquid had a rich brown color, there was a floating piece of fruit inside, and the label was covered in Spanish superlatives.

"Well… ok," I said. "Thank you…"

"Sure," she replied. "I hope you enjoy it."

We looked at each other for an awkward moment before I said, "So… have a safe trip."

"You, too."

At saying this, she kind of half-smiled, turned and hurried off. I looked down at the bottle again and when I looked up, she had already blended into the crowd.

Hesitantly, I took the bottle from her…

Shaking my head, I wheeled the cart over to Jarmila, who asked what had happened. I told her the story and showed her the bottle.

She listened intently and then asked, "Did you give her any money?"

"Uh… no. Should I have?"

"She had to pay for the bottle, no?"

"But she would have thrown it away otherwise."

"Yes, but it looks expensive."

"Hmm."

So now, in addition to my confusion, I felt vaguely guilty about not paying the woman. We headed over to wait for the luggage and as the situation processed itself, out of nowhere, paranoid, obsessive Jim manifested himself.

"What if it's a bomb?"

"It's not a bomb," responded Jarmila.

"How do you know that?"

"Well, look at the bottle - it's still sealed."

"No, it's not. The top is just kind of melted together. You see how it's a little black and discolored there? You could do that with a cigarette lighter. Plus, you can't

see inside the top of the bottle because of the label. And who knows – maybe there's a detonator there. It might explode once we open it or something. Or maybe it's got enough Anthrax in it to infect Europe."

"No…"

"Well, I ain't gonna open it. In fact, I'm going to leave it in the bathroom."

"But what if it really is a bomb – then it will cause big damage. And they'll see you putting it there on the security cameras."

I looked around and spotted about 10 cameras strategically placed throughout the hall.

"Shit."

"Here," she said. "Give it to me – I'll take a drink to prove it's not bad."

"You will not!"

"Why not?"

"Why not. You're funny."

"Fine. Throw it in the garbage outside if you don't want it."

"But I'll still have to take it past security guards."

"You will have to do that in every case."

"Man! I feel like I'm trapped here. But yes, we'll throw it out. I can't believe I even took it."

Just then a group of policemen appeared from the crowd. They had the woman I had been talking to in handcuffs and were walking straight at us.

No, just kidding. We ended up throwing the bottle away in the garbage before we took a taxi, and in the following days we didn't hear anything about an explosion at the Madrid airport, so hopefully nothing happened with it.

But that bottle – that situation – sure affected me. Looking back, I consider myself a naïve fool for taking the bottle in the first place, and a skeptical reactionary for eventually throwing it away.

Such a simple situation, really, but it twice reduced me to my worst.

I wonder if that lady knew what she was doing to me.

A sort of homecoming
Spain, 2008

The surly Immigration Officer couldn't care less that we were coming back to the States for my 10th, 15th, and 20th year homecomings – the only thing that concerned him was the status of my wife's green card. We'd been out of the country for more than 6 months (apparently a no-no) and either he was just doing his job or he was being a first-rate jerk. Sometimes it's hard to tell with those guys. Anyway, without really listening to our explanation, Officer Happy referred us to the secondary interview room. The secondary room is never a fun place to be, as your presence there indicates that you're gonna have to do some fast-talking. And after flying over the Atlantic, one is rarely at the top of one's rhetorical game.

We walked into the low-ceilinged room just as one of the officers, exhibiting the twitchy signs of chronic over-caffeination, began to browbeat a college-aged French girl. From the look of her gigantic luggage she had gone back to France to fetch some things, taken longer than planned, and was now facing this guy's wrath.

"So why you wanna live here anyway," he demanded.

"I am studying."

"Why not study in France?"

"I… I'm sorry?

"I SAID: Why not study in France?"

"I have another year, and-"

"YOU'RE NOT LISTENING! I SAID: WHY NOT STUDY IN FRANCE?"

"I… I…"

And then she began to cry.

My wife Jarmila and I traded looks as the officer continued.

"Listen, honey, you keep playin' this game and you're gonna find yourself in front of the judge real quick. And believe me, he'll be harder on you than I'm being."

"The… the judge? <sob> But-"

"Look, I'm only gonna ask this one more time and you better get it right, because-"

On and on this went, with my wife and I feeling terrible for the girl and fervently hoping that we wouldn't have to deal with the cretin.

Luckily, when our turn came the browbeating wasn't yet finished. We got the other guard, who was calm, collected, and who *almost* seemed like he disapproved of his colleague's behavior. He opened my wife's folder, typed some things into his computer and asked why we had been gone so long. I told him I'd been doing research for a book and my wife had come along for the trip.

"Ok, fair enough," he said, still not looking up. "But you been listening to my partner, right? It's not a good idea to be gone for so long. Next time it might be a problem. You need me to repeat any of that?"

"Nope."

"Ok."

He stamped our passports and handed them back to us.

"Welcome home."

The five-year plan

A lot of American college students do exactly what society tells them to and end up graduating in four years. Others, like me, prefer to stay in the womb as long as possible: I took a light academic load each semester and filled the rest of my time with campus journalism and the odd semester of rugby. Throw in a semester of student teaching a bunch of teenage girls (there were probably boys in the classes as well, but I don't remember much about them) and you've got the five years that separate my high school graduation in 1987 from my college graduation in 1992.

The five years that separate the completion of undergrad and grad school are a bit more complex: a stint in California; returning to school and falling for a lesbian (her switching teams was revealed only after we'd been together for awhile, and was actually less of an ego-boost than one might think).

But the point is that 2007 held the prospect of a unique set of homecomings: 20 years for high school, 15 for college, and 10 for grad school. I had it pegged a year in advance: Jarmila and I would take a month off work and hit them all. I took it as good karma to discover that my three alma maters' homecomings took place on consecutive weekends. It was to be a *tour de force* of old friends for me and new acquaintances for Jarmila.

I just had to lose 10 pounds first.

What's wrong with the speakers?

What I remember from high school: cheap (sometimes warm) beer before football games; weightlifting; dropping pencils to look up skirts; random intimidation; hanging out at the video arcade; boners at the most inopportune times; working for the school paper; the Beastie Boys; being one of two fat kids in our class; the warm glow of friendship and belonging, liberally spiced with a bit of the old ennui.

It was the warm glow of friendship, I think, that drove me to the delusion that I would return, 20 years later, to a homecoming game and be surrounded by dozens of old high school friends – perhaps many of whom had traveled there for that very occasion.

The Friday night game was also to be Jarmila's first exposure to the glory of my plan, to which she had thus far been amenable, if vaguely skeptical. The Czech culture, you see, does not place importance on school reunions unless they are of the sort organized by smaller, closer groups of friends. Moreover, Jarmila does not share my enthusiasm for American football, so three straight weekends of homecoming games was not a selling point. Rather, I had to argue (not altogether untruthfully) that in American culture, the games are merely an excuse to get together with former classmates, a sort of comfortable background noise that can be used to fill in the gaps of conversation that naturally arise between people who haven't seen each other for years. This line of reasoning passed muster and I was at last able to convince her to come out on a frosty October night to watch our Blackhawk Cougars take on the Moon Tigers.

Problem was, all this convincing meant we arrived late, and we missed the obligatory pageantry of the Homecoming Queen and her Court (though we did later spot the queen parading around in her crown, and my goodness was she *hot*). Another problem: my classmates from 1987 apparently hadn't considered our 20th year homecoming to be as significant as I did – we didn't run into a single one. We did, however, run into my older brother. He was standing near the band, where he could watch over his 11 year-old daughter as she ran around with her friends, and also keep a suspicious eye on his 15 year-old with the cuddly boyfriend.

In 1987, Playboy magazine named Slippery Rock University number five on their list of top party schools in the nation… But as any student at the time will attest, achieving number 5 was by no means due to The Rock's lively bar scene. Indeed, back then, Slippery Rock was a dry town.

The bored, I-suspected-as-much look on Jarmila's face was almost too much to bear, but I soldiered on, using the opportunity to catch up on family matters. And I really did enjoy the game, which featured a hometown running back who bowled over the defense for no less than three touchdowns. After nearly every play it seemed, the loudspeakers would blare a distorted cougar's roar to encourage the crowd.

"What's wrong with the speakers," Jarmila finally asked. "They keep making that terrible noise."

My brother and I giggled, then explained its significance.

The high point of the night, surprisingly, was the band's halftime performance. Jarmila had never seen the scale of a marching band's halftime show, and was full of questions: where do they practice; do they have to pay for their uniforms; do they all really go to band camp? It was another illustration that the most random of things can catch a cultural sojourner's attention.

Alas, once the second half started, Jarmila's shivers came on full-bore, so we left my brother to attend his daughters and headed home. Far from disappointed, Jarmila was happy to have been exposed to this "cultural experience", as she put it. My take, however, wasn't quite so positive. Yes, I was happy that she had enjoyed herself. But the first of the homecomings had come and gone and I hadn't yet seen any of my old classmates.

A dry town

In 1987, Playboy magazine named Slippery Rock University number five on their list of top party schools in the nation. This feat was naturally a source of great pride for the students and likely boosted the school's word-of-mouth recruitment for years. But as any student at the time will attest, achieving number 5 was by no means due to The Rock's lively bar scene. Indeed, back then Slippery Rock was a dry town. As in, no alcohol was sold in any restaurant, and no bars existed within city limits. From time to time some forward-thinking student or businessmen would enter into the political fray and put the liquor question on the ballot, but it always failed.

Luckily there were ways around this prohibition. There were some seedy bars within driving distance, for example, The Shed (which was perfectly named). Also, a place just outside the city limits sold beer by the case and keg and did an absolutely roaring business (there was also a state-owned liquor store for when the bank account was flush). Thus, obtaining booze was never a problem, and in the absence of bars, house parties or the legendary Keister Apartments were the favored places to get sodden. Weekends were epic: if you had a plastic cup, you could wander from door to door, party to party, and you were welcomed like a Viking returning to Valhalla.

Nevertheless, it was heartening to learn that in 2001 Slippery Rock became a "wet" town: students there can finally meet and mingle like normal people do all over the world – over a beer. So what if it took until the 21st century to attain age-old amenities? At least now returning alumni have a proper place to spend our cash.

These and other SRU-related topics prevailed in Jen and Murray's SUV as we drove over to the Slippery Rock campus for the second portion of the homecoming holy grail. Murray had somehow talked his wife Jen into being our designated driver that day, so much emphasis was put on how Murray and I were gonna get "faced" (our old drinking vernacular having bubbled up from years of dormancy).

As Murray, nowadays a teacher, sagely commented, "It's funny, with good friends the years are brushed off like dust on a coat that's been hanging in the closet too long and the old stories are soon intermingled with new."

Indeed, embarrassing rugby stories were jousted with, new tales were shared, and before we even parked we'd regained that easy intimacy of old friends and teammates.

A walk through campus illustrated the degree to which things have remained the same at SRU: it was absolutely deserted. There was nothing going on anywhere, save for a sparse gathering near the stadium. A ten-minute walk later (during which Jarmila again grumbled at the folly of my plan) and we were at the only show in town – a large tent had been erected to house those (few, aged) alumni who had made the trip back. A nominal entrance fee got us a pair of party beads, a beer cup, and all we could eat burgers and fries. We made a beeline for the tap.

The last time I'd had a beer on the Slippery Rock campus I'd gotten arrested for it, so it was something of a vindication to be able to fill my cup and walk around in plain sight of the coppers, which I made everyone do just because we could. Upon our return to the tent, however, we were shocked to discover that the place was already closing down; apparently the start of the football game signaled the end of the tent's usefulness.

A short buzz-kill ensued, but my carefree beeriness was not to be overcome: I moved behind the vacant but still serviceable beer table and filled my cup as the tent was pulled down around us. Never one to pass up a chance to pour his own, Murray joined me and soon thereafter so did the girls.

During the next thirty minutes of cadging beers I fell into exactly the type of dreamy languor that one would expect of a middle-aged alumni at homecoming. The years melted away to reveal those dazzlingly beautiful, funny, young selves that reside within all of us, and it made no difference that Jarmila wasn't around back then – we saw her as she would have been, and she belonged. That short episode, those all-too-real glimpses of youth, made the whole trip worthwhile.

So naturally it was too good to last. Cue my niece, a straight-laced A-student, a sophomore at SRU, calling to meet up. Could we meet her in her dormitory?

Disclosure: I had really been looking forward to seeing my niece, to meeting her friends, to again smelling the distinct aroma of a university dorm. But what I wasn't ready for was the ratcheting down of my enlarged and now careless beeriness. The f-bomb, something that I hadn't yet dropped in front of the niece, reared its head at least three times before Jarmila gave me a little talking-to. Now, did I need the talking-to? Certainly not. But did I *need* it? <Sigh.> *Yes.*

Anyways, trying perhaps a bit too hard to make conversation, we walked to the shiny new brew house where we made fast-friends with the waiter, who had a delightful way of bantering with half-drunk knuckleheads. Some absolutely fantastic beers (and food, I think) later, we ended up at the next bar to discover that my niece, her boyfriend and her roommate were underage. No problem, said the gorilla doorman – they had non-drinking wristbands for them to wear. Still, they were obviously out of their element, and no amount of fun that Murray and myself were having could convince everyone to stay. We soon said goodbye to my niece and her friends, and on the ride back to Murray's we decided that next time – relatives or not – it would be wise to leave the underage girls at home.

Changed name, changed plans

When a snobby East Coaster dismisses everything between NY and LA as flyover territory, chances are they've never actually *been* to the Midwest. But the thing is, if a New Yorker parachuted into, say, Warrensburg, Missouri, it's likely their negative opinion would only be reinforced. Oh, the people are kind as can be and the place is livable enough: there's a heap of bars and restaurants, a notary public, a farmer's supply. But when a town's historical high point is the "world-famous" Old Drum, the statue of a dog honoring Senator George Graham Vest's 1870 speech titled "Tribute To A Dog", well, it would be hard to convince the New Yorker that the parachute in had been worthwhile.

Things don't change an awful lot in the 'burg. The freight trains that run directly through town still lean on their whistles in the middle of the night; the bars still sell hard-boiled eggs to go along with your beer; and the university is still the largest employer around.

One thing that *has* changed over the years is the name of the university. When I was attending school there in the 1990s, it was called Central Missouri State University (CMSU). Someone must have finally told the administration about its more informal name (Call Me Stupid University), because in 2006, the name was changed to the University of Central Missouri (UCM).

In truth, the time I spent at CMSU/UCM was excellent (aside from the lesbian girlfriend): I studied and worked with a number of intelligent and likeable people, expanded my worldview, and forged some knuckleheaded friendships that I expect to keep for many years. But the sheer, bloody distance that separates Warrensburg from the rest of the world was just hard to *deal* with: the nearest town of significance is almost 30 miles away, the nearest city over 60 miles distant, and my parents' home in PA upwards of 840 miles removed.

That last one didn't always present a problem during my 20s, when I was still open to popping a handful of trucker's little helpers and driving straight through. But now, with a wife who (oddly) doesn't appreciate my 220-volt self, an 840-mile round trip pretty much translates into four nights in various hotels, and an equal amount of days in a rental car – an unappealing prospect all around.

So there was that. Another reason we ultimately decided against the trip to CMSU/UCM was that my friends all ditched at the last minute: the flight from Chicago was cancelled, the Floridian suddenly couldn't take off work, the Missourian's sister was having an important shindig.

But the prospect of bailing on one of my alma maters seemed too much to bear, and up until the day of departure I fully intended to drag Jarmila out there anyway. Ultimately though, her last-ditch argument hit home: "There's no use traveling all that way without having a crew of friends to spend time with. Otherwise it will be the Blackhawk game all over again."

Though I still wonder where she picked up the word "crew", I nonetheless had to agree. Aside from completing the homecoming holy grail just on principle, there didn't seem to be much point in spending all that time and money for the trip out west.

Still, I regret not having made it, you know?

The coup

In March 2007, one of my high school classmates discovered my website and emailed me: "Hey, is the Jim Curtiss that stalked all the cheerleaders in high school? Signed, Denise."

After confronting several repressed episodes, I realized that in fact I *was* that Jim Curtiss, and soon Denise and I were trading emails. Our discussions centered around shared memories and updates of our current lives, until one day she mentioned our upcoming 20th year reunion. Specifically, she couldn't believe that nobody had stepped up to organize it. *Ah-ha*, I thought, *Here's my chance to alter the course of events in my favor.* I soon posted a letter on our high school's website:

> *Dear Members of the Blackhawk Class of 1987,*
> *Our class officers have abandoned us. The President is nowhere to be found, the Treasurer made off with the funds, and the last organizer of a reunion vowed never to organize anything again.*
> *Thus, I, Jim Curtiss, am staging a coup for the Presidency of the Blackhawk Class of 1987. Though I'm hoping this is a purely ceremonial position, I nonetheless understand that my main duties will include organizing a 20th reunion party.*
> *And because your President lives in Spain and will not be in P.A before then, I hereby declare that the reunion will be held in mid-October.*
>
> *Signed,*
> *Jim Curtiss, New President of the Blackhawk Class of 1987*

As far as coups go, this one was entirely bloodless and met with no resistance. In fact, it was welcomed: apparently nobody wanted anything to do with organizing a reunion.

Some parts of my character aren't what you'd call presidential

I never planned on being a figurehead President cut from the Zaphod Beeblebrox mold, it just turned out that way. Because there was absolutely no way I was going to fly home from Spain in order to case out banquet halls, test bland buffet food, audition clowns, etc., the newly-appointed VP (Denise) did practically all that work while for months I wrote emails and drank coffee. And while it's true that, when done properly, writing emails takes both time and effort, if there's anything more *me* than email writing and coffee drinking, I'd sure like to know what it is and whether it pays.

At any rate, it was startlingly simple to get back in touch with friends I'd not spoken to or heard from in so many years. There was so much to relate and question that some days I would spend three or four hours on emails alone: to Mindy, who works for a university press; to Missy, a teacher; to Dan, a big-shot in the glass industry; to John, an oil-refinery wrangler.

I rationalized these many hours spent online by telling myself that I was doing *research*.

For my *article*.

This made me feel much better.

Still in the closet after all these years

Despite his ongoing and eloquent arguments to the contrary, John, the oil refinery fellow, was the instigator of most of our adolescent schemes. The party we planned to hold when my parents were out of town – the one that was discovered beforehand? John's idea. All those plans to skip school that were foiled? John's idea. Driving his parent's car before we had a license? John's

> The hostess rushed over and threw the curtains open fast enough to see the boys running away. This was repeated until it became routine, at which point John convinced one of his accomplices to moon the girls.

idea. In fact, John's schemes were so infamous that my mother, upon seeing him in our kitchen for the first time in 25 years, exclaimed, "I remember you – you're the one who always skipped school by hiding in the closet until your mom left for work!" John reddened and rushed to his own defense, "Did Jimmy tell you to say that? Because you know, your son was the worst of us all. Heck, did you know about the time when he and Robby got the physics test beforehand and-"

This is when I hustled John out the door and took him over to the bar for a few beers and stories, of which he seemed to have a never-ending supply. My personal favorite, which I re-told at least five times over the following days: John's girlfriend at the time was hosting a sleepover with 5 other girls, so John and two buddies thought it would be a good idea to go scare them. The girls were in the basement when they arrived, so the boys laid down on the grass, knocked loudly on one of the ground-level windows and watched, giggling, through a crack in the curtains as the girls became concerned. They knocked again. The hostess (who'd probably been expecting such a prank) rushed over and threw the curtains open fast enough to see the boys running away. This was repeated until it became routine, at which point John convinced one of his accomplices to moon the girls. So the guy dropped his pants and put his butt up to the glass. Meanwhile, the hostess had organized all the girls to stand right in front of the window; apparently the plan was to scare the boys right back when they returned.

Cue the knock, the curtain gets flung open and not six inches from the girls' faces is our buddy's hairy rear-end. A collective scream filled the night air, the curtains were quickly closed, and the boys got the hell out of there. The capper: John swears that amid the screams, he heard a girl yelling over and over, "Oh my God! I saw hole! I saw *hole*!"

Countdown to the big show

Activities planned for the reunion weekend included a Friday night meeting at a local watering hole, a Saturday picnic to show off the kids, the reunion itself, and Sunday morning golf. To Denise and I, the point was to maximize the amount of time we'd have together. Some of the attendees didn't appreciate that tack, however. My friend Michelle put it like this: "When I saw what you had planned for us, I thought, 'I haven't seen these people in 20 years and they wanna spend 48 straight hours together? Get real!'"

In truth, on the Friday beforehand I was feeling much the same way. Yes, I had fielded dozens of phone calls from forgotten classmates and collaborated with Denise on last-minute dilemmas. But still, I had nagging doubts that our efforts had all been for naught. After all, we'd only registered 80 people from our graduating class of 270. Would that be enough?

When we showed up at the local watering hole at 8 p.m., my fears were confirmed. Only *six* of us had turned up. My nerves skyrocketed. Was this the right bar? Had we forgotten something? Where *was* everybody?

John took me up to the bar and consoled me: "Relax, Jimmy. It's ok you're still a loser."

Three hours later, though, the bar was absolutely *jammed* with classmates and I was being overwhelmed by scores of people I hadn't seen in years. I was being prodded and judged and asked questions that I couldn't answer, teasing and being teased, laughing at old jokes, looking at pictures of loved ones (children, spouses, cars, houses) lamenting the time that had passed.

My favorite interaction of the night came after Chris and I had exchanged our stories. Another friend, Steve, who I keep in regular contact with, joined us and asked Chris what he'd been up to. Without missing a beat, Chris replied: "I'm a writer. I live in Spain."

Puzzled, Steve looked at me and I shrugged my shoulders in agreement. We looked back at Chris, who continued: "I also lived in Prague and married a Czech girl."

Steve's lost expression was priceless. "But…"

"Her name is Jarmila. That's her." Chris pointed to my wife, who was over talking to John.

Steve looked between Jarmila and Chris at least twice before we cracked. And while Chris and I thought it was hilarious, Steve simply shook his head and walked away.

I tell this story to illustrate the kind of easy camaraderie that many of us fell into that first night. We were ribbing each other, flirting, confessing past crushes, and telling long-forgotten stories. And truthfully, it was almost enough of a reunion to stand by itself. It was just that good.

The big show

As an abstract concept, I don't find public speaking to be a daunting task. This is probably why I had no concerns when Denise said one of us should deliver a welcoming speech and no way was it gonna be her. Further, she reasoned, as a writer I could whip something up in no time. I agreed, and then spent six months writing the thing, picturing myself getting laughs in the right spots, thoughtful nods in others. You know, a little something for everyone.

Confession: While I very much enjoyed writing the speech, the closer the prospect drew of actually *delivering* it, the more I became a festering, obsessive mess. I memorized it a month in advance. Constantly worked on delivery. Tweaked it. Asked my wife for advice. If anyone asked how I was doing, I'd say, "Shitty. I have to give a speech at my reunion."

"Don't worry," they'd reply, "you'll do great. Public speaking should be no problem for someone like you."

Which is the approach that pretty much everyone in the world takes when it's not *them* that has to give the speech, and it never helped relieve my nerves.

Anyway, here's what eventually made it out of my twitching mouth that night:

Welcome everyone, to the 20th year reunion of the Blackhawk High School class of 1987. <self-congratulatory applause>

Sometime last year as Denise and I mulled over the idea of putting this reunion together, I got an email from her that I'd like to share with you: Quote: Hey, if you still have your cowboy hat from 5th grade, please bring it with you in October. <laughter>

My cowboy hat from 5th grade? Now who in the world but Denise Peel would remember that she wore my cowboy hat all that week at Camp Kon O' Kwee? <laughter, no longer thinking I would puke>

But that simple sentence brought back such a flood of memories, and I thought, YES, this is what the reunion thing is all about – re-connecting with those people who helped form all those memories in the first place. <thoughtful nods>

Now I'm sure there are a thousand more memories buried around here somewhere, and our hope is that this weekend will help you stir up some of the better ones… and maybe exorcise some of the worse ones. <smiles>

In closing, I'd like to thank – in turn – the lovely ladies who worked so hard to put all this together. We simply wouldn't be here without them.

First – Stacey for all her research and organizational work…< applause, an embarrassed Stacey stands up>

Michelle for cooking the books… <laughter, applause, Michelle stands and shakes fist at me>

And finally, Denise for doing pretty much everything else- <huge applause, so much so that my punch-line, which was planned to get myself some applause, was no longer relevant>

I handed the microphone to Denise, and she began to speak about the photo montage that she had created: "Let's all direct our attention to the screen, shall we… Jim, could you…"

Now, I know it shouldn't have bothered me, but what about *my* round of applause? What about a little love for *el Presidente*? I walked over to the computer with a gob of resentment lodged in my throat and started the photo montage. It beamed up on the giant screen and I sat down nearby. The montage was nostalgic and terribly absorbing, and two minutes into it, a surprise: my fat-boy senior photo appeared on the screen with a red heart drawn over it. Big laughter, applause… and my resentment was supplanted with gratitude. Denise had delivered after all.

Finally, with quite possibly one of the most stressful events of my adult life behind me, I felt myself relax. It was time to enjoy the night that I had helped put together.

Panamama

Paul and myself were never buddies in high school, but we now have a great deal in common: He also has a wife from outside of the United States. Paul is married to a Panamanian woman, and they ended up sitting next to Jarmila and myself at dinner. Conversation was thus right up our alley – lots of travel-related topics, language-oriented dilemmas, difficulties with adjusting to foreign families and customs.

At one point we discussed the simplicity of dating a woman from a foreign culture, specifically, how there's very little of the "I'm-not-gonna-treat-him-*right*-until-he-gets-me-a-ring" approach that we've seen with some of our American women friends.

Sitting across the table, our friend Tom chided his wife.

"That sounds familiar."

"Well it worked, didn't it," asked his wife. She held out her hand and sure enough, she had a gigantic rock that drew appreciative coos. "And it was worth it too, wasn't it, honey?"

"Oh, definitely," he shot back. "And really, who needs a fishing boat anyways?"

The laughter was infectious, and the line of discussion lasted well past dinner.

But back to Paul, it was interesting to make such a profound connection to someone whom I'd really never known in high school. Heck, even our wives got along famously.

Open bar

Mark, a lawyer, was under the impression that the open bar policy would only last until dinner. Thus, early on he was seen at the bar throwing down vodka and cranberry drinks and ordering more straightaway.

Holding Samantha's hand, my friend barged into a conversation that my wife and I were having. "Tell Samantha how hot we think she is," he demanded. Both Samantha and my wife looked at me expectantly; one in a positive sense, the other less so.

Midway through the night he slouched over to me, drunker than he ought to have been, and demanded to know why it wasn't announced there would be an open bar all night. His slurred speech blended seamlessly into a disclosure that he always knew I had a crush on his older sister, and that further, we had never, as I recalled, gone shopping together for shoes.

"Mark, look at your feet," I suggested.

He was wearing a pair of the same Penny Loafers I claimed we'd gone shopping for in high school.

He considered them and then looked up at me with a crooked grin.

"Circumstantial evidence at best," he replied, and steered me toward the bar.

Call my wife

Michelle and I were good friends for a long time. She was sweet, pretty, laughed at nearly all my jokes – and what more does a high school kid need, really? However, back then she also had a long-distance boyfriend who she insisted on being faithful to. Despite this, I'd often ride her home from school and in return she'd allow me to ride her family's quad – all in all a good trade. As so often happens, though, we drifted apart when I went off to college, and in the intervening years we rarely spoke.

So it was a bit of a surprise when a man I'd never seen before (her husband, it turned out) walked up to me at the reunion and said, "You need to keep in touch with my wife more – she always talks about you."

Blink. Blink.

"Uh... ok. Is she pretty?"

My big, lovely, perfect house

Drinks in hand, my good friend and I stepped back to render judgment on our women class-mates. We were pretty much in agreement: x had put on a lot of weight, y had stayed much the same, z had lost a little something. What was absolutely obvious, however, was that Samantha had matured into something special. She had a glowing loveliness that every man present had to admire.

Fast forward two hours of an open bar later: holding Samantha's hand, the same friend barged into a conversation that my wife and I were having.

"Tell Samantha how hot we think she is," he demanded. Both Samantha and my wife looked at me expectantly; one in a positive sense, the other less so.

Apparently I'd had just enough booze to silken up my tongue, because I responded, "Samantha, we were saying earlier that you've turned into a very attractive woman – not that you weren't in high school. But you have a different shine to you now."

I turned to my wife: "At least, that's what the other guys are saying. I haven't really noticed."

After seven years of marriage my wife no doubt recognizes my brand of bullshit, but in this case it worked: I talked myself off the hook and Samantha was dragged elsewhere for further forced avowals of her beauty.

Ten minutes later, the same friend happened by: "Man, that Jennifer is *such* a bitch. First she wouldn't talk to Samantha. Then she just gave me some polished monologue about her three kids and rich husband and how she lives in a big, lovely, perfect house. And then she excused herself! Didn't even ask me a question."

"She did the same thing to me earlier," I answered. "I'm surprised she's not wearing her bank statement instead of a name tag."

Proud to be *el Presidente*

A few moments later Dan came over. He said he'd been skeptical about coming to the reunion because 5 months prior, his wife's class had organized *their* 20th reunion, and it had been filled with a bunch of snooty prigs. He said he and his wife had left early because of all the falsity and disinterest. This brought us to Jennifer and her story, and we shared a laugh at her expense because she'd basically told Dan the same thing: that she had a rich husband, three kids and lives in a big, lovely, perfect house.

In defense of my class, however, there were only a handful of people who behaved like Jennifer – either because of how cool they think they were in high school or how cool they think they've become. But as I said, that group was very small. For the most part, the night was about transcending our old cliques and speaking to everyone, including classmates that we really didn't know back in the day. And as an organizer who felt partially responsible for everybody enjoying themselves, that made me quite proud.

Another thing that made me proud was that we were able to keep an open bar policy the whole night – keeping the attendees well-lubricated seemed to keep them happy and mingling. In fact, everyone was so into their conversations that the expensive DJ's music was just so much background noise. My iPod would have served the same purpose.

Indeed, had we planned everything just perfectly, there would have been no surprise when, just as the party was hitting its stride, an unfun-looking man (the supervisor, it turned out) approached me and told me they were kicking us out at 11p.m. Something about state regulations for banquet halls, he said. Try as I might, I could not argue, cajole, bribe or plead the man into bending the rules, and at 10:45 I had to make the hassled announcement. This was not the news that people were ready for, and the next 20 minutes were rather empty now that I look back on it – no one wanted the night to end and we all pretty much dragged our heels on the way out.

I somehow ended up being the last one out of the banquet hall, both jazzed up with the discovery of vital, rejuvenated friendships to pursue, and disappointed at how the evening had been cut short. Cocktail napkins with earnest scribbles bulged my pockets, and as Jarmila and I made our way to the room to collapse after the overload we'd experienced all day, I fully intended to keep in touch with all those wonderful old friends.

Six months on

Despite my best intentions, I have yet to email anyone from that night. I don't know why this is, exactly. It could be that the areas of my life which my old classmates once occupied have been filled with new friends and pursuits. Or perhaps that dusty jacket Murray mentioned no longer fits… I'm not sure.

And though two portions of the homecoming holy grail didn't come off nearly as well as I'd envisioned it, I did get to show my wife my old stomping grounds and reconnect with some great folks, which is the main point, really.

But the reunion – wow – it was one of those experiences that are so intense they're instantly rendered into the nostalgic portion of one's memory, and looking at the photos from that night makes me realize I haven't yet attained the proper distance from it. Instead, I can only watch Denise's photo montage and hope that at the next reunion, I will think I look as good now as, looking back, I think I looked then.

And who knows, maybe *el Presidente* is an office I can appropriate from my other alma maters as well. I'll have find another hard-working VP to shoulder the workload, of course. I'll also have to convince him or her to deliver the speech to spare me the stress of public speaking…

Hmm.

Come to think of it, perhaps I should just forget my political aspirations, count myself lucky for staging one successful coup in this lifetime, and re-brand myself as a Reunion Planning Consultant.

Surely there's more money in that than in email writing.

It's Those Foreigners
Podcasts
2005-2008

Foreigner mojo
Germany, 2005

One of my best buddies during grad school was a Swedish kid named Bjorn. Equal parts funny and smart, Bjorn was a popular figure on campus, and I was always impressed with how people were drawn to him; he always seemed to be the center of attention, and he always seemed to be dating the best-looking girls.

Knowing him as well as I did, I never questioned his popularity – he was a great guy and it was natural that he should be well-liked. But one particular evening when we met in our favorite pub, I came to realize that Bjorn had something extra going for him – some intangible quality that made him inherently more interesting to people – he had the Foreigner Mojo.

The scene that really helped me understand the dynamic was this: I walked into a crowded bar and saw Bjorn surrounded by a group of four sorority girls. Hot damn, I thought, and worked my way over. Seeing me approach, Bjorn interrupted his story to introduce me. And to a girl, they gave me the iciest reception they could muster before closing ranks and turning the charm back in Bjorn's direction. Seeing my puzzlement, Bjorn just shrugged, resumed his story, and left me to my own devices, during which time I slunk to the bar and tried to figure out his secret.

In the 10 years since then, most of which I've spent in Europe, I have – to varying degrees – experienced the same type of unexpected goodwill associated with being an expat that Bjorn enjoyed, and what follows are a few situations that upon reflection I can only attribute to Foreigner Mojo.

The first situation occurred on the campus of the Czech Agriculture University after Jarmila and I had been dating for awhile. One day I was picking her up from her campus office and her supervisor happened to be there. It was the first time that we had ever met and while not exactly ingratiating, the professor was very deferential even though I was just 28, and he was in his 50s. At any rate, after exchanging pleasantries, the good doctor excused himself and Jarmila began to collect her things. We were about to leave her office when Jarmila's supervisor returned, carrying a set of tall beer glasses which he presented to me with great ceremony. The glasses were beautiful, each decorated with the Czech Agriculture University logo, and I felt terribly awkward accepting them – I mean, what had I done to deserve them other than being American?

The second experience requires some background: In the Czech Republic (indeed, in most European countries), private language lessons are a common way for expats to earn money. As it happened, one of my private students had a brother who played guitar in a jazz/funk band; my student told me that the band was very good and that I should go see them play sometime. Fine. So when an out-of-town friend came to visit, we turned up to a scheduled show and were about to buy our tickets when the guitar-playing brother suddenly appeared and said no, no, no we don't have to pay. Surprised but grateful, we thanked him profusely, but he just kinda waved us off. He led us inside and up to the bar, where we overheard him tell the barman that we were his personal guests and that we were not to pay for any of our drinks. Dumbfounded, my friend and I could only giggle at our good fortune, but it wasn't over. The guitarist led us to a table filled with the band's friends, half of which were women interested in practicing their English with us. The evening was fantastic, didn't cost us a penny, and oh yeah, the music was good, too.

Later that year, Jarmila introduced me to a Czech woman who worked for Radio Free Europe/Radio Liberty, an American organization that broadcasts uncensored news into most of the former Soviet countries. Anyway, this lady was ultimately able to arrange a tour – given by the director himself – of the whole broadcasting facility. For those of you who have been to Prague, Radio Free Europe is housed in the boxy socialist building at the top of Wenceslas Square. If you're still having problems placing it, it's the one next to the National Museum. At any rate, the building itself was, during Soviet occupation, the parliament building and as befitting such a structure, is not only imperial inside, it is also afforded with fantastic panoramas of the Prague Castle. It was an amazing visit, was completely and totally undeserved, and I enjoyed every minute of it.

The capper to these Foreigner Mojo episodes took place during the 2006 National Football League playoffs. Being a native of Western Pennsylvania, the Pittsburgh Steelers have been my team for years, and that they were playing so well in the playoffs was of course thrilling. However, being in Germany, I had no way to watch the games on television – or so I thought.

As it turned out, a kid I sometimes play basketball with gave me the email address of a man named Jan who was supposed to have Sky Sports, an English sporting channel that was showing the games. So I wrote Jan a letter asking if it was possible to watch the games and he said sure, you can watch it at my apartment if you'd like – I'm not going to be there <pause for effect>. So here's this guy I had never met before offering to let me watch a football game in his flat while he wasn't even there. Awkward or not, we still took him up on the

offer and when we got there were stunned to discover that he had a gigantic plasma television with surround sound to boot! It was simply beautiful watching the Steelers thrash the Broncos, and the only explanation that I can think of for a stranger letting me into his home is another healthy dose of that Foreigner Mojo.

But what if...
Germany, 2005

I don't know how or why we let it happen, but last night we had a visit from a life insurance saleswoman.

She must have weighed 300 pounds easy, and was as intense a woman as I've come across. No friend of the soft-sell, Frau Elke stayed with us for over two hours, often stooping to the worst-case scenario pitch.

In response to any of our reservations, however slight, Frau Elke would put things into perspective for us:

"But Frau Curtiss, what happens if your husband pokes his eye out? How will he be able to write if he's blind? Who will pay for his glass eye? Who will do the shopping?"

Or:

"But Herr Curtiss, what happens if you both get into a car accident and have to have your legs removed? Who will pay for your wheelchairs? How will your wife do research with no legs?"

Finally, after entertaining thoughts of the nastier side of life, I said, "Ok, ok, enough with the worst-case scenarios."

"But Herr Curtiss," she replied, "I'm serious. What happens if you break your hands, for example. How will you write?"

Oh, she was relentless.

I was proud that I listened to her the whole time, but then remembered I didn't actually manage it: when she was talking her nonsense, I was mentally picturing positive things happening so she didn't get her dirty negativity into our chakras.

Ok, ok, I don't know the first thing about chakras.

But I do believe that speaking and thinking about negativity breeds negativity, just as speaking and thinking positive thoughts breeds positivity.

As I wrote that last paragraph, I thought of a perfect comeback to the saleswoman's many terrible scenarios: "But Frau Elke, what happens if you break our stool and fall on your healthy butt? Are you insured for that?"

But come to think of it, she probably was.

Paranoid? Who, me?
Germany, 2005

My preferred Sunday routine is simple, really: it consists of coffee, *The Economist* and brunch with Jarmila.

Last Sunday we were on the third leg of this triad and I was feeling good. The sun was shining and the fresh bread I'd bought at the bakery was almost too warm to eat.

And then the doorbell buzzed.

I made no move to get up, so Jarmila answered the intercom. She spoke German to someone and then I saw her put on her shoes.

"Where are you going," I asked with mild surprise.

"Someone is taking a survey. I couldn't say no to him so I'm going downstairs."

I blinked. "We're eating."

She shrugged her shoulders. "I couldn't say no."

"But you're not bringing them in, right?"

"I'll just go down and see what he wants."

"Hmph."

I'm normally not a grumpus when it comes to such things, but I had just read an article in *The Economist* about identity theft.

It seems that more than 10 million (!) people have problems with it every year, and two big personal data firms recently had major breaches of security during which, among many other details, their clients' social security numbers were leaked. Hundreds of thousands of the people who had been compromised had to take precautions against the suddenly huge problem they faced.

Down the stairs went Jarmila, leaving me to scarf my bread alone before I got the idea that we were alone in the building. There are just three apartments in the old villa we live in, and I knew our neighbors weren't there. What if the man thumped her?

I hustled out and eavesdropped from atop the stairwell.

I couldn't hear their words, but everything seemed fine and, relaxing, I started walking back to the apartment. Then I heard them coming up the stairs. I returned and leaned over the rail and there they were, one flight below.

"Why are you bringing him up here," I demanded in English, banking on the fellow not understanding my words.

"It's a survey for the UN," said Jarmila, somewhat taken aback by my aggressive paranoia.

"Why not do it out here, on these chairs?" (We have a couple of decorative chairs on the landing). She suggested this to him in German.

"But I need a tabletop for the computer," he said in German.

I turned on my heels and said, "I don't want him in our flat."

To myself I said, "I can't believe this is happening."

My paranoia was churning – I remembered the recent news article about the Iraqi man living here in our provincial town of Halle. He was wanted by the police and the army because he knifed a man and a woman.

We all came into the apartment, Jarmila trying not to look at me, and took off our shoes. The man was in his late 50s and had brought a pair of slippers with him. He stood up after putting them on and said to me in German, "I'm sorry. I don't want to cause a problem."

"Ok," I said gruffly.

I wasn't being a very good host.

Jarmila asked him if he wanted to have some tea and, disgusted, I went into the living room and parked on the couch with a couple of mundane tasks. I eyed the man suspiciously as he came into the room and set up his notebook computer on our dining room table.

Jarmila came in with the tea and they sat down to work. I read the identity theft article again, then listened intently to the questions he was asking.

Some foreign organization now has the following information about us:

Names
Ages
Address
Education
Nationality
Marital status (how long together?)
Employment history
Renting or buying
Where we plan on moving next
Which language is spoken at home?
Do we plan on having children?
Can we be happy without children?
When did we arrive in Germany?
Who cooks?
Who does the dishes?
Who does the shopping?
The chores?
Pays the bills?
How often do we argue?
How often do we argue about money?

How often do we discuss decisions?
How satisfied are we with our home life?
And so on.

This went on for an hour and a half. By the end, I had calmed down and realized there was no reason to be meanly paranoid.

But still, I didn't like that Jarmila let a stranger into the house – I thought her momma had taught her better than that.

We talked after the man left because I wanted to know what she had been thinking. She said that after conducting her own scientific survey last year in which she spoke to dozens of farmers for hours at a time, she felt obliged to help out other people's surveys.

It's a karma thing, she was implying, and just didn't agree with me about the dangers of an organization having so much information about you.

Later that evening as she was preparing for the work week, she asked me where her wallet was.

"That surveyor took it, I bet," I said.

"Stop it. Haven't you seen it? It was by the door the last time I saw it…"

"I knew it was a mistake letting that guy in our apartment," I said.

The wallet wasn't by the door. We stood in the hallway, facing each other.

"You really don't know where it is," Jarmila asked, looking troubled.

"No, I haven't seen it," I said.

Then came her epiphany – "Oh, you know what? It's in my jacket pocket," she said, and happily fished it out from the coat rack.

And like a freak, I was half-disappointed it was there.

You don't need it
Germany, 2005

Last November I went to the dentist in our building with symptoms very similar to what one feels when chewing on a bit of aluminum foil.

"Oh, that tooth has to come out," said my dentist, in German.

I didn't doubt it, but I still asked why.

"Blah blah blah," she replied as I struggled to understand her. And then, "Very expensive and painful."

Well, that sounded like something to avoid. But I wanted to keep my tooth, y'know?

When I told her I wanted to keep my tooth, she stood and walked over to a poster of a refrigerator-sized human tooth and showed me how much of my last molar was gone. It seemed only the salad crisper section remained.

"The root is in danger," she said.

"Please, just fill it," I said.

She shook her head at me and said a lot of stuff I didn't understand, but the gist was, "I'll fill it, but you'll probably be back in a day or two and we'll have to pull it anyways…"

"Please, just fill it," I repeated.

She filled it, and for five months I had no problems.

Until her stupid filling came out.

I made another appointment.

"Oh, it's that same tooth, isn't it, Herr Curtiss?"

"The tooth is fine. It's your filling that's coming out," I replied in the sentence I'd practiced ten times in front of the door.

"Hmph," she said, and sat me down.

Of course it was stupid of me to anger someone who's got license to jab me in the mouth with sharp objects, but there you go.

She asked me whether she could drill without Novocain.

"What!?" I asked. "Why?"

"It's just the filling. Not your tooth."

I remembered how strange it is recovering from a numb mouth, and reluctantly said ok.

So she drilled.

And drilled.

And then it suddenly wasn't the filling anymore. I writhed around, almost scattering her tray of instruments.

"Oh, did that hurt, Herr Curtiss" she asked.

> So she drilled. And drilled. And then it suddenly wasn't the filling anymore.

No smartass, I thought, *it felt good*.

"Well, Herr Curtiss. The hole is bigger. That tooth should come out. Blah blah blah."

"How big is my hole," I asked.

I guess that's a funny question in German too, because she giggled and then went over to her wall chart again.

Blah blah blah, she said.

All I caught was that a root canal was very expensive and painful, and that I didn't need that last molar anyways.

But I wasn't really listening.

"Please, just fill it," I repeated.

"But Herr Curtiss, blah blah blah… and with private insurance it will be very expensive."

"Money isn't a problem. I want to keep my tooth."

She harangued me further, and finally, I don't know why, I just relented. It was the very last one, after all. And I don't eat much meat anyways.

"Ok, take it," I finally said.

And boy did she light up! It was like Christmas morning for her, the little sickie.

She gave me the shot of Novocain I should have had in the first place, wrestled the tooth out, and stole it away. It was surprisingly quick and simple.

Afterwards, as she was hustling me out of the office, I asked if I could have my tooth. She seemed a bit disappointed as she put it in a little baggie for me – there was still blood on it.

We had a party that night and after I was half-drunk I broke out the tooth as a party favor. Strangely, though, I seemed to be the only one laughing.

Let's have a ball
Germany, 2005

Many of the goings on in rural areas are just not my cup of tea. For example, while I very much enjoy looking at farm animals, I have little desire to touch them, to ride them, to smell them, to clean up after them, or to listen to them while I'm trying to sleep. Heck, I even have just a slim, bordering on negligible, desire to eat them.

Thus, when our Czech friends invite us over because, as they say, "We kill pig," I always steer us clear. (We did drop by once – on accident – during such a spectacle, and lemme tellya, seeing sausage being made that one time was enough for me in this lifetime. Possibly next.)

Anyway, it was in this spirit – this snobbery of rurality I suppose – that I approached a visit to my wife's home village of Zdeslav last year. We were going there for a long weekend, and as Jarmila mentioned while packing, the annual Fireman's

Ball was to take place on Saturday night in the village pub.

I had known for awhile that dancing balls are an important tradition in the Czech Republic. While we were at the Czech Agriculture University, Jarmila even dragged me along to one. Made me wear a tie and trip the lights fandango to waltzes and other such dances for an evening before I started to step on her feet, not really intentionally, but neither regretfully.

Outgoing Czech high school seniors also have Balls, and instead of the student-only affairs that Proms are in the U.S., the Czechs invite the whole family along to celebrate. We missed our Czech nieces' Graduation Balls, much to Jarmila's regret (and my relief) and I thought that was the end of the Threat of the Balls.

Alas, I knew as soon as she mentioned the Zdeslav Ball that we were going. The usual excuse of being elsewhere was nullified. Instead, the lack of interest on my part was outweighed by the pull of the whole family planning on attending, the possibility of Jarmila's long-lost friends being there, and the fact that once we arrived in Zdeslav, the Ball was THE topic of conversation.

The whole village would be there, they said. Live music. Cutting down the May tree. A chance to win *Tombola,* which is a type of lottery where the villagers donate an item to a pool and then the firemen sell chances to win the stuff.

In short, it was to be a proper Czech hoedown.

Saturday night then, along toward 8 or so, people started converging on the pub. Jarmila had convinced me to bring along a nice shirt and khakis, and she was going to wear a dress. But everyone we saw were wearing jeans, and I started lobbying for Jarmila to dress down a bit, maybe wear jeans as well.

Which was a mistake.

"Jim doesn't want me to wear a dress," she tattled to her mom.

Mom's disbelief was palpable.

"What?! Why not?! It's The Ball! Everyone will be there! What's wrong with a dress?! *I'm* wearing a dress!"

The tension I created was enough for me to drop the matter. We would dress for our respective parts: Jarmila would be the Belle of the Ball, and I would be her American husband escort.

I have been to the pub for lesser events, you see, and it is always the same. I am the curiosity of the village, because Americans in Zdeslav are about as common as muscle cars or pet therapists.

Now, my sociable self enjoys being the center of all this attention, but my introverted self agonizes over it and so I slinked away for a pre-party beer while the makeup was being applied. I was debating the merits of a second when Jarmila emerged. She of course looked wonderful, and I felt sorry to have tried to talk her into dressing down. We walked up the street to the pub.

The pub in Zdeslav, called the Tiger, has seen better days. Though not rundown exactly, even I can recognize that it needs a good scrubbing. But this *was* the Firemen's Ball, so everyone ignored the surroundings. We weren't inside the crowded hall for five minutes before the village boy named Wenceslas (Vaclav for short) collared me. I had met him once before, on Easter, the week after he had hacked up his right forearm and hand in some sort of chain saw accident. The wounds had been unbandaged and angry-looking when we shook, but his right was still the hand he extended to shake with.

Back to the ball: drunk as hell, never having been beyond the biggest hill in sight, and as honest and strange as the day is long, Vaclav insisted we do a shot of rum together. Got in my face in an innocent drunk way until I relented. Wouldn't hear my objections to the rum. Wanted to talk at me

"The whole village will be there! Live music! Cutting down the May tree!"

even though I couldn't understand the bulk of his slurred Czech. Jarmila finally came to the rescue and dragged me to the dance floor, but it only lasted for awhile. Soon after we sat down, Vaclav came over and made a big show about asking Jarmila to dance.

One does not turn down dance requests at the Zdeslav Firemen's Ball, so off Jarmila went to politely endure the reminisces of her childhood buddy with the drunken breath.

After their dance, Vaclav dragged a reluctant Jarmila up to the bar, so I followed after. When I got there, she was objecting to the insisted-upon shot and I was volunteered as a replacement. But I was feeling tough and protective, so I declined the drink.

"Then dance with my wife," said Vaclav.

"I don't want to dance," I said.

"Jim can't dance," Jarmila added.

"Well," said Vaclav, "you can either dance with my wife or do a shot of rum with me."

"Where's your wife," I asked.

"That's her over there." He pointed her out. Short. Black hair. 230 pounds easy.

I looked back at him. "I'll do the shot."

Jarmila giggled and Wenceslas looked at me for a moment wondering whether to be offended. Then his thirst overcame him.

Jarmila was dragged somewhere by someone else, and after we did the shot, I agreed to do another and listened to Wenceslas talk. He wasn't very interested in what I had to say, so no problem with my language. Instead, he just seemed happy to tell me about his childhood time spent with Jarmila. From what I gathered, she was quite the athlete. Best soccer player in the village when she was young.

After a bit, I extricated myself and found Jarmila selling tickets for the *Tombola*. They'd set the price too low for the tickets and people had bought them all up before I'd gotten there, so I had no chance at the jar of olives, the shot glasses, or the large ceramic beer jar.

The big winner of the *Tombola* was an older couple who won a deer.

Not a pet deer, but a dead, frozen deer. It was without head and hooves, and was folded up to fit into a big banana box.

And they *loved* it.

As did the people who won the cord of wood.

And the shot glasses.

And yes, even the olives.

Which made me realize something: there are simple joys to be found in Zdeslav that I should perhaps stop resisting.

Football
Germany, 2006

Being an American expat in Central Europe is easier, I suspect, than being an expat from say, Korea or Venezuela. For while Koreans and Venezuelans themselves may be most welcome and treated with hospitality in their adopted countries, it is unlikely that they would be able to come across the same amount of cultural influences from their respective homelands as would an American.

To test this hypothesis, I took a walk through my hometown of Halle, Germany last weekend with an eye out for the English language and a side order of American

influence. My stroll yielded the following results:

- Up the street from a nearby (American) English language school is the bistro "American Food", which serves a selection of hot dogs, hamburgers, French fries and ice cream.
- Big Daddy's USA Sportwear, a hip-hop/sporting apparel store.
- There are three skateboard shops within a five minute walk.
- We have a McDonald's AND a Burger King.
- There is a Subway sandwich shop on the market square.
- There are several upscale bowling alleys around town.
- There are various newsstands which sell National Geographic, Rolling Stone, and many other English language periodicals.

And lastly, if my taste buds ever get a real hankering for American fare, I can shop in the upscale supermarket on the Market square. A little investigation revealed this partial list of yummies: Newman's Own salad dressing, Hellman's Real Mayonnaise, Strawberry Fluff, Peter Pan and Snicker's peanut butters, respectively, Heinz tomato soup, Hidden Valley Ranch dressing, Frank's Red Hot Sauce, Bisquik, maple syrup, Doritos, more than a few types of barbecue sauces, and, praise be, original Oreo cookies.

As far as entertainment goes, around the corner from our flat is the local video rental store, which has an ample and ever-growing supply of the latest Hollywood releases on DVD. We may be two months behind the release dates, but they get here eventually.

Television is another area in which the American influence is noticeable, and not always for the good. Among the bright spots for me are Hogan's Heroes re-runs (in

Germany, mind you!) which I watch, and Desperate Housewives, which I do not. These are all dubbed in German, by the way. All German television is, which I find a bit sad. Because when I was in Copenhagen awhile back, I noticed that Danish television showed the English language version – with subtitles – of the Discovery Channel, the History Channel, National Geographic and even the Cartoon Network (How better to teach kids a foreign language than with cartoons?).

So as you can see, being an American expat in Halle isn't the most difficult of things, and what I'm about to say shouldn't be considered complaining.

It's just that life here would be *so much better* if only American sports were shown on television. American sports aren't shown here because there are just too many other fascinating sporting events going on all the time: the Eurosport channel frequently devotes prime time to ski jumping, biathlon, snooker, horse jumping and other equally gripping sports.

DSF, the very German version of ESPN, occasionally devotes time to soccer matches, which for lack of an option I have come to grudgingly enjoy, but otherwise they show random activities like poker, darts or curling.

Now, I *could* shell out 150 Euro for a contract, another 100 for the equipment, and then 60 Euro per month thereafter for the premium satellite TV packages that include North American sports, but there we run into problems with length of contract. That is, if we leave the country before the 3-year contract finishes, we would be obliged to pay it anyway, which could end up gouging us for more than 700 Euro if we bolt early.

<Sigh>

So with these options, I have to very much rely upon the finicky Internet to keep up to speed. Which works for the most part:

> It's just that life here would be *so much better* if only American sports were shown on television.

If I want to listen to NFL games, for example, there are several outlets, including nfl.com, which has live broadcasts as well as some really neat game ticker graphics.

But while I have been able to find many video highlight shows - after the fact - for my favorite ball games, live broadcasting seems to be a thing of the future.

My vote for the best innovation of the year goes out to the iTunes people, who were clever enough to come up what they call "Bowl Blasts." Essentially highlight reels of the Bowl Championship Series games, bowl blasts are downloadable for 1.99 each and run between 15 and 25 minutes. And since I couldn't see any of the live action, believe me, they're worth it.

But stop the data stream! I recently learned that - praise be to the Terrible and Benevolent God of Football Majesty - a pub in town will be showing the Super Bowl this weekend. And with my hometown Steelers playing, what could be finer?

I suppose the answer to that is a kickoff time earlier than 1 in the morning.

Weekend adventure
Germany, 2006

A whole weekend of Springtime freedom stretched in front of me. The chestnut trees were blooming, there was less and less need to heat, and the days stretched until 20:00.

Jarmila had a big presentation in England, for which she had to leave at 04:30 Friday morning (poor kid) and after I finished up my own work on Friday, I packed and was off.

I'd originally planned to travel down to the Thuringia Wald in search of two things: the village where a Christian mystic named Meister Eckhart was born, and the perfect Thuringia Bratwurst. Alas, the distance – six hours by VW Golf – finally dissuaded me. I only had two days, after all.

Plan B was the much closer Harz National Park, two hours away and very near the Brocken, the highest peak in the Harz mountain range.

After an idyllic alpine drive, I arrived at the huge parking lot from which most people hike the two hours up the Brocken. But the rain had decided to turn to snow and I found that admiring the Burg was best done from behind the wiper blades.

Which was impressive, but it was also getting along towards dinnertime, so I headed out of the park and down to Bad Harzburg.

A spa town, Bad Harzburg was understandably peaceful, and even had a stream running through the pedestrian area. After parking, I walked the streets until I spotted what must have been the best room in town – it was on the top floor of an old villa, and had a huge balcony that overlooked the highest mountain around, the Burgberg.

I rang the hotel's doorbell marked for guests and after a few moments an attractive older lady with short red hair and high beams answered.

I asked for a room, specifically the room with that balcony, and luckily it was unoccupied. As she led me upstairs, the woman complimented and then inquired about my pidgin German, and this led to a long conversation about my background and what had brought me to Europe in the first place. It was great practicing my German, and she seemed genuinely interested. My being the only guest for the night likely also afforded her the time.

Next morning, as I helped myself to the prodigious breakfast buffet, we traded opinions on the Pope's funeral, Prince Charles and Camilla's wedding, Bush and Cheney, and then ultimately the weather.

It was still sleeting, and the coffee hadn't overpowered my mild hangover nearly enough to climb the mountain I had stared at from my balcony.

So I paid my hostess, Heidi – I insisted she not call me Herr Curtiss, and in return she insisted I use her first name – and hit the road. It was 10:00 on a Saturday and I had nowhere to go but home.

I took the most direct secondary road I could find and it led me through all sorts of quaint towns, including one that had a dreamy beer store with at least 50 varieties I'd never heard of. I bought as many as I could carry, and later took notes on their respective qualities – all done in the name of research, mind you.

The most remarkable town along the way though, was Quedlingberg. The medieval old town is all narrow, cobbled streets, carved timber store fronts that make you wonder about the lousy place that you're living in, and in the center of it all is an imposing castle fortress that UNESCO decided to protect.

Despite the cold, it was a rewarding two-hour jaunt and I was on my way back to the car when a sign enticed me: coffee and chocolate cake for Euro 1.50.

Well, just yum.

I walked in and ordered a cappuccino and cake from the graying waiter/owner, but somehow flubbed my German grammar. Recognizing me as an English speaker, he seized on the chance to *Englisch sprechen* – which is cool, it makes my life easier – and then smugly repeated my order back to me in English.

He bustled off and as I sat looking out the front window, a tour vehicle shaped as a train, with separate cars even, passed by. It was full of older people, and I returned their good-humored smiles and waves.

The waiter eventually brought my cappuccino and cake and both looked artistically and deliciously prepared.

"Enjoy it," he said.

I thanked him and thought, *How could I not?*

And then I spooned what I thought was unrefined sugar but was actually parmesan cheese into my cappuccino.

I tried to spoon out the floaters and choke it down, but no way. I had to ask for another cup. I offered to pay extra, but the waiter wouldn't hear anything of it.

I think he understood full well that the mileage he'd get out of the story of the stupid American was worth much more than the price of a replacement cup.

Notes on a trip to America
Germany, 2006

For international travelers, going through immigration at JFK is very similar to what the first day of army boot camp must be like – one is alternately yelled at or ignored, then herded through an oppressive room only to be belittled by the border official until that precious passport stamp is begrudgingly granted. Welcome to America. But lucky for us, this year we passed through the immigration facility at Newark International Airport, which to our surprise is MUCH more welcoming than that of JFK. A bright, airy space awaited us there as we made our way to the waiting area. Then, once in front of a U.S. border guard, we were smiled at and made to feel at ease. In fact, after the transaction was completed, the guard even gave me a warm "Welcome home." Such simple things, but they made a huge difference. Whereas we normally complain about the JFK immigration experience for a good week after we pass through it, this time it was all puppy dogs and ice cream.

- Americans are nothing if not an open people. Whereas in Germany, most people employed in the service sector maintain a professional distance between themselves and the customer, here in America, that distance is drastically reduced. Three experiences illustrate my point:

1. At the drugstore, the cashier told us that her purse had been stolen, that she was pregnant, and that she had three kids.

2. At the liquor store, the clerk's explanation of why he didn't have the bottle of wine that we wanted spiraled into how the State of Pennsylvania is the single largest buyer of wine and spirits in the world. He then told us that Pennsylvania purchases over 1.5 billion dollars worth of liquor each year. He went on to speculate that a recent lawmaker's raise that they had voted themselves had been skimmed off of this money in the form of the 6% sales tax that is slapped on all sales (except food) in the state. He would have continued, but there were four people in line behind us.

3. While assisting dad on a service call last Tuesday, I was introduced to a man who works in the boiler room of a hospital – the boiler room being where all the water issues are dealt with (very hot in those places). Anyway, within three minutes of our introduction the man told me that he once had a very big problem with alcohol,

that this problem made him knock around his wife from time to time, but that since he found his savior in Jesus, he had straightened out and now can only think of how wonderful his wife is and how he cannot wait for his work days to end so that he can go home and spend time with her and his new little baby. Then he broke out the pictures.

- Though many European cars are impressive in their own way, most American cars – especially muscle cars – are simply much cooler. One may argue that Italian sports cars are the finest in the world, but those cars are unaffordable for the average person. Here in the States, one can purchase an old Mustang, Corvette, Thunderbird or GTO and be King of The Road for far less than a new car costs.

- Hidden calories are everywhere here. At a coffee shop the other day, hoping for a low-calorie snack, I ordered a pretzel and was surprised after biting it to discover that it was filled with cream cheese. There goes my diet.

The mob
Germany, 2005

During last-minute preparations for my birthday party, I heard a ruckus from the street below and went to the window to investigate. It was 7 p.m.

Looking through the window of our rotunda, I could see that my strange neighbors – all nine of the children are cut from an overweight, nearsighted, not-very-bright stock – had congregated on the street in front of their dilapidated first-floor balcony. There was much yelling and gesturing – I couldn't help being reminded of a troop of

Big action on Lafontainestrasse Halle, 2005

agitated primates – and several of them were yelling at someone out of my field of vision.

I moved to the other side of our aerie and looked down. Lying on the sidewalk was a boy of about 15. His shoes were off, and he was surrounded by a group of 10 kids who were yelling and gesturing back at my neighbors.

About a minute later, the first police car showed up, parking on the sidewalk between the two groups. The yelling died down a bit and I ran to get the camera and a beer.

Over the course of the next five minutes, four more police cars showed up, with none other than the Chief of Police emerging from the last car. Everyone seemed suitably impressed, and the mood turned cooperative. The ambulance showed up shortly thereafter.

Interviews between the principals ensued, and from what I overheard from two floors up, the youth lying on the ground had spray-painted the neighbors' door. One of the family's boys had caught him in the act, chased him down, and thrashed him.

Which, though I am against violence, seemed proper to me. Because even though most of the neighbor family are strangies, they are fundamentally nice strangies, and I hate senseless persecution of people just because they're odd.

Anyway, the drama concluded when the boys who had fought reluctantly shook hands. I suppose it was hoped that this would help deter future problems, but two days later one of the neighbor boys showed me how all of the cables on his bicycle had been cut while he was at school.

"But that's all right," he said. "We'll get them back."

A trip to Naples and Amalfi
Germany, 2006

Day 1

We live here with more passion," said Nicolas, the adult son of our Italian host Giovanna and her English husband Albert. It was Sunday morning and we had just arrived at their bed and breakfast in the Naples suburb of Posillipo.

"The soil in Campania is so fertile," he continued, "that it fills the foods grown here with extra flavor, extra..." he searched for the correct word, but couldn't find it.

"You know what I mean, don't you," he asked, giving me a double-handed, shrugged shoulders gesture.

It is often said that Italians punctuate their speech with their hands, but in Naples I observed that they actually punctuate their speech with the entire upper body. Shoulders shrugs, head movements and hand gestures all complement their words, as if the English language is simply not adequate to convey the richness of their ideas.

Anyways, I wasn't exactly sure what Nicolas meant, but I still agreed with him. Pleased at our mutual understanding, he placed his hand on my shoulder.

"Now you simply must try this," he said, leading us into the kitchen. He rummaged through the refrigerator and took out a plate of freshly caught shrimp, bright red and with all their appendages. He peeled two

for Jarmila and me as he explained that Mount Vesuvius not only makes the soil extremely fertile, but the sea more nutrient-rich as well.

He placed the uncooked shrimp on a plate, followed by a touch of olive oil, salt, and fresh pepper. The delicacy of the flavors were immediately recognizable, and Nicolas loved that we appreciated it.

We retired to our room to freshen up and when we returned, Giovanna, who we later learned had appeared on American cooking shows, had prepared a meal for us: bruschetta smothered with olive oil, fresh basil, tomatoes, mozzarella and garlic. Wine. Cappuccino. Fresh orange juice. Sweets. Fruits.

It was simply divine, and with apologies to my mother and mother-in-law, it was the best food I've eaten in years. Nicolas was right about the flavors of the food – the tomatoes were bursting with ripeness, the mozzarella was made from buffalo milk and so had an extra dash of... *something*, and the olive oil was more flavorful than any I'd ever had.

We had stumbled into a gourmet's kitchen, and for the rest of our stay enjoyed not only lovely food, but Nicolas would later break out his stock of fine white wine from the cellar. It was stored in a 10 liter jug which he lovingly poured into smaller jugs, bottles and a carafe which he shared with us on our last night as we spoke about life.

And though I realize I'm raving about the yummies, it was only a small fraction of the hospitality that we enjoyed with that family. They were extremely open, friendly, funny, and helpful, which added to our overall sense of well-being.

Giovanna even spent two afternoons with us, showing us places in Naples that non-natives rarely venture to, for which we are extremely grateful.

If you ever plan a trip to Naples, do your-self a favor and try to arrange accommoda-tion at www.posillipodream.it.

And please, tell them Jim and Jarmila said hello.

Day 2

While giving us very useful advice on what to do and see in Naples, Nicolas scribbled so much information on our map that it was rendered almost unusable. An idea would come to him and somewhere on the map he'd write a name, draw an arrow, circle an area, list what kind of fish to eat or what kind of wine to avoid, which muse-ums were worthwhile... In short, he was an overflowing fountain of information, and with the options presented to us, we felt badly we had only two days in Naples.

One of the pieces of advice that we did manage to take was to visit the island of Procida, visible from Giovanna's spacious and elegant balcony. We were advised that the island, while not the most spectacular in terms of scenery, had resisted the onslaught of tourism and retained its age-old tradition of fishermen leaving every morning and returning with their catch in the evening. There was also a lovely abbey to visit.

To get to Procida, we first took the slow-est train in the history of locomotion from Naples to the end station Pouzoulli, and then hoofed it down to the harbor. When we arrived, a huge ferry was being loaded with vans and trucks. We approached the harried head honcho and asked if we could take his boat out to Procida.

"No! No space," he barked, shooing us out of the way of an onloading semi-truck.

Disconcerted, we lingered around for a few moments before deciding to approach someone else. The second man welcomed us aboard and asked for our tickets. We didn't have any. He pointed to the ticket kiosk about a kilometer away and then looked at his watch. We'd never make it.

He talked to the head honcho, who looked us over and then waved us aboard. Con-fused, we looked at the ticket-taker, who waved us past. Score one for the stupid tourists - we got a free boat ride!

The most telling point regarding the lack of tourists on Procida came when we got off the ferry in its harbor. We were the only two to disembark, and the head honcho yelled at us in a commanding voice – "Hey, this is Procida, not Ischia!"

"*Si*," we yelled back. Seems we were in the right place if we wanted to avoid the noisy crowds.

Unfortunately, it was a bit too quiet. All the stores lining the harbor were closed for siesta, so we headed to the beach and over-paid for some beach chairs on the seaside. I pushed the deal through because I didn't want to sit on the sand with just one towel between us, and the price we paid – €16 for two hours – still gets Jarmilka fired up.

We rested on the beach for a couple hours and then headed back to the harbor to rent a scooter. It was such a simple affair – no security deposit, no credit card number – just my driver's license number and the cash up front. The woman asked €25 for two hours, but I gave her the silent treat-ment for a moment and she countered with €20. (A very cool thing about Italy – most prices are open to negotiation.)

Boom, we had wheels.

We headed up the cobbled streets and away from the harbor, wrong-turning our way through historic districts hundreds of years old, children running in front of us, old men and women watching the goings-on from their stoops beside the road, stray dogs, dented cars, girls dressed up for a stroll, all in the late-afternoon heat of southern Italy.

The Abbey of San Michel, the archangel, lies at the top of a very steep, two-sided cliff overlooking the sea. And though our scooter was relatively powerful, it almost petered out when faced with the last climb (Jarmila nearly had to bail off).

We ignored the no entrance sign (only with a permit could motor vehicles enter) and were rewarded with a trip into the past. The Abbey, which dates from 1026, has been continuously inhabited since then, a fact illustrated by the trappings of both antiquity and modernity - the buildings are roughly hewn but wondrous, and the cobbled streets are dotted with cars and scooters. A woman carrying a basket of laundry ambled by, chatting away on a mobile phone. There were satellite dishes on balconies and on the sides of buildings.

We found an overlook and sparred over who would get to take photos, and then we had to hustle to get the 20:30 ferry back to the mainland.

The sunset was divine, and once we arrived back at Giovanna's, Nicolas broke out his coveted white wine and we enjoyed a lovely evening of conversation on the terrace overlooking Naples' islands.

Day 3

"She is so beautiful, she needs three men!"

This is what a Naples dress shop owner said about Jarmila as we browsed through his wares.

I wasn't present when he said it, else I would've said this one man is more than she can handle, or something similarly macho.

But the ladies in that store simply fawned over Jarmila, bringing dress after dress for her to try on. She even modeled dresses that she herself didn't like because the ladies just wanted to see how she looked in them – their Barbie doll brought to life.

The store was one that Giovanna frequents, and as a matter of logistics Jarmila and I were accompanying her before she dropped us off at the port for the ferry ride down to Amalfi.

In the end, Jarmila bought a cool and unique dress that she'll always have as a souvenir. After the dress store, Giovanna had to run an errand so we split up and agreed to meet at the car. Ten minutes later we returned to find a Sri Lankan man waiting for us. He told us there was a problem with our car, and sure enough, there were scratches, scrapes, and large dents on the rear of Giovanna's auto.

We nervously waited – our ferry was leaving soon – until Giovanna arrived. We showed her the dents but she waved them off, saying, "Hah! Those are old. No problem!"

(Indeed, the Neapolitans are so unconcerned about their cars because fender benders there are exceedingly common. In fact, on the first day as we taxied to Giovanna's, our driver ground the front fender of his new taxi into a parked car. He cursed, but it was of such little concern that he didn't even leave a note on the car he had dented.)

At any rate, we caught the ferry with time to spare and sadly waved goodbye to our wonderful hostess and the town of Naples.

Positano, Italy

Days 4-6

Once aboard the ferry to Amalfi we were treated to a spectacular view of Mount Vesuvius lording over Naples. We stood outside snapping pictures and after a time, Naples was but a faraway city.

We eventually rounded the peninsula and headed to our destination – the Amalfi Coast.

If you are not suitably impressed by the name, don't worry. I hadn't heard of it either, but after having visited, I now know where paradise is found.

And I'm not the only one – for most of the 20th century, the gentry flocked there, movies were filmed there, and writers took up residence to soak in the beauty and the quietude.

Our ferry trip down the coast was filled with dozens of open-mouthed "Look at that's", and mere words are not capable of conveying what an absolute marvel Amalfi and Ravello are. You simply have to go there yourself.

We spent an amazing time there, saw beauty unparalleled, and if you are ever presented with the opportunity, please, *just go*.

Because it is very likely you will remember it for the rest of your life as the most beautiful place you've ever been.

State College for a month
Germany, 2005

After three weeks of running around with drunken students, disgruntled Inauguration Day protesters and various academics here at Penn State, I still hadn't found time to visit the family cabin in Elk County.

It's hard, even when you don't have an office to go to, to find a whole day free of commitments. A day you can just slip off and head for the hills. But finally, yesterday I did just that. I dropped Jarmila off at work and turned dad's gigantic Ford Expedition northwards.

It took about an hour of silent driving (something about the bleak January day made me switch off the radio) to reach the portion of State Road 150 I was looking for. Just north of Lock Haven, 150 begins to trot next to the Sinnemahoning River and between the stately, majestically rounded mountains of Central PA.

FALLING ROCK, NEXT 5 MILES warn the signs, as the road skirts blasted-out cliffs decked out for the winter in icy dreadlocks. I kept my eyes open for incoming boulders, but later realized they were probably frozen in place and wouldn't be a problem until the spring, by which time I'd be long gone, back to European living.

Around midway through my planned driving retreat, I stopped seeing other cars. At first this made me feel courageous and slightly reckless, but then it occurred to me that people were probably not driving for a reason.

But what the hell. I had a 4-wheel drive with huge tires and nothing better to do but visit my old stomping grounds.

I sallied forth. The trees were black. The snow was white. The only real color was the frigid blue of the river as it washed over the smooth frumpiness of its lower icy layers, or where it peeked around the jagged corners of the broken ice floes gathered in the river bends.

Overlooking the river at one such bend was a sturdy log cabin, built 200 yards up the hill from the water. It had a massive rear deck which must have provided a panoramic of the pine-forested, 2,000 foot-high peak across the river valley. As I sped by, I longed to have such a place.

The longing stayed with me and as I drove on I found myself feeling slightly depressed, which was odd because I'd been more upbeat lately than not.

Then the nature of my malaise dawned on me – I was *halfway through* my day-long adventure. My big day of freedom was half-over, and I was looking back with sadness at the time gone instead of looking forward with happiness at the time to come. Or even enjoying the moment that I was in.

These musings put me in mind of midway points, and I slowly realized that among all things, it is mid-way that I dislike the most.

- When I was midway through my novel, I was petrified that something might happen to me and the world would never know the book. I was also afraid that I might never muster the will to finish it.

- In the best of times I am a nervous flyer, but midway over the Atlantic, a point I pass over all too frequently, is a place that truly freaks me. It is then I begin to worry in earnest. What would happen if the plane went down in the middle of the Atlantic? How soon would the rescue teams make it there? If we survived a landing, if we were able to get out of the plane before inhaling ocean, and if we were able to wrest them from under the seats, would the puny floatation devices even work?

- It is halfway through our trips back to the States that I begin to dread the upcoming return flight and the subsequent distance from my American family and friends.

- Lastly, I am 35. Mid-life crisis, anyone?

PS: As I wandered through our rustic cabin, I finally gave up the dream that I'll ever be able to convince my wife to spend another night there. The photo of the gigantic, frozen spider on a background of moldy ceiling was just too good – I had to show her.

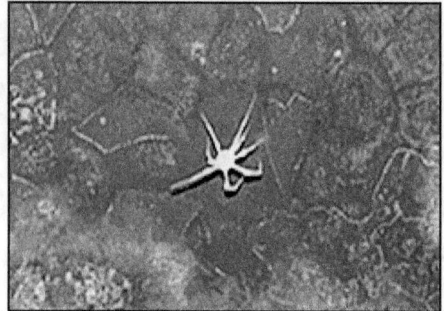

Medix Run, Pennsylvania

Urine trouble
Germany, 2005

My wife Jarmila has a number of stories that she enjoys telling about me, but I believe her favorite one is this: An international academic project she was involved with was winding down and we were at a party celebrating its successful completion. The mood was jovial and I was introduced to many people, among them the director of a prominent research institute in Prague. As he and I spoke, it came out that I had lived in Prague for a few years, and he wanted to know my overall impression of his hometown from a foreigner's point of view. The way Jarmila tells it, I looked off in a concentrated way for some moments before turning back to the director and saying: "In all my life, I've never seen as many people urinate in public as I did in Prague."

The director coughed up half his drink and both he and Jarmila looked at me slack jawed as I explained that I had spent a great deal of time walking through Prague – often up to three hours a day – and that along the route I had walked, I would normally see *at least* five people urinating in the bushes or down alleyways. And that wasn't counting the small children, who are routinely pointed business-end into the gutter by their parents no matter where the urge may strike.

Jarmila tried her best to change the subject, but I continued on because as an American, seeing people urinate in public is just a trifle scandalous. Funnily enough, the director was keen on the topic and we happily discussed scatological issues over two or three drinks.

The punch line to the story is this: two years later at a World Agricultural Economics Conference held in some faraway country, Jarmila happened to overhear the Prague director *repeating* this urine story to a group of like 10 people, most of whom – to her surprise – took up the subject. My impressions of Prague and its habits had apparently struck a nerve.

In the intervening years, I have been lucky enough to visit some of Europe's great cities, and in so doing have come to think that public toilets are among the most obviously necessary issues out there, but they are also paradoxically taboo in polite discussion. Yet the fact of the matter is that one's impression – especially a tourist's impression – of a country is based, to no small degree, on that host country's toilets.

Take Copenhagen for example. A lovely Scandinavian city in every sense of the word, in the city proper you will find *some* public toilets – for men only – but these tend to be trough affairs where, if it's crowded, you basically have to jostle your way in. But in such close quarters, if you've got stage fright or that nicely-worded but very likely unpleasant condition called shy-bladder – you'll have to wait until the coast is clear and then move in for a strategic strike.

To remain in northern Europe for the moment, in my experience the Dutch are an amazingly accommodating and – related to that – a strikingly liberal sort of people. But as an exchange student in the city of Eind-hoven a few years ago, this liberalism pushed me into uncharted territory when, for the first time, a group of us went out to the pubs in Stratumseind, Eindhoven's nightlife area. After having a few beers at one of the popular pubs, nature summoned me and I headed toward the back of the bar in search of a loo. I looked everywhere but couldn't find one, so I asked Ralf, one of the nearby Dutch students, where the toilets were. To my dismay, Ralf told me – though it seems as if it should be illegal – that most of the pubs in Stratumseind do not, in fact, provide such facilities.

Briefly dumbstruck, my growing urgency helped me recover and I asked him in an alarmed voice what I was going to do with all of the beer I'd been swallowing. Ralf just smiled and led me onto the street.

He looked left and right – and here I must confess that I briefly thought he was going to tell me to do my thing right there. In-stead, he pointed to a gray, plastic structure standing off to the side of the street but nonetheless in plain view. There was a line of men leading to it, and after pointing me in this thing's direction, Ralf returned to the pub.

Thinking that a joke was obviously being played, that pissing in plain sight of passersby was simply not done, I stood there for a few skeptical moments until I saw a man step away from the structure and zip up his pants. I tentatively walked closer, and in so doing, began to grasp the system - it was a men's urinal all right. Incredulity

The director coughed up half his drink and both he and Jarmila looked at me slack jawed.

slowly gave way to necessity, and I joined in the line and took stock of the thing's construction: shaped like an upturned Phil-ips-head screwdriver, each patron was allot-ted an open, v-shaped platform with tapered partitions on both sides and a receptacle between the legs – in this sort of exposed privacy the user was expected to do his thing.

When my turn eventually came I nerv-ously stepped onto the thing, and as I un-zipped I took a look around me, which was a silly mistake. I had been anxious enough, but the sight of people surrounding me – some of them even watching me – was simply too much to bear. I just couldn't make it happen. I gave up and rejoined the line, hoping for a better outcome at my next go. Instead, after the second fruitless at-tempt, I loitered around the urinal – draw-ing many disapproving looks – until the whole deal was vacant, and then I moved in for the kill, which I'm happy to report was relieving.

Overall, it was an embarrassingly silly first encounter with the Stratumseind uri-nals, and though each subsequent use be-came easier, by no means did I ever be-come comfortable with those exposed Dutch contraptions.

Still, Northern Europe is by no means the only region to provide inadequate toilet systems. Because when it comes down to it, *most* urban toilets – if they exist at all – are simply unpleasant. For example, in two of the world's most cosmopolitan of cities – New York City and Rome – it's ridiculously difficult to find any toilet, let alone one that the maître d', concierge or cashier will permit you to access.

On the other hand, both Paris and Berlin employ a sensible system, though it's perhaps not as widespread as it might be. Scattered around those cities' sidewalks are a smallish sort of structure that might be mistaken for a telephone booth were it not for the lack of windows. These coin-operated public bathrooms are both secure (the door locks during use) and clean (they go through an automated cleaning cycle after each use) and if you aren't too concerned about who you do your thing in front of, you can easily fit in two or three friends.

So urban toilets don't have to be all bad; indeed, one might follow the lead of the Japanese, who have developed a technologically-superior version of our western-style latrines; their versions are outfitted with built-in seat-warmers, bidets, wipers, and even air-dryers… all of which seems to take away the fun.

Interestingly, however, the Japanese aren't the only Asian country developing better and better commodes. According to the Associated Press, the Chinese capital of Beijing has, in recent years, spent some $29 million on building or renovating roughly 750 bathrooms at tourist spots around the city. It seems that the Chinese have come to grasp the idea that being a developed country also means providing proper bathrooms.

Now, all of this potty talk might seem a bit too much for the average John, but some people consider commode issues to be serious indeed. Take, for example, the World Toilet Organization, or WTO, which was founded in 2001. According to the WTO website, anyone interested in studying scatology need look no farther than the World Toilet College in Singapore. Jack Sim, president of the WTO, was quoted by news provider Agence Française de Presse as

saying the World Toilet College "…aims to train toilet cleaners to upgrade themselves to a level where he or she can take care of the whole toilet, including changing bulbs, repairing leaky taps… technical cleaning, taking away urine salt inside the toilet, etc.".

The WTO's website says the Restroom Specialist Training Course will help address the 2.6 billion people worldwide that do not have a toilet, which seems like a fine aim. WTO's website goes on to claim that "at present, there are no toilet educational institutions that address both urban and rural toilets' needs in a continuous manner."

Hence, ladies and gentlemen, I give you the World Toilet College, located within Singapore's Republic Polytechnic, which seeks to fill this gap. A full-time residential program, World Toilet College is by no means cheap. But not to worry: for those who cannot afford the $2,300 tuition fee – plus living expenses – there are options.

First, you might visit the World Toilet Summit and Expo. Then there is the Annual World Toilet Expo & Forum.

Lastly, if you aren't in a position to travel, you might try your hand at the surprisingly educational video game, Urgent!, featured on the WTO website. The game's description follows:

"Imagine the possibilities of your personal toilet layout. You design the way it looks, ensuring customers enjoy the ambience setting you provide for them. Imagine strategically positioning toilets and utilities in the toilet to be used by customers even if they are normal users, elderly or handicapped. Unlike reality, it does not take much to amend a mistake, just sell anything you don't like off, and start to build again! Learn from your mistakes and reap the profits! So what are you waiting for? Start playing!"

So I did just that, and amused myself with toilet planning issues when I should have been working. Among other challenging tasks, I was forced to choose toilet models with which to decorate my space, and in the end, as it were, my toilet featured the following products, accompanied by their original description.

1. The Ultimate Poop Sucker Toilet. Your customers will definitely be empty when they come out new. Just as their wallets will be.
2. The Standing Coffin Urinal: Fire at will and never mind that you can't aim. Everything will fall into place.
3. The Box Cup urinal: let its bigger ceramic build shield away sinful eyes.

Alas, even with such colorfully-depicted choices at my fingertips, bathroom design was more difficult than I'd bargained for. Three of my virtual customers became infected by herpes, and as the game's instructions tell you, herpes can only be transmitted when toilet conditions are "really horrible".

So perhaps I should cut all those toilet planners some slack and instead of complaining about lousy urban toilets, I should spearhead a campaign to send them to the World Toilet College in order... to freshen up.

Expatriatism
Germany, 2006

A quote from Ernest Hemingway's The Sun also Rises: "You're an expatriate. You've lost touch with the soil. Fake European standards have ruined you. You drink yourself to death. You become obsessed with sex. You spend all your time talking, not working. You're an expatriate, you see? You hang around cafés."

Life here is easy, holidays are frequent, and stress, along with polio and malaria, has been virtually eradicated.

I read this quote to illustrate what I think is a common American view of Europe – that life here is easy, holidays are frequent, and stress, along with polio and malaria, has been virtually eradicated.

Indeed, most of my friends and all of my family members believe that my expatriate lifestyle is not only exciting, but also deeply relaxing, culturally rewarding, and virtually free of the normal hassles of daily living.

To a degree, they've got a point. For example, in my professional life I can walk or bike to my classes, I do most of my editing and writing at home, and aside from my mother-in-law, I don't really have a boss. So yeah, I see what they mean.

But when it comes to one's personal life, things can be challenging for an expatriate. And with apologies to all the lucky students who go on foreign exchange programs, I'm not talking about a semester spent studying abroad. Because while these are highly beneficial and expanding in many ways, the challenge of striking out on one's own is largely taken out of the equation when one deals with two cooperating institutions that take care of housing, living permits, classes, excursions, etc. Heck, sometimes they even feed you.

Instead, the challenge I'm talking about here is day-to-day LIFE abroad. The daily grind, but with that added foreign twist.

We have friends, for example, who are also expatriates and have a year-old baby. The mother has had to maneuver through the complexities of *child care* in a foreign context for the last year and a half. Can you imagine your baby having a fever and during a hospital visit you only understand maybe ½ of what the doctor is telling you? How's that for stress?

Indeed, if you're looking for a courageous undertaking, try working your way through a foreign bureaucracy to secure a living permit.

Looking for adventure? Try finding a decent, affordable place to live in a foreign city.

But I don't mean to complain. I chose this lifestyle and I very much enjoy it. I merely want to illustrate that life can get stressful no matter where one may be.

Case in point: we are going to move from Germany to Spain, and of course both my wife and I are deeply excited about it. We've been speaking about virtually nothing else since she was offered the job there, and we are beginning to realize just how complicated a move between foreign countries is actually going to be.

A partial list of stressors that will feature heavily for us in the near future:
- Learning a new language.
- Both of us changing jobs.
- Selling our car.
- Having to vacate and paint our apartment.
- Either selling *all* of our stuff, or driving a rental van, with all our stuff in it, the roughly 2,000 miles to Seville. And then back.
- Finding an apartment in Seville.
- And lastly, we have to get our living and working permits sorted out, which spells hours and hours of sitting in shabby waiting rooms for the privilege of being condescended to by surly paper-pushers with veto power over your future.

Sigh.

All of this naturally begs the question: is it really worth it? I mean, one only undertakes such a move to improve one's lot in life, and we're fundamentally happy where we are. In the five years that we've lived here in D-land, we've jumped through all the hoops and now it's just a matter of coasting along as if we were normalized citizens, even if I'll always speak pidgin Deutsch.

Anyway, to apply some external criteria to the question of whether or not expatriates suffer from stress, I Googled the Holmes-Rahe Scale, a sociological instrument based on the premise that "good and bad events in one's life can increase stress levels and make one more susceptible to illness and mental health problems."

Holmes and Rahe came up with their scoring system nearly 40 years ago to test the observation that their patients tended to have experienced several life events in the months before the onset of illness.

Moving to a foreign country wasn't on the list of choices, though I imagine it would have put me well above my final score of 294 points, just five shy of the major stress threshold of 300.

Which is ironic, because when we first considered moving to Spain, I reckoned that the dry, warm climate there would be good for our health. But the way the Holmes-Rahe Scale sees it, I should be in the hospital pretty much any day now.

Bearly related
Germany, 2006

A pair of seemingly unrelated topics have occupied Germany of late. The first is the Soccer World Cup, which is allowing the German national team – and the country itself – to present their best face to the world. Across the board, critics are lauding the German organizers, football fans and overall population for their ability to put together such a world class event.

Columnist Steve Richards of British daily *The Independent* wrote this week that Germany had already won the tournament off the pitch with, "the ease of travel from city to city, the cleanliness of its towns, the class of the accommodation, the cycle-friendly paths… and the ability of its cities to stage late-night festivals without them ending in a drunken brawl."

In addition, German flags, once a source of shame due to the grim specter of German history, are again being waved proudly. People are happy, and a previously lacking sense of community has formed. All of which are surely bright spots and worthy outcomes of the World Cup's slogan "A time for making friends".

The second engrossing topic of late is related to the World Cup only in how it illustrates what one might call the flip side of German efficiency.

About a month ago, you see, the first brown bear since 1835 was sighted in Bavaria after having raided a beehive.

Soon after that first spotting, Bavaria's Environment Minister Werner Schnappauf said the bear, dubbed Bruno, was "Welcome in Bavaria". Schnappauf went on to tell people they had nothing to fear from Bruno, who had been released in Italy in an attempt to repopulate the northern Alps with brown bears.

A few days later, however, Schnappauf was in the news again. He was now describing Bruno as "a problem bear" because, as bears are wont to do, Bruno had taken to killing sheep. A lot of them. And not just killing to eat, but killing to kill. Bruno ran through a couple of herds of sheep like, well, like the adolescent bear that he was, excited to try out his God-given hunting tools on such easy prey.

After pronouncing him a nuisance and possibly a threat to humans, the same minister predicted that a man-bear encounter could occur at any time and that the bear could not be allowed to roam freely. "We will ask hunters to shoot the bear," he said.

"Hysterical," pronounced Bavaria's animal rights groups, who, in cooperation with the World Wildlife Fund, decided to employ alternate means. A special bear trap was flown in from the US State of Montana. A team of Finnish tracking dogs and their handlers, confident they would find Bruno and deliver a dart into his considerable backside, were presented to the media with great aplomb.

But the bear was wily and for weeks eluded all attempts to capture him. He crisscrossed the Alps, leaving the hounds far behind, and was even seen, in perfect Yogi Bear style, sitting in front of the police station in the town of Kochel.

Meanwhile, entrepreneurs created a Bruno teddy bear, on sale for 120 Euros a pop, and a website sprang up where you could shoot darts at a virtual Bruno. In short, the country had Bruno Fever until Bavaria's government bear expert, Manfred Woelfl, faced the cameras last Monday and announced, "The shooting has happened. The bear is dead."

Almost immediately, Austrian animal rights group Four Paws called for a police investigation into Bruno's ursinicide. They also released a statement that perfectly captured many people's opinion on the matter.

It read, "We are extremely dismayed that Bruno had to die."

Farmers and sheepherders couldn't believe the fuss over killing the big varmint. He was a nuisance and a threat to their livelihood, they reasoned, and in the cosmic struggle of man versus nature, well, man has to come first.

A blogger from Canada summed up this idea when he wrote, "We occasionally have bears in our backyards. We live with it and accept that they too have a right to be on this planet. It seems the Germans only have room for one species - *Homo sapien*. So sad and so narrow a viewpoint. In many ways, I believed European countries were more "mature" than us savages of North America. Perhaps not."

To come full circle, how is it, exactly, that the soccer World Cup and the handling of Bruno the bear are related? In my opinion, they both serve to highlight the inherent strengths and weaknesses of two well-known German characteristics: detached logic and straightforward efficiency.

A time for making friends
Germany, 2006

Billboards proclaiming the FIFA World Cup soccer championship as a "Time for Making Friends" appeared all over Germany months before the actual event.

This struck me as a wonderful campaign slogan, because I've lived in the Saxon-Anhalt city of Halle for more than three years, and while its inhabitants are not exactly hostile, they will never rate much higher than "Prussian" on the friendliness scale.

Indeed, this campaign for making friends seemed like such a good idea that I immediately concocted a plan: I would use this World Cup campaign to expand my circle

of German friends. I would be open and friendly to every person I met, and if rebuffed I would cite my adherence to the "Time for Making Friends" campaign as an explanation for my odd, i.e., friendly behavior.

I decided to start close to home and work my way outwards. The victim of my first random act of kindness was the woman who had just moved in next door. When I ran into her, it was in our building's foyer. She was struggling through the entrance with a bike, so I hustled over to hold the door; she said a curt "thanks" as we passed.

> It occurred to me that perhaps my self-conscious German was the problem, that instead of saying, "Nice bike," I'd really said, "You ignorant cow."

Noticing that she was wheeling the expensive mountain bike I had been admiring, (she also drives one of those cool Minis), I said, "Oh, so that's your bike. It's really-"

"Of course it's mine," she spat. "Why?"

I raised my eyebrows and said, "Uh... Because it's nice?"

She just grunted and went about locking the bike, so I went out to check the mail. When I returned she was gone, leaving me to wonder about the encounter. It occurred to me that perhaps my self-conscious German was the problem, that maybe instead of saying, "Nice bike," I'd really said, "You ignorant cow," so I decided to ratchet down my friendliness to a non-verbal level – I embarked on a waving campaign.

My first setback occurred in the bedroom. For through that window and across the courtyard, one can see a lovely and spacious terrace brimming with foliage. Occasionally I am in the bedroom at the same time as the terrace people (whom, I confess, I envy intensively). Prior to my friendliness campaign I had played along with their I-ignore-you, you-ignore-me charade. But this time when I saw the four terrace dwellers lounging in the sun, I opened the window, called out a friendly hello to get their attention, and waved.

To a one, they stopped talking, looked at me briefly, and then turned away deliberately, as one might turn away from a bedraggled street beggar. Chuffed, I called out, "Hel-loooooo, Hel-loooooo," while waving both arms in an attempt to break through their willful ignorance.

After a tense minute of my gesticulations being offset by their snootiness, however, the effort became just too embarrassing. Defeated, I stammered at them, "I thought it was a time to make friends," and gave them the finger.

Somewhat darker of mood, I trudged down to pharmacy, and in the checkout line recognized the guy from the video store where I've rented videos weekly for the last three years. Though we're not buddies, we're definitely friendly. Here was my chance! I waited until video man happened to look my way, then smiled and waved at him, and damned if he didn't jerk his head the other way! He did it so quickly I was worried he'd sprained something. He was clearly shunning me, and when I asked him about it the next weekend as I was renting a film, he testily replied – as if there are any

other goofy-looking Americans in town – that he hadn't recognized me.

Dejected, I walked towards home musing on my failures to connect with the people of Halle until I happened to pass by one of the "Time for Making Friends" billboards. I stopped in my tracks – the slogan was in *English*! That must be the explanation: people didn't get the thrust of the campaign because it was written in English, not in German!

That night, I snuck out with a can of spray paint and grafittied in German underneath, "A Time for Making Friends. This means YOU, Crabapples of Halle!"

Weeks have passed and oddly enough, the results of this new campaign have not yet been discernible.

The friendly skies
Germany, 2005

What do David Bowie, Mr. T, and the Dalai Lama have in common? If you guessed they all like fancy clothes, guess again. If you guessed that they all dislike flying, you get yourself a pair of shiny plastic pilot's wings.

I too, dislike flying. And although I accept it as a consequence of living across an ocean from my homeland, I am nonetheless a reluctant flyer. My aversion to the friendly skies could possibly be in the genes, as mom is nearly phobic when it comes to flying. But dad, on the other hand, is a cool customer in planes.

So if my parents represent opposing ends of a joy of flying scale, I suppose I would tend toward my mother's side. It might just be a control thing, that is, my fear of putting my life into someone else's hands, or it could be the totally understandable fear of heights. But more likely these days is all the nonsense that's been going on in the world when it comes to aviation.

Just two days ago for example, 19 suspects were arrested, and some remain at large, for having planned to blow up as many as 10 airliners. Such a plot is obviously atrocious, and my hat is off to the UK security forces for spoiling it. Great work, M15.

But step back from the hellishly unsavory prospect of such an attack for a moment, and one can understand why terrorists would want to attack planes in the first place – it's not jealousy of freedom or even cowardice, as the governments or the media profess, but rather an evil shrewdness on the part of the plotters.

Perhaps one of them even read the article titled Do We Fear the Right Things?, by David G. Myers, a professor of psychology at Hope College in Holland. In that paper, Myers states that psychological science has identified four influences on our intuitions about risk. First, we fear what our ancestral history has prepared us to fear. Human emotions, he says, were road tested in the Stone Age, and flying may be far safer than biking, but our biological past predisposes us to fear confinement and heights, and thus to fear flying.

Second, he says, we fear that which we cannot control. Even though it is far more dangerous, driving is something we can control, whereas flying we cannot.

Third, we fear what is immediate. Much of the plane's threat, he says, is telescoped into the moments of takeoff and landing, while the dangers of driving are diffused across many moments which range from completely safe to potentially life-threatening.

Fourth, we fear what's most readily available in memory. One needs only an instant, for example, to envision the World Trade Center attacks.

The main point that Myers makes is this: availability in memory provides our intui-tive rule-of-thumb for judging risks. Small wonder then that most of us perceive plane accidents as more lethal than car accidents. For when we see a plane crash, the flames, the drama, the unfulfilled promise of those countless lives lost are truly horrific. They are no more so than car crashes, but the scale is what makes the difference.

And I *know* that it's illogical to be afraid of flying, that the numbers say it's safe, that I have a better chance of choking on a doughnut than dying in a plane crash.

Nevertheless, the odds of some lunatic smuggling a vial of liquid explosives into my back seat and then detonating it is far, far less than it seems to be in today's friendly skies.

Which only confirms my opinion that after we sort out global warming, we should do away with flying completely by simply moving the continents back together again.

Long live Pangaea!

Yeah, I'm the tax man
Germany, 2005

Strangest thing happened to me the other day. I was working away at the computer when the doorbell rang, so I shluffed to the front door in my slippers and pressed the intercom.

"Hello?"

"Herr Curtiss," the tinny voice said. "I'm from the German Tax Bureau."

"Pardon?"

"I'm from the tax bureau," he repeated.

"Uh... Ok. I'll be right down."

What is this all about, I wondered as I put on my shoes and walked downstairs.

I opened our building's front door, and standing there trying to look tough was a well-muscled kid, tanning booth brown, wearing a tight, short-sleeved shirt.

I puffed up my chest. "Yeah?"

He was holding a huge leather case like the airline pilots carry, which allowed his arm to be continuously flexed.

"Herr Curtiss, I'm from the tax office and blah, blah, blah," he said in German.

"Uh... I'm sorry, I don't understand."

He gave me that look – the one where he clocked me as a foreigner – and then he handed me an official-looking document from the tax bureau.

"Can you read German," he sniped.

"Of course," I replied as I snatched the paper from him. I looked over the official-looking document and understood maybe 25% of it.

I handed the paper back to him testily. "Yeah, and…"

"You must pay this money, Herr Curtiss, plus a penalty," he said. "Do you have it?"

"Wait. I have to pay you right now?"

"That's right."

"And you're with the tax bureau?"

"Yes."

"Do you have any identification?"

He sighed deeply, obviously peeved, but hey – should I pay every random guy who comes to my house claiming to be the tax-man? I don't think so.

His ID seemed legit, so I asked him, "I have to pay you how much? And why?"

"Forty Euro. For your *taxes*."

He'd had enough of me already.

"So do you have it," he asked.

"Uh... I don't know..."

"It would be bad if you don't."

"Uh-huh." I still didn't want to believe the situation I was in, but he was legit so I invited him up.

"So this is all about my taxes," I asked as we walked upstairs.

"*Yes.*"

'But I paid my taxes last month."

"Yes, but not all."

"Uh-huh. You have the documents for this?"

"*Yes.*"

> "So I don't pay you, and what – you take my television?" "For example," he shrugged, looking around in a what-*else*-they-got kinda way.

We got into the apartment and I led him into our living room – and then I remembered that it looked like a clothes and paper bomb went off in there. My wife had just overhauled our bedroom and the spillover made its way to a pile by my desk. A pile of shirts awaited someone to give them ironing attention. My desk was littered with papers. There were dozens of CDs on the floor by the player. Our laundry was drying on the rack. In short, we were trailer trash.

Anyway, we sat down at our rotunda table and I tried to make sense of the situation.

"Ok, now could you tell me again what's happening here?"

He took out a file and showed me that I hadn't, apparently, paid all of my taxes for the first quarter of the year. I'm scheduled to pay a certain amount by a certain date and I had missed the deadline by one day. Big deal, I thought. But then, two days after I had paid my taxes in full (a significant amount, mind you), a letter arrived saying that I owed this full amount plus a 40 Euro late fee.

Being me, and since I had already paid, I threw the letter in the garbage and forgot about it.

But now here was Mr. Savage Tan come to collect these 40 Euro. As it fully dawned on me that he was some thug from a collection agency, and since I knew I had the money, I asked him what would happen if I didn't pay him.

He said a word I didn't understand, so I asked him to write it down.

"Pfändung" was the word.

I ran for my dictionary and looked it up.

"Seizure" was the translation.

I looked up at him.

"So I don't pay you, and what – you take my television?"

"For example," he shrugged, looking around in a what-*else*-they-got kinda way.

I blinked at him.

Shaking my head, both amused and scandalized, I said, "That's unbelievable."

He shrugged. "That's how it works here in Germany if you don't pay your taxes, Herr Curtiss."

Don't wave for me, Saxon-Anhalt...
Germany, 2005

The Golden Rule of living abroad is to keep quiet about your host country's drawbacks. But sometimes one just can't help it.

The seed of my discontent was planted a few weeks ago when I was grocery shopping. Near the checkout line I recognized the bakery lady who I've bought bread from pretty much daily for the last two years and who's always ready to give me a good-natured German lesson.

So when baker-lady looked my way, I gave her a wave and damned if she didn't jerk her head the other way! She did it so quick I was worried she'd hurt herself. Her turn of the head was a clear shun, and when I asked her about it the next week, she testily replied – as if there are other such goofy-looking Americans in town – that she hadn't recognized me. Yeah, right, I thought, and lined her pockets some more.

Anyway, the shun would be no biggie if it were just an isolated case. She's just a provincial-city bakery store lady, right?

But then, last week on my way to the institute where I teach, I was waiting at a red light when a young researcher (who I've taught and even partied with) walked by with a group of his colleagues.

He looked in my car, this kid, we made eye contact, and I waved at him. But guess what? He gave me the sourpuss face and kept walking.

I honestly don't know what prompted his reaction, because when I later asked him about it in class, he said he didn't remember the situation. Yeah, right, I thought, and gave him extra homework.

And then yesterday as my wife and I were walking home after work, one of her colleagues was coming the other direction on his bike. When we were about 20 feet away, I said his name and hello, and he looked right *at* me as he rode by without greeting.

So what the heck is it about this country's waving customs?

Three possible explanations for my shunnings come to mind:

1. Germans don't wave.
2. Germans don't wave to foreigners.
3. Germans don't wave to Jim.

But frankly, none of these possible explanations sit quite right with me.

The laser pointer
Germany, 2005

On the Czech side of the border with Germany, along a mountain road that overlooks high pastureland for miles and miles, there are dozens of Asian-owned shantytown shops peddling booze, cigarettes, pirated CDs and knock-off designer label clothing including the most popular soccer and Formula 1 brands. The clientele for these stores are mostly Germans who do their shopping on the Czech side of the border because it's cheaper, or expats (like Jarmila and I) who pass by on their way between homes.

So last week as we drove to Jarmila's village in the CZ for Christmas, it occurred to me that I could really use a laser pointer during my English classes. Jarmila pointed out that I *didn't* really need one because I had taught fine for years without one. But since I jump at any chance to upgrade our technological standing, we pulled into one of the snowy shantytown parking lots. As we slowed to find a parking place, we both looked through the windshield in surprise as no less than five of the parka-wearing shopkeepers hustled out through the ankle-deep snow, each waving at us to park in front of and shop at *their* booth. They must have seen our German license plates.

As an act of protest, Jarmila stayed in the car, and I hustled over without a jacket to the nearest overcrowded booth. Like the ten that flanked it on either side, this one was overflowing with the most random of junk, and as I stepped in I was surrounded by three small Asian shopkeepers hassling me to buy various objects, including a pair of sunglasses, a children's backpack, and a pair of jeans. I looked back at Jarmila, who was giggling in the warm car. What had I gotten myself into?

One of the shopkeepers was speaking pidgin German, one was speaking pidgin Czech, and the last was speaking in an indistinct Asian tongue. Alas, my mind was working in English and I was freezing my butt off, so once I was able to cut through the din and tell them what I wanted, I rushed into buying the first laser pointer that looked unassuming. It was 100 Crowns, roughly three dollars, and once back in the car I was pleased I had purchased something so useful and necessary so cheaply. Plus, Jarmila had enjoyed the show and it gave us something to speak about as we made our way home.

After we had arrived and said hello to Jarmila's family, virtually the first thing I did was tear open the laser pointer box. Pointing it at the wall, I pressed the button and the laser itself shone in red wonder. The problem though, was the hellish, high-pitched laughing noise that came out as well. It's aggression stunned me, and I immediately stopped pressing the button. I furtively looked around to check if anyone had seen, and sure enough there was Jarmila, standing in the doorway with her jaw hanging.

I looked at her meekly and smiled, then pressed the button again to make sure that the hellish noise was really there. It was, and we burst out laughing at its strangeness.

As humor gave way to my being deflated at having such a crappy new toy, I placed the pointer back into its box because I was determined to exchange it when we next passed the shantytown.

This turned out to be a week later as we were returning home from our Christmas holiday. I stopped in the exact same shanty and went through the same song and dance of parking and being hassled before I explained, in Czech, that I wanted to exchange my laser pointer because it was for business and it had that stupid voice thing happening.

Again surrounded by three smallish people jabbering at me in three languages, the upshot of the conversation was no way would they exchange it. I'd have to buy a new one.

I tried to haggle, but in the end I lost my patience and told them there was no way I was gonna pay for another one. Huffily trudging back to the car, I told Jarmila what happened. She thought it was just my poor Czech causing the problem, so she took the pointer in hand and tried her luck. As I sat behind the wheel watching the four of them haggle, it occurred to me that the three dollars I had spent were well worth the show I was watching. They were all gesturing heatedly and I wasn't surprised when Jarmila came back without having exchanged the thing.

Which means I'm stuck with a devilishly-laughing laser pointer that's only good for one thing: Jarmila thinks the laser will burn her if I point it at her too long, which has provided me with hours worth of good-natured tomfoolery.

Power distance
Germany, 2006

According to Professor Emeritus Geert Hofstede of the Maastricht University in Holland, there exist five key intercultural dimensions that can predict how a person from a particular country will behave in any given setting. These factors are the Power Distance Index, Individualism, Masculinity, Uncertainty Avoidance, and Long-Term Orientation.

Of the five mentioned factors, differences between American and Central European societies' Power Distances have recently been exemplified in my circle of acquaintances, and I'd like to share some of the anecdotes which illustrate those differences.

But first, let's examine the term power distance itself, which in short refers to how much a culture does or does not value hierarchical relationships and respect for authority. Thus, if those in authority in your country openly demonstrate their rank, through either dress or behavior, or if class divisions within your society are accepted and reinforced, you can be pretty sure that your country has a high power distance score. That is, the gap between ordinary folk and those of a higher social status is rarely bridged, and co-mingling between the classes is virtually unheard of.

Countries with high power distance scores include China, India, Arabic speaking countries, as well as Russia and its former satellite states.

At the other end of the power distance spectrum, officials in countries with a low power distance score might not flout their power or influence, and in general terms, the society tends towards egalitarianism. That is, people from all societal levels are theoretically seen more as just plain human beings, and how they earn their living is of secondary import. In these countries, you might even see political leaders biking or walking to work.

The following country scores are only guidelines, but the power distance differences between the United States and the Czech Republic, and by extension Eastern Germany, are rather telling.

In the United States, for example, the power distance index score is 40 of a possible 100, while in the Czech Republic it is closer to 60. The higher the score, the higher the distance between normal folk and the upper classes. Thus, 20 points is a considerable difference and perhaps explains a few variations between my own behavior and that of my Czech wife.

For example, a few years ago Jarmila and I were at a conference in Prague called Forum 2000, which was founded by then-Czech President Václav Havel, Japanese philanthropist Yohei Sasakawa, and Nobel Peace Prize laureate Elie Wiesel. Anyway, during the final portion of the conference there was a round table discussion of distinguished guests, including Havel himself and ex-U.S. Secretary of State Madeline Albright.

As these guests concluded their discussion and arose to leave, I realized there was an opportunity to go up and meet them or take their photo, and I tried to convince Jarmila to come along with, but nothing doing – she got a haunted look and flat-out refused. So I shouldered my way past the media and right up to Madame Secretary. I shook her hand and got an autograph as well – no problem.

Afterwards, when I asked Jarmila why she didn't want to come with me to meet Madeline Albright, she said – somewhat uncomfortably – that she just didn't feel like it. My hunch now is that it was a power distance thing – that is, she didn't feel comfortable approaching someone of such a high social rank.

Another illustration of power distance was brought home to me this last week when a German family that we know returned from the United States after having lived there for a year. Keeping in mind that egalitarianism, that is, equality between people, is a mainstay of lower power distance societies, this German couple had so gotten used to the approachability of people in the United States that returning to the higher power distance society of Eastern Germany was a bit of a shock.

"The people here in Halle are so nasty," said the woman. "Ok, sometimes the friendliness in the US can be cosmetic. But here in Halle, I've actually been scolded by cashiers for not packing my groceries fast enough. And I had my four kids with me!"

For those of you who think this might have nothing to do with power distance,

please remember that in the former Eastern, that is, Socialist Germany, the store clerks were actually powerful people and could act nasty if they wanted to, and you couldn't do a thing about it because they were the ones with the goods that you needed.

But the recently-returned German woman actually stood up to this nasty clerk, saying "Apparently you don't want or need my business here."

Unaccustomed to the customer being right, the clerk got simply furious as the mother of four collected her children and left the groceries unbagged and unpaid for.

To switch gears, a somewhat more pleasant effect of the power distance phenomenon is continuously manifested here in Halle at our favorite pub, Object 5. Actually, Object 5 is more of a cozy concert hall than a pub, and so far we've seen approximately 10 concerts there. And of those 10 concerts, on the three occasions where the bands were readily approachable, all three of them were American, or at least American-influenced bands. Indeed, we were able to get chatty and chummy with the bands each time.

The first was with Stan the Man, a bluesman originally from Scotland by way of Louisiana, who talked like he had marbles in his mouth. After an hour of speaking to Stan, Jarmila told me that to her, he basically sounded like this: rarrea areae aaeahasd Prague rarrea areae aaeahasd New York rarrea areae aaeahasd Berlin rarrea areae aaeahasd…"

Which is true – he did talk like that: but at least he was approachable.

Then there were the Tiptons, a female group of saxophonists who embodied an entirely unique style and sound. After the concert they came out into the crowd and we were able to speak to them for a long while.

And then two nights ago the Japanese-American jazz trio of Makoto Ozone came to town. Jarmila, myself and another Czech girl went to the concert and between sets the drummer happened to walk behind me. He was wearing a hipster hat over his shaved head and as he passed by, I said, "Hey man, you guys are really cookin'!"

He stopped and looked at me, the ice in his glass tinkling, and said "You sound American."

"Yeah, I am," I replied.

I'm not kidding, this guy threw his arms around me in a big hug and said, "Man, I miss home!"

This hug started a conversation that ran the whole of the band's break, and the pianist even joined in as well.

To return to the power distance thing, though my wife Jarmila is now used to me being involved in such situations, our other Czech companion said, "I think it's sometimes useful to have an American boy around. Because while I enjoyed the conversation, I would never have started it in the first place."

Indeed, I'd also like to think that a low power distance score, and not my own stupidity, explains why, when the pianist after whom the jazz trio was named joined in our conversation, I introduced myself and asked, "And what's your name?"

Semana Santa
Spain, 2007

At the mention of Spain, one typically thinks about bullfighting, flamenco dancing and sunshine. Looots of sunshine. However, chances are that one overlooks a significant and impactful aspect of Spanish culture. And no, I'm not talking about the wine. Rather, I'm talking about Catholicism. Because with approximately 37 million baptized Catholics, that means roughly 90% of the Spanish population is Roman

Float from Semana Santa
Sevilla, Spain

Catholic. And perhaps nowhere else is their religiosity more evident than during Holy Week in Sevilla, which we were lucky enough to experience this past April.

With a tradition that dates back to the 1600s, Semana Santa features long processions of hooded brotherhoods, the focal point being the *pasos*, or floats.

The processions – 57 of them this past year – are organized by various brotherhoods that are aligned with a certain church, two floats per brotherhood being the norm. The floats themselves are wooden sculptures of people and events from the Passion of Christ, and most of the processions also include floats of the Virgin Mary, who is very much venerated here.

The objectives of these processions seem to be three-fold: first, they provide the brotherhoods a chance to serve penance. That is, they walk – often barefooted – for up to 12 hours through the city in the hope that their sins will be forgiven. Secondly, it allows the brotherhoods to show off their sizes, and thus their economic and political import. Indeed, some groups boast over 3,000 members. And most importantly, the processions make their way to the Cathedral so that the float can be blessed.

Usually weighing more than a metric ton, the floats are carried on the backs of the *costaleros*. These men are hidden under the floats' platform, giving the impression that the float is… well, floating. Historically, dock workers and manual laborers were hired to carry the floats, but nowadays, the task is carried out by members of the brotherhoods, who train all year round. The largest float requires 64 men to carry it.

The brotherhoods of Spain are essentially religious organizations, though membership rules vary. Some people, like my friend Ines, are members of not one, but multiple brotherhoods. When I asked her the reason for her multiple memberships, she said that one of the brotherhoods has a procession that is serious, that is, people cannot speak during the walk, and everybody around keeps silent while the procession passes. The second brotherhood earned her allegiance because she has always liked the image of their Virgin. Also, she bought an apartment very near the church, so she decided it was something like "a sign". So she wanted to say thank you, and to collaborate with the brotherhood, so she decided to join that one too.

At any rate, the members of the brotherhoods can appear… a little scary during the processions. This is because most are required to wear penitent's robes, which include masks and pointy KKK hoods, though the brotherhoods' robes can be black or blue or gold or white. Ostensibly, the robes are worn to allow the members to show penitence but not reveal their identity. The history of these costumes by far predates their usage by the KKK, so it's a pity that most North Americans associate the Spanish brotherhoods with that group.

Sevilla is a city of roughly 700,000 people, but during Semana Santa, that population swells immensely. Hotels and pensions are booked out and people roam the streets until well past midnight, wandering around with folding maps or books illustrating the processions' routes.

We were among the crowds this year, and for us, Semana Santa was one of the

most interesting extended experiences of our lives. The peaceful coming together of millions of people, the non-stop action visible from our living room balcony, the spiritual discussions that the processions sparked – they were simply a marvel.

A force to be reckoned with
Germany, 2006
This story first appeared in
Stonefreemagazine.com

Two guys are sitting in an attic on a hot summer day trying to write a song.

That may sound like the beginning of a seedy joke, but the punch line is that the two guys were Jack White and Brendan Benson, both of whom had already enjoyed considerable musical success, and the song they wrote that day eventually led them to form a band called The Raconteurs, who, by the way, kick ass.

The culmination of a late-night, boozed-up promise made by members of two Midwestern American garage bands, The Raconteurs could easily be thought of as a one-off band, because each of its members are involved in projects they will return to after their current tour. Which begs the question: does the advent of The Raconteurs toll the bell for The White Stripes? Jack White insists no, that isn't the case – he's merely concentrating on something else for now.

Which is great for his fans, because now they can enjoy a more dynamic version of White than previously available. Not to say that The White Stripes lack either talent or creativity – far from it – but The Raconteurs' May 2006 release titled *Broken Boy Soldiers* is simply a more varied collection of musical styles than any of The White Stripes albums have thus far been.

As far as The Raconteur's music itself goes, one cannot tell exactly what kind of mutt this album is. The song *Broken Boy Soldiers*, for example, starts off all cowbells and honky-tonk but morphs into a Deep Purplish operatic movement. The track *Call It a Day* has the catchy simplicity of The Beatles but with garage band tendencies. And the song that inspired them to form the band in the first place, *Steady, As She Goes*, is a rousing, guitar-driven song, one you wouldn't be all that surprised to find on a White Stripes album.

However, instead of coming across as a band that can't find musical direction – or one that is dominated by White – The Raconteurs give the impression that they are just terribly curious about making sounds, and while they hope you like it, they're more concerned about making good music than making good money (though come to think of it, that might be debatable).

As Jack Lawrence (bass), Brendan Benson (guitars, vocals, keyboard), Patrick Keeler (drums), and Jack White (guitars, vocals, keyboard) themselves say on The Raconteurs website, they are happy to take on any genre they encounter. And above all else, this is the one aspect of the band that indeed makes them a force to be reckoned with.

Googled
Germany, 2005

As part of my ongoing efforts to avoid working on my novel, last week I Googled myself to check my website rankings. My usual stories appeared at or near the top of the list, followed closely by a number of links for a Mayor Jim Curtiss of Montevideo, Minnesota, links to the historic Curtiss-Wright aviation company, and links to Jim Curtiss the real estate agent, who, apparently, is also quite a fellow.

But jimcurtiss.com was nowhere to be found, so I trolled through a few pages of hits looking for signs of it until I came across this little gem from the Film Makers' Cooperative in New York City: "... this movie tells the story of Jim Curtiss, a man now detached from reality. His fantasies and realities are out of connection; he struggles to join his dreamlife with his realife; he goes through a series of adventures which underline his isolation..."

The blurb hit me like a Manhattan in the face because in the weeks prior I had been doing no small amount of dream research in an attempt to construct a blurred frontier between the realife and dreamlife of my novel's protagonist.

Of course, reading that "Jim Curtiss was a man detached from reality" made me wonder if it was really true, so I held a hypothetical conversation with my wife while she was not present.

"Is it true," I asked Jarmila, "that I'm detached from reality? And be honest."

She puffed out her cheeks and said, "Well, that depends on your definition of reality."

"Because," she continued, "you've certainly rejected the *economic* realities of life. Or, at the very least, you ignore them."

I rushed to my defense. "But-"

"Also," she added, "you spend more time philosophizing than is probably good for you. Most people don't deal with – or care about – what you care about. Religion and so forth."

"But people don't care about it because the wool has been pulled over their eyes," I said. "This whole economic construction leads us to materialism and not a wholesome relationship with the earth… or with the universe, or the things which are ultimately important."

"You see," she said. "That's just what I mean. For most people, having a full-time job is the most important thing."

"Yeah," I barked. "Because they're confused about their self-worth! They think that having a job for 40 hours a week is the only way to betterment and it's just not. *Man*. If I were unemployed-"

"You *are* unemployed," she said.

I sized her up for a moment. "I work full-time at least."

"You're not paid for it, though," she sniped.

"So?"

"So, society doesn't value your work. That's the reality."

"And I accept that reality," I said. "I'm not complaining that I'm not paid, though of course I'd like to have a larger audience. But back to the point – do you really think that I'm detached from reality?"

"Let me put it this way," she said. "Look who you're asking."

The conversation wasn't turning out the way I'd hoped, so I sent her away. If anything, I was even more concerned. I sat there wondering about this movie starring me and my out-of-connection fantasies and realities. If it *were* all true, I mused, where the hell were my royalty checks?

So I wrote an email to the producer of the film, mentioning my dilemma and asking for some form of compensation for his using my life as the basis for a film.

His response? *Dream on.* Which apparently should be doable.

Batminton
Germany, 2005

The August heat wave swept through Europe like a Roman conqueror, leaving hordes of miserable victims in its wake. Daytime temperatures battled up to 38 Celsius (100 F), and the nighttime wasn't much cooler. Hoping to coax a breeze, we kept every window and door in our apartment open.

Lying on my back and sparring with my sweaty sheets during one of these oppressive nights, I heard a disturbance ripple through my sub-conscience. I opened my eyes and looked around, but could see nothing in the dark bedroom.

Then a bat flapped over our bed.

And then another.

Suddenly wide-eyed, I played opossum as they circled above us before flying out the bedroom door and into the hallway.

I jumped up and hustled around the bed, savagely stubbing my toe on the way.

"Got dammit," I cursed, crouching down to hold it while waddling toward the door.

My wife bolted upright. "What's wrong," she demanded.

Just then one of the little buggers flew back into the room.

"Aaaah," I answered, and jumped onto her side of the bed.

"What are you doing," she yelled, panic in her voice. Apparently she hadn't seen the critter.

I lay next to her as it circled and went out into the hallway again, then I jumped up and slammed the door shut.

When I turned the light on, we both squinted against it as I tried to calm her down.

"Relax, honey. It's only a bat."

"A WHAT?!?"

A quick mental scan of our neighborhood cleared up how a bat had come to be in our abode: we live in an attic apartment and there are dozens of abandoned buildings in our vicinity. The varmints had probably wandered into our belfry by mistake – simple.

But simple or not, our hypothesis did nothing for our need to pee. Drastic measures were called for: in order to clear the way, I was to go out in the hallway, herd the bats into the living room, and shut the door on them.

Unfortunately, these were no ordinary bats. They were cunning, I tell you, because when I gingerly opened the bedroom door, one was suddenly in my grill trying to get by! I haplessly swatted at him and in fact screamed like a little girl before slamming the door shut.

My wife and I looked at each other with huge eyes and then broke into the type of laughter often exhibited by those under great duress. We doubled up with it until we were out of breath.

Wiping away my tears, it occurred to me that we had two badminton rackets stashed under the wardrobe. I fished them out, brandishing one dusty racket in each hand, and my wife prepared to open the door for me.

Slow motion time began.

My wife opened the door and stood behind it.

A bat came into view.

The dust from the racquets made me sneeze.

My wife squealed.

I sneezed again.

The bat was joined by another.

She squealed some more as the bats fluttered around.

Slow motion jammed into fast forward and, snot-nosed and teary-eyed, I was finally able to draw a bead on the circling bats. I swatted at one, missed, and they taunted me with a couple more circles. My wife huddled behind the door as I swatted at the air until they winged out into the hallway again.

I ran after them, swatting away like Johnny Mack on speed. I kept low to the ground, sometimes on my knees swatting at the air around me. When I had at last advanced to the living room door, I peeked around the corner and there were AT LEAST ten bats circling around chaotically.

"Holy Moses," I intoned as the heebie-jeebies commenced.

Still crouched down, I'd lash out like mad when one of the things would get too close, i.e., within ten feet of me.

Confession: I'd always scoffed at people who worried about having a bat become tangled in their hair, but at that moment I developed a whole new understanding of the issue.

Problem: in order to create a bat-free zone, I'd have to go *into* the living room with just one racquet – half of my defense – because I needed a free hand to pull the door closed. I grudgingly laid a racquet by my feet.

Taking a deep breath, I edged out, feeling that if I acted nonchalant, they'd leave me alone. And then something grazed my left ear and swooped away. I shrieked, dropping my racquet in panic. Defenseless, I quickly leaned for the door handle as another bat took a collision course with my face.

I flinched left, and the bat skimmed my head, but the resulting wind on my neck started a nasty bout of convulsive willies. From my dog's-eye-view, the living room was thick with bat as I groped around the floor for my weapons.

Another near-miss to the head, followed by loud shriek (don't know if it was me or the bat) completely deflated my courage. I scurried back to the bedroom, bats no doubt clinging to my back baring their thirsty diseased fangs.

I turned the door handle, pushed, and bashed my face into the locked door. Panicked, I banged until my wife opened up and this is no shit: just as she closed the door behind me, one of the crazy bats ran into it!

My wife jumped back under the covers and pulled them over her head.

A bat landed outside the door and scratched around the bottom – I could see its dirty little wings as it fished under the door. I giggled, feeling myself creep closer to the edge of hysteria.

We both still had to pee, but decided the bats were just going to have the run of the place for the night. No way I was going out there again. We tried to calm down and sleep, but every 5 minutes or so there'd be a crash or bump that got our imaginations working and my adrenaline gushing again.

We didn't get to sleep until about 4.

When the alarm went off at 7 a.m. we were groggy and warily padded out the bedroom door, fully expecting to be attacked or to see bats hanging from every available space.

I saw an old stain on the wall and jumped, thinking it was a bat.

My wife laughed at me until she saw the black mobile phone charger and jumped, thinking it was a bat.

A thorough but cautious inspection of the apartment revealed no more bats, but they did leave us plenty of guano to clean up.

Not that we were afraid the bats would return, but that day we bought a fan for the bedroom and slept with the windows closed tight.

Easter Monday in Zdeslav
Germany, 2005
This story first appeared in Glimpse Abroad magazine

During my English classes the week before Easter, my students asked me if I was going to Zdeslav for the weekend, and they laughed knowingly when I said yes. When pressed for an explanation, they said things like, "Oh, you will to enjoy our traditions here," or "Do you will hit your girl?"

Confused, I moved into the lesson I had prepared. Later, I asked Jarmila what my students were talking about and she explained that in Czech tradition, the Willow tree possesses the Vitality of Spring, and in order to pass on that vitality to Czech womenfolk, the men weave willow whips in order to, uh, transfer it into the women.

The system goes like this, she explained: first, men and boys cut branches from a Willow tree, about 3 feet long will do just fine for the men, shorter for the boys. The branches are then weaved together, with the resulting wider end acting as the handle, and the thinner end, which is adorned with a festive ribbon, acting as the whip. Then on Easter Monday, groups of men and boys go through the villages, stopping at each house to sing a song, lightly whip the womenfolk, and then collect decorative eggs and sweets from the women.

Uh-huh, I thought. *Sounds like something else I'll have to politely endure.*

On Saturday and Sunday of Easter weekend, the house was a flurry of activity: springtime had arrived, there was plenty to do outside, and there was also Easter Monday to prepare for. The younger women in the family spent hours decorating eggs. And when I speak about decorating eggs, I'm not talking about dying eggs various colors and putting stickers on them. No, their system was to boil the outside layers of onions until the water was brown, and then dip the eggs into it. This created the egg's base color. Then beeswax, dyed with food coloring, was melted by placing it in a teaspoon and burning a candle under it. The wax was then used as a sort of paint for the eggs – for a brush they used the head of a pin.

The resulting eggs, which take perhaps 10 or 15 minutes each to prepare, are beautifully intricate and reflect traditional designs. I tried doing one myself, and the technique requires a lot of concentration. After one egg which I titled *Abstract Czech Egg*, I'd had enough.

Not only did the eggs consume hours in their preparation, so did the food; at each house that the roving gangs visit on Easter Monday morning, they are offered a feast of food and a bevy of drink, and not water, either.

At 9 a.m., I was taken in tow by my brothers-in-law… The exact procedure was worked out over shots and beers, which I was not at all ready for. Of course this brought jeers from the whole group, and they immediately saw the day's game; peer-pressure the American into drinking.

So the weekend was all a lead-in to Easter Monday, and I was a touch leery of it, especially after realizing how much the men and boys in the village were looking forward to the day.

As my brother-in-law explained it to me, "*To je bez kontrol, Jime! Bez kontrol!*" (It's without control, Jim! Without control!)

Great, I thought, picturing my fiancé getting whacked at by gangs of out-of-control drunks.

Anyway, on Monday morning Jarmila hurriedly rose at 7a.m., because men were already knocking at the door, singing their song and looking for someone to deliver the Vitality of Spring to. She had to rush downstairs and let in a group of 5 or so older men, all of whom already reeked of alcohol. I dressed and went downstairs amid a ruckus of laughter and lashes and screeches, and then the men bellied up to the kitchen table and waited to be served. Some of them took shots of Becherovka, some of them took Slivovice,[1] and some of them took coffee. But all of them ate the *chlebicky*, little open-faced sandwiches the womenfolk had prepared the day before.

After the first wave cleared out, it was already 8 a.m., and the house was abuzz. Even the brothers, who had been drinking the night before, were up and at 'em. At 9 a.m., I was taken in tow by my brothers-in-law. The plan was that our group would meet at the pub and then proceed through the village systematically. The exact procedure was worked out over shots and beers, which I was not at all ready for. Of course this brought jeers from the whole group, and they immediately saw the day's game; peer-pressure the American into drinking.

After leaving the pub, we walked up the street and without knocking entered the house of a distant friend. The men sang their song, which began, "*Hody Hody, Dobra Vody, dejte vejce malovany...*" (Hey Hey, give us some colored eggs…)

When the group spotted the woman of the house, they all took turns gingerly patting her on the bottom with their whips, which impressed me completely. Here I thought they would be hacking away like Huns, and it was all about pats instead. Fine, I thought. Jarmila will be ok after all.

---

[1] The direct translation of Slivovice is fruit brandy, but I find that misleading. Brandy in my understanding of the word is dark-colored, drank from snifters and is normally considered to be a highbrow liquor. Slivovice, on the other hand, is clear, and while it can be bought from the store, is best and smoothest if it is homemade.

We were given our shots of booze or beers (I had coffee) and everybody shot the breeze until the troops were rallied – there were a bunch of houses to get to before noon![2] So off we went, gathering our eggs as an afterthought as we filed out the door.

At the next house, we barged in while singing the song. There were a couple of younger girls there, in their twenties, and the willow whips had a little bit more swagger to them this time – still in the patting range, but with a sting thrown in there at the end. And as our group numbered seven or eight, that added up.

We sat down and most of us were given shots. There was snacking and talking, and my water drinking was met with dismay by the women who were serving us. There followed a concerted effort to get me to drink, and it went on for awhile. Reasons cited to drink were tradition, everybody else was doing it, and politeness. I refused all of them, and I'm sure they all thought I was a prime example of a big fat loser.

This scene was repeated five more times before we arrived at Jarmila's house. The boys had taken, say, six or seven shots by this time, and the clock had yet to ring 11 bells. The boys sang their song and whacked Jarmila pretty good, but she was wearing jeans, so no harm done – a couple of "YOWs", but that was all.

We still had like seven houses to get to, so I continued along with the group after our house, and even though the pressuring to get me to drink had diminished, it was still present. At 11:30, after visiting three more houses, I finally relented. Everybody around me was wholesale drunk and giddy, and I was hating the fact that I wasn't really having much fun. I thought a couple of shots might help – and they did.

In fact, when I downed that first drink, the group took to me like a long-lost brother; finally, I was *with* them. Lots of arms-around-the-shoulders, drunk breath, not-understanding-each-other-but-happy-anyways situations.

Still, the whipping thing was bothering me. What had started out at the first house as a friendly pat had in fact degenerated, in direct proportion to the amount of booze that the group had taken in, to a full-bore whipping. No one was spared, and the men seemed to genuinely enjoy hitting the women – one could see it on their faces and hear it in their laughter.

Around mid-day, when our drunk group was walking down the street towards the next house, an unlucky group of girls who had been camping happened by. They were all in shorts, all were carrying backpacks and sleeping bags, and the men literally descended upon them. The girls screeched and cursed, trying to cover up their bottoms, but to no avail. Their only option was to run like hell to get out of that strange situation, and the youngest boys were the last to give up the chase.

Somewhat disturbed by what the day had become, I told everyone I'd had enough and suffered the resulting tongue-lashing, which was the end of my Easter Monday with the boys. I went home and lounged around, half-drunk, picking at leftover sandwiches until Jarmila drove us back to Prague.

For her part, Jarmila was glad that I finally participated in the tradition by drinking a couple of shots with the boys, and truthfully so was I.

But you know, I'm still a little unsure about the things I saw that day.

---

[2] After 12, if the men arrive at a house and sing the song, the women can have their revenge by dumping a bucket of water on them. Believe me, the women are good and ready for revenge by the time it's all over. But as far as I saw, none of the boys got hit with water because they gave up the whips well before noon and made friendly again.

The mad Russian
Germany, 2004

The Mad Russian was probably not Russian, but in our ignorance we called him that anyways. His beard, a bushy Dostoyevsky affair, and his demeanor, skittish and sideways-glancing, gave him the air of a strange philosophy professor on a leave of absence from reality. We never got to know him very well – in fact, as he didn't speak English and we didn't speak Czech, communication was difficult. But for our purposes at the time, verbal communication wasn't necessary.

Milo and I would meet in Prague's Kampa Park at least once a week to play catch with the baseball gloves I'd brought from the US. It was great fun, and since a lot of people had never seen baseball gloves before, we were approached nearly every time we played. That's how we met the Mad Russian.

As we were playing one day, this bearded man of energy approached Milo and spoke to him in a Slavic language. Of course Milo didn't understand a word, but from the gestures the man was making, Milo reckoned that he wanted to have a catch.

So Milo took off his glove and handed it to the man, who was clearly elated. Even putting the glove on the wrong hand was funny and interesting for him, and it was with great excitement that he punched his hand into the mitt and beckoned me to throw the ball to him.

Milo stood back, grinning and happy to be an observer of this fresh new comedy.

Because Milo and I are old hands at playing catch, we were standing about 30 or 40 yards apart – for this fellow, I figured I should move up a bit. So I walked towards him, but the closer I got, the more agitated he became – he didn't wanna play little kid catch, he wanted to start out in the big leagues!

So I threw the ball to him, lightly and with a good bit of arc so he had time to react to it. As soon as the ball left my hands, this fellow began dancing, trying to gauge the ball's trajectory. The nearer the ball got, the more anxious and jittery he became, and at the last second he decided to abort the whole operation and held the glove over his head. The ball plopped on the grass next to him, no damage done aside from his nerves. All three of us were laughing.

I decided to move closer to him so he wouldn't be so scared of the ball, and this time, he didn't object. However, it was his throw, perhaps the first of his life, and he wasn't about to throw it short. The ball went sailing 10 feet over my head.

Which is fine, until you consider that Kampa Park is crowded in the afternoons. The ball went rolling through the people lying on the grass and came to a stop about 50 feet behind me. No one made a move to pick it up and throw it back, so I trotted over to get it.

When I picked up the ball and started walking back, I could see the Mad Russian gesturing at me – he wanted me to throw him the ball from 80 feet or so!

Right.

I jogged back to within 30 feet, his smile growing smaller and smaller the closer I got, and threw the ball to him. He still danced wildly under the ball – Jerry Lewis Plays Catch – but this time he managed to get his glove out and actually hit the ball before it plopped to the ground.

Perhaps peeved at our continued laughing, this time when the Mad Russian had the ball he acted like he was going to throw it at me as hard as he could – a mighty windup and full follow-through – and I jumped like someone said boo, glove up and protecting myself. But the Mad

Russian didn't throw the ball, he was just clowning around and he and Milo fell all over themselves at my indignation.

When he finally did throw the ball, I caught it and sent it back to him lightly. He still did that tap dance under the ball, but this time he actually caught it – he was really making progress, and was completely entertained and happy.

Milo was also entertained as the game went on and the Mad Russian sprayed ball after ball over my head, way left, way right, at the same people again and again.

The Mad Russian must have seen a baseball game somewhere in the past and was imitating it: he tried to throw every ball as if he were a pitcher trying to pick off a first base runner. He'd face sideways and look at me over his shoulder before exploding in a fury of flailing arms. Of course the ball hardly ever came towards me, and I was getting a huge workout shagging his misdirected throws. Finally I asked Milo to trade places.

"No way, Jimbo. This is too good."

So I was stuck with the Mad Russian for about 20 minutes that first day before he very theatrically rubbed his shoulder as if the throwing hurt him – and it probably did, what with the pickoff moves he was attempting – and handed the glove back to Milo. Very earnestly, the Mad Russian shook both our hands before disappearing back into the park.

Milo and I sat down together and discussed our strange experience, enjoying its retelling already, and that's when we came up with his nickname. The Mad Russian became a regular and comedic addition to our games of catch after that. When we'd see him coming, Milo and I would play rock, paper, scissors to see who would watch the other run after the Mad Russian's misguided throws.

Later, after Milo moved away and took our games of catch with him, I saw the Mad Russian on the street and said hello, but he didn't recognize me and kept on walking.

Boundary conditions
Germany, 2003
The audio version of this story first appeared on tellyouatale.com

The scruffy Utah landscape occupied my attention through the passenger-side window as Bjorn, my Swedish traveling companion and fellow graduate student manned the wheel. It was the first time Bjorn had driven my flashy little Pontiac during the trip and I had just relaxed enough to take in the darkening sky.

"I like twilight," I ventured. "It's just so… *neat*," I concluded, feeling I had captured the entirety of the human condition.

Bjorn looked sideways at me, his upper lip bulging with Swedish snus, and said, "Yes James, that's brilliant. Thank you for your wise words."

I had grown used to Bjorn's verbal jabs and pretended to ignore him, but he was right – I was being superficial. Thus spurred on to think about what I really enjoyed about twilight, I continued staring at the blurred middle-distance until it came to me; it wasn't twilight itself that I felt poetic about – what intrigued me more was the boundary between day and night. The boundary condition that twilight represents – the ambiguous mixing of light and darkness – is what I really enjoyed.

I shared this thought with Bjorn, noting how all boundary conditions are inherently fascinating – the ocean pummeling the land, the mountains clawing at the sky, the past sneaking up on the future…

Apparently satisfied with my revised observations, Bjorn grunted, turned up the music and I was left to my musings once again.

Leaning my head back, thoughts of boundaries pulled me back to the summer I had spent next to the Pacific Ocean trying to overcome the differences between me and a blonde Kansan. Geography and religion were the boundaries that we explored that summer – she an ardent Christian from the Midwest and I a transplanted Californian atheist. In the end, those boundaries were more than enough to drive a wedge between us.

The sigh of the wheels, the floating clouds and the rolling waves of the Pacific carried my thoughts back to a nearly-forgotten weekend in Canada, and somewhere along the way the ocean's calm was replaced with the relentless crashing of the Niagara Falls.

I remembered with a shudder that late one night after many beers I had climbed over the railing and scrambled down onto a huge stone block not ten feet above the Niagara River. Standing on the edge, my ears were assailed by the cacophonous roar of water rushing downward and I swayed in vertiginous fascination. I was at a boundary between primary elements – air and water and earth – indeed, at the boundary between life and death had I been lulled into jumping.

I stood there atop the Niagara Falls in awe until I regained my senses in Utah, where it occurred to me that this spring break road trip Bjorn and I were undertaking was also about boundaries. Aside from being on our way to perhaps the most profound border area of them all, our various cultural boundaries kept springing up. This was illustrated just moments later when the radio announcer mentioned some important fact about the World Champion New England Patriots, an American football club.

Upon hearing the "World Champion" turn of phrase, Bjorn launched into a rant on the arrogance of American sporting teams who win a *league* title and declare themselves *world* champions. The tirade went on for awhile and after he had exhausted himself, he declared, "America is *not* the world."

Bjorn's rant had made me fidgety, partly because I knew he was right, but also because I wasn't able to muster any defense for the "world champions" custom. Left with nothing else to do, I ejected the cassette and played with the radio. Clean signals were hard to come by on the FM side, so I switched over to AM and hit scan. The digital numbers ran completely though their entire spectrum – a new experience for both of us – before locking onto something. We were in luck – folksy philosopher Paul Harvey was in the middle of telling his listeners about the various talents of the world's countries. We listened to a few half-truths about central Europeans before Harvey boomed, "And the Swedes, of course, are terrific at woodworking."

I looked over at a grimacing Bjorn.

"It's true," he said solemnly. "We Swedes are all *great* woodworkers."

"Yeah, right," I said. "The only wood you're well-acquainted with is the bar top at Barney's Pub."

We laughed and continued to ridicule Harvey's generalities until we pulled into a sleepy roadside motel for the night.

As we dealt with the room transaction, the hotel clerk – a roundish young kid wearing bib overalls – detected Bjorn's accent and asked where he was from. When Bjorn said "Sweden," the clerk just grunted. Then, as we handed over the cash for the room, he asked, "Do they have money over there in Sweden?"

As we handed over the cash for the room, the boy asked, "Do they have *money* over there in Sweden?" Bjorn hesitated until he saw that the boy was honestly asking the question, and then he said of course we have money, and pulled out some Swedish bills and coins.

Bjorn hesitated for a moment until he saw that the boy was honestly asking the question, and then he said of course we have money and pulled out some Swedish bills and coins. At first the whole scene was fun, but after the kid gave us five *That's so cools* in a row, Bjorn paid his way out of the conversation with a Swedish coin.

We found and settled into our room, and after we had occupied our respective beds, another of those unexpected cultural differences manifested itself: even though we were on the ground floor, Bjorn insisted on keeping the windows wide open. Obviously he'd never heard of "Psycho" or the Bates Motel, and while he slept like a baby, I slept with one eye open.

Next morning we were on the road early. We had to make Arizona by noon if we were to make our destination by sundown. The late-March day was sunny and temperate and we drove with the windows down but our jackets on. Every now and then we spoke, but for the most part we were quiet. We were both looking forward to getting to the Grand Canyon.

My first visit there years before had been so overwhelming that I had dreamt of it for months afterward – sometimes flying deep inside the gorge, so near the muddy Colorado River that I was afraid I'd fall in, and sometimes just standing near a lookout, peering over the abyss.

Anticipation hovered as Bjorn drove – he was all keen on the destination now, and sitting there with little to do, I tried very hard not to build up the canyon too much. I didn't want to spoil it for Bjorn by talking it to death – but in the end I just had to hold forth.

"I've been thinking about boundary conditions," I said.

"Uh-huh."

"And I think the Grand Canyon might be the ultimate one. I mean, not only does it violate the laws of space and relativity-"

"What the hell are you talking about," he interjected, "'*violates space and relativity*'?"

I shook my head at him. "Things are all distorted there, man. The thing is, you're looking at something ten miles across and your mind just can't *grasp* that it's so large and so far away. Like you'll be looking at some rock, wondering what kind of puny insect is milling around it, and then you get this blast of recognition – it's a group of *people* walking around it, and the rock that your mind originally thought must be quite close suddenly goes through this terrible vortex shift of distance, and you actually feel... I don't know if *dizzy* is the right word, but definitely disoriented... It's just a strange place."

"Well, stop telling me about it and let's get there," he said. "I'm gonna get it up."

I raised an eyebrow at him. "Uh... do you mean *giddyap*?"

"Yes! Giddyap. I'm gonna giddyap!"

He looked over at me for permission to speed up and I shrugged my shoulders; he had been driving well, so why not?

The answer to that question came in the form of an Arizona Highway Patrolman, who clocked us doing 85 in a 55 zone.

"Where you boys headed," asked the husky officer as he ticketed us.

"The Grand Canyon, sir," responded Bjorn.

"Well," the cop shot back, "it ain't goin' anywhere, so how 'bout keepin' it to the speed limit?"

Bjorn nodded and after the cop eventually pulled away, he turned to me and said, "You drive."

So we switched places and continued on our way in relative silence, our destination drawing ever nearer. I tried not to ponder the boundary conditions that were haunting me, but in the end they were too compelling. I thought of both the vast distances involved in our road trip and the relatively short time Bjorn and I had before we would eventually go our separate ways that summer. I pondered the relative importance of the cultures that spawned and separated us, as well as the geography that had brought us together.

We arrived at the North Rim of the canyon an hour before sunset, at that magical time when the Grand Canyon starts to show off its rose and auburn glows, and after parking we took a short walk to a lookout. Being together in the car so much had made us appreciate our privacy, and I sat on a picnic bench enjoying the sunset while Bjorn walked off somewhere.

Sitting next to the Grand Canyon, blissfully noting how it toyed with my senses, I suddenly saw myself five years older, already looking back with nostalgia, knowing that the most important remnant of the trip would be a vision of the Grand Canyon glowing with a poetic twilight radiance.

But even more than that, I suddenly realized that I wanted to be like the Grand Canyon. I wanted to overcome boundaries such as time and geography. But then, looking at the majesty of the prehistoric cliffs formed over millions of years, I came to see that's not how the Grand Canyon does it at all. Instead of struggling against boundary conditions, the Grand Canyon has just been. And perhaps the trick of it is just that – to just *be* and to somehow proactively allow ourselves to be shaped by the forces that act upon us.

These were the thoughts running through my mind as Bjorn reappeared. I looked at him there in his hiking boots and white Scandinavian sweater, a ruddy, long-haired photograph come to life.

"This," he said, smiling and sweeping his arm over the already nostalgic view, "is why we are here."

I smiled back, already missing him, and wondered how long it would take me to embody my realizations.

The best offense is a good defense
Germany, 2005

For better or worse, most of the world has at least *some* knowledge of the United States, and here in Europe you will find many people who have visited America and have come away with strong impressions. These impressions can be a good start to many a conversation and therefore many a friendship, but frequently, being an American expat carries with it an unexpected onus: having to assume the role of Defense Attorney for the United States of America.

As an English teacher, I have taught in a handful of European countries and have thereby nurtured an interest in intercultural issues. Periodically, this interest draws me to seminars that have titles like "Intercultural Issues and How Everybody Can Just Get Along," or "How to Understand and Master Intercultural Issues."

I use artistic license with the seminar titles, but you understand my point – these seminars are designed to stimulate thought about the difficulties of intercultural communication, even if they tend to aim a little high. And indeed, humans being what we are, discussions that touch on these issues often generate a lot of friction. But friction or not, I always try to approach the seminars with an open mind, and, if they have enough free snacks, a genuine interest.

A few years ago I attended a Young SEITAR seminar in Amsterdam, Young SEITAR being the youth-oriented version (cheaper membership fees, more parties) of SIETAR, the Society of Intercultural Educators, Teachers, and Researchers. Anyway, one of the sessions consisted of a discussion on cultural differences (take off your shoes inside the house here, don't be surprised at being groped in the tram there) which was lively, interesting, and funny, but in the end it turned into a chance for people to get in a little America-bashing. The diatribes were full of all the American issues one would expect a European to complain about – guns, violence, haves and have-nots, a lack of traditions, etcetera, etcetera, *ad nauseum.*

Alas, I had just arrived in Europe and was completely True Blue, and I took offense not only to the content, but also the style in which my country was being criticized. Thus, perhaps predictably, when I spoke up it was with a defensive tone, and I remember my defensiveness being interpreted as capital A American Aggressiveness – a perfect example of how Americans are neither polite nor well-educated. Further, I was baited into arguments which I was ill-suited for because I had little knowledge of the countries that my tormentors hailed from. I mean, how does one point out the inadequacies of, say, the Latvian society?

Oh yes, they pummeled me in Amsterdam, and I left that conference with a violated taste in my mouth. I was the token American whipping boy for all the seminar participants to grouse at, and if it wasn't for that Dutch girl I met, the whole conference would have been a net loss.

As it was, I walked away from Amsterdam that weekend with a slew of questions. What was this anti-American stuff, anyway? Why were they attacking *me*? Why couldn't I have been more convincing in my pro-American arguments? Where did I put that girl's number?

In the years since I have learned that many Europeans consider it fine sport to point out the inadequacies of the States while in the presence of an American. Oh sure, it always starts benignly enough. Yuri the European starts with, "I was in the States before..." which generates the standard question, "Oh, yeah? Whereabouts?" And then comes the listing of visited states and cities, National Parks. Sometimes they even manage to speak about the positives, which never seem to include the beer or coffee.

The American educational system does precious little to prepare the roughly 3 million Americans who live overseas to verbally defend our country.

But then Yuri starts in with the inevitable negatives – bad public transportation, eating with plastic utensils, the middle-of-nowhere hicks that they take as representative of a typical American, and so on.

To be fair, some of the statements and questions are interesting and show genuine thought, but more often than not they are designed to allow the other person to share his or her very insightful, clever, and anti-American opinion. To illustrate this, I present an excerpt from one particularly irksome discussion I had during a conference workshop in Berlin:

Thomas, a native of Hong Kong: "In high school I stayed in an American family as part of an exchange program and I couldn't believe how the family simply exploited their grandmother! She was retired but they had her minding the children and sometimes even cleaning house! In return for this, they paid her! In *my* country we would never demean our elders in this way!"

Me: "Demean her? How much were they paying her?"

Thomas, ignoring the laughter: "That isn't the point. The point is that we have respect for our elders in Hong Kong, which you in America do not."

<Nods of agreement from the crowd.>

Me: "I think it's more complicated than that… in American we take pride in our ability to contribute to society through our work. And our reward for that tends to be money. When I was younger and cut the grass for our family, for example, I generally got paid for it."

Thomas: "In Hong Kong we just contribute with no thought of reimbursement!"

Me: "Uh-huh… well, I don't know about this grandmother you spoke of, but perhaps she was happy to have a feeling of accomplishment that might even have helped keep her mentally fit. *And* she got paid for it."

Thomas: "That's ridiculous. It's simply disrespectful."

Me, getting fired up: "You know, I thought the goal of intercultural exchange was to avoid this type of generalizing."

Thomas: "But when we come across something negative, we must point it out."

Me: "But you just said that based on this one experience, we in America don't respect our elders. Doesn't that seem like an over-generalization?"

Thomas: "And what about your country's habit of placing old people in nursing homes to die? Does that seem respectful of one's elders?"

Me: "That's a whole other-"

Thomas: "In my country, we take in our elders when they are sick. We care for them ourselves. Doesn't this seem more proper than placing them in the care of strangers?"

At this point the rest of the participants got into it, agreeing with Thomas and generally supporting his view with several anti-American anecdotes of their own. I myself was left to simmer and occasionally rise to the bait with rebuttals that were swiftly shouted down.

All of this negativity may have been a bitter pill, but it did make me reflect on how the American educational system does precious little to prepare the roughly 3 million Americans who live overseas to verbally defend our country.

Indeed, according to the American Citizens Abroad website, "As highly visible "ambassadors" of the United States – economically, politically, and culturally – US citizens overseas play a key role in advancing America's interests around the world."

Which is too true, because if you think of it, the millions of us Americans who live abroad are the front lines of the American diplomatic corps. And if we foot soldiers appear uneducated, the world sees America as uneducated. If we are uninformed, the homeland will also appear as such.

So I propose a sweeping new initiative, to be paid for with money that would otherwise be flushed down – diplomatically speaking – the toilet that is the American defense budget: before receiving a passport, each citizen considering moving abroad must attend what would effectively amount to law school boot camp. There, we would be trained in the arts of logos, pathos, and ethos; we would be shown the downsides of other countries in order to better twist and spin arguments; and perhaps most importantly, we would be trained to coolly accept the sad truth that other countries simply don't think as much of us as we tend to think of ourselves.

The shocking true story of why socialism really failed
(*This article first appeared on www.jimcurtiss.com, and a portion later appeared in Impressions Magazine, May 2006*)

The reasons behind the demise of socialism in Russia and its satellite states depend on your nationality. Many Americans think that Ronald Reagan, in pouring so much money into the arms race, simply drove the Russians into bankruptcy while attempting to keep up. For other countries, however, the reasons are more varied.

When I asked my Kazakhstani friend why she thought communism failed, she replied, "Well, the planned economy was unsustainable, for one. We couldn't get things we wanted at the stores, for example."

A thought struck me as I slurped at my third cup of go-juice.

"What about coffee," I asked. "Was *it* affordable?"

She looked at me like I was a Stalin supporter.

"No, no, no," she replied. "Coffee was *very* expensive, unless it was instant. We drank tea. Maybe one cup after a meal."

"That's it? Three cups of tea per day?"

"No more."

Which got me to thinking: caffeine is surely mankind's favorite drug. According to the International Food Information Council Foundation, based in Washington, DC, it occurs in over 60 naturally-occurring plants and is found across the globe in products such as tea, coffee, chocolate, energy drinks, pain relievers and diet pills.

So why wasn't strong coffee available behind the Iron Curtain?

I emailed my Polish friend – a faculty member at the University of Warsaw – and asked her about it. She replied that real coffee was very rare and precious during socialism. In fact, if you ever had any left over after giving it as a special Christmas gift, it was more useful as a bribe for the store clerks than for drinking. Instead, they drank tea. Lots of tea. But after the beginning of 1990s, she said, consumption of coffee increased dramatically.

That last point was verified during a conversation with my older East German friend. I asked him about coffee consumption during communism and he bellowed at me, "We didn't live in communism! What is that, anyways? It's better to say "so-called socialism"! The point is, some old men, they forgot the world around them and wanted to create their own playground under a cheese-box. But nobody who thought differently than them were allowed to play!"

"Uh-huh," I nodded, wondering what the hell he meant by cheese-box. "And what about the coffee?"

"Coffee? We had only instant coffee powder – very weak – it was better to drink tea."

Hmm, I mused. Three former Soviet satellite countries, three tea drinking countries; maybe I was onto something.

Fact: According to the UK-based food safety watchdog group Food Standards Agency, a cup of tea can contain up to a mellow 90 milligrams (mg) of caffeine, while brewed ground coffee can have up to a buzz-inducing 254 mgs. That's a big difference.

I asked my dad, a veteran coffee-drinker, about his consumption. It was mid-afternoon and he was pouring himself a cup from his thermos when I walked into his office.

"Hey dad, how many cups of coffee do you drink per day?"

Dad's wary of frontal attacks, and I could see him tense up.

Is it happenstance that Starbucks has enjoyed worldwide success during the same time that Microsoft has grown and thrived? Or can it be that the e-conomy is actually wired with caffeinated IVs?

"Eight or nine," he snapped. "But it doesn't affect me! Why do you wanna know?"

"Uh, no reason…" I said, and slowly backed away before he could do any damage with the letter opener.

Being over-caffeinated is something that most Americans can readily identify with. As a nation, Americans ingest an average of roughly 3 cups of coffee or tea per day. Heck, many companies even supply the stuff for free. And for good reason – the more you drink, the more effective and energetic you'll be, right?

The sordid truth is that we're all complicit in America's dirty little secret – our famed productivity isn't a result of the Yankee Work Ethic or pursuit of The American Dream – nowadays it's all about the caffeine, man!

Take a look around yourself. Who doesn't have a coffee or tea mug on their desk? Who doesn't have a cup holder filled with some caffeinated drink in their car? Who hasn't choked down that last cup of coffee after it's baked in the pot all day? Slackers, that's who!

The Finns, the world leaders in caffeine consumption, take in about 145 grams of the stuff per year – which, at about 40 mg per day, is one full cup of coffee more than Americans. Is it coincidence that Nokia, a Finnish company, is also the world's most prosperous mobile phone producer? I think not.

And what about Microsoft, the Seattle-based computer giant? Is it happenstance that Starbucks has enjoyed worldwide success during the same time that Microsoft has grown and thrived? Or can it be that the e-conomy is actually wired with caffeinated IVs?

I realize some may call my arguments as weak as the instant coffee they had to drink behind the Iron Curtain. Still others may call me a historical relativist for saying it, but I can't help thinking that today's world would be a lot different if the "so-called socialists" had kept the proletariat properly hopped up on the caffeine.

Here and now
Germany, 2006

Many religions and philosophies extol the idea of the Here and Now. And though they may have different expressions for it, each respective philosophical doctrine essentially entreats us to be completely aware of the present moment, for only then – free of distraction – is one able to concentrate upon doing the right, that is, the altruistic thing. A Taoist might call this spontaneous goodness *tzu-jan,* a Buddhist might think it's a combination of karma and metta, and a westerner might simply refer to it being a good Christian.

Whatever you want to call it, I found myself in this particular state of mind for much of my visit to Rome in November, 2005. Jarmila was there on business and I had tagged along, pleased to be gifted a week of discovering Roma. I did the usual tourist things: overdoses of cappuccino, the Colosseum, cheeses and wines, and of course far, far too many churches to mention.

At the end of day four of tourism, the sky was dark when I boarded the bus for the return back to our hotel. My rucksack was bulging with gifts and since the bus was rush hour crowded, I unshouldered my bag and held it between my legs as I held precariously onto a strap. Packed in like Mediterranean sardines, we weaved our way out of the town center through dozens of look-alike residential neighborhoods.

It should be mentioned that I had just given confession – an uncommon practice for me – and at St. Peter's Cathedral to boot. Thus, while not feeling exactly holy, I was certainly feeling good about things, like I was residing in that mythic Here and Now mentioned earlier. I seemed to be less *me* than normal – or was it *more* me than normal – and I was noticing a lot of details that would normally escape me.

Anyway, at one particular stop, as a good portion of the crowd moved toward the doors, I noticed that the kid directly in front of me was trying to pickpocket an old man as they shuffled towards the door.

As I said, I was in this altruistic state of mind, plus the pickpocket was a head shorter than me, so I poked him – *hard* – in the back. His hand jumped away from the man's wallet and thus startled, he turned to look at me. I wagged my finger at him as the crowd swept him toward the door, and the further away he got the louder he yelled at me. I smiled to myself, thinking how cool I was for helping that old fella keep his wallet, when two gorillas materialized from the crowd and got in my face.

I couldn't understand their Italian, but I sure got the gist of it and my fight or flight mechanism kicked in. I hastily picked up my bag and shouldered past the gorillas to join the exiting crowd. The gorillas continued hazing me as they followed me onto the sidewalk and towards the waiting, thwarted pickpocket. It was a confusing scene of people moving in every direction, and as the gang of three tried to surround and stop me, I just kept my head down and stepped around them by using other people as blockers. I got a few steps ahead and followed close to three or four able-looking adults until I rounded a corner and spotted a brightly-lit café.

There were half a dozen people sitting at sidewalk tables, and I hustled inside. The hazing in my ear had stopped but for all I knew, the gorillas were waiting for me around the corner. I went to the bar and asked the black-haired woman behind the high counter for a taxi. She didn't know the number of a taxi and called out to her colleague across the café – did *she* know the number for a taxi? No. The colleague raised her voice to include the sparse patronage – does *anyone* know the number for a taxi?

No response.

The woman in front of me – she was wearing a yellow-and-white striped apron – shrugged at me. "No taxi. Bus," she said, and pointed to where I had just been chased from.

"I *really need* a taxi," I said, gesturing at her in typical Italian style, all five fingers of my hands held upright and together.

The force of my words pushed her eyebrows up and she wiped her hands on a towel before moving to the end of the bar where there was a public phone.

The woman pantomimed that I needed change for the phone and I handed her the only one I had – it was a one Euro coin.

She shook her head at me. It was too much. She wanted a smaller coin. I tried to communicate that I didn't have anything smaller and didn't care – I just wanted her to use the coin to get me a taxi. Overpaying for a phone call was of no concern and certainly better than being stabbed.

But she refused to put in the Euro coin and went back to her register to break it into smaller coins.

Impatient as only someone in danger can be, I looked out the window and saw threatening shadows everywhere. Assessing the café now, I decided that if the gorillas came in after me, I'd grab the nearest wine bottles to fling at them, and if that didn't work, I'd bust open another two. I hadn't decided whether to throw the broken remnants or use them as knives when the lady returned, smiling.

She showed me the 50 cent coin and put it into the phone. She dialed a number while I alternated between watching her and the threatening shadows outside.

After 30 seconds of no one answering she began to lose patience and eventually hung up. I looked at her with raised eyebrows and upturned hands. She shook her head and said something negative.

And there in the middle of the street, menacingly lit up by the taxi's headlights, were the gorillas. They had been waiting for me.

A helpless feeling enveloped me: I had no idea where I was, no idea how to get home, and a bunch of gorillas were waiting for me outside the door.

"Please," I begged. "Try again. Please."

She looked at me for a long moment and then dialed the number again.

Ten seconds passed. Twenty.

She shook her head at me.

Thirty seconds.

She shrugged. And then, gloriously and at last, she was speaking to information. She wrote down a phone number and hung up the phone – and then, smiling and giving me a "You see?" gesture – she used the other 50 cents to call for the taxi. Eventually she hung up.

Smiling, she held up ten fingers and said, "*Ten minute, si*?"

"*Si, si,*" I gushed. "*Grazie, grazie.*"

She returned to her duties and I stood there with my nose in the specialty item shelves beside the phone, because when I would steal a glance at them, the patronage would all be staring at me. In fact, once when I looked up, a middle-aged man dressed in a rumpled and threadbare sports jacket motioned for me to join him at his table. I gave him a half-smile and shook my head.

After inspecting the shelves for what I gauged to be ten minutes, I ventured toward the door. Shadows were still lurking, but there was nothing to do about it, so, heart racing, I stepped outside and sheepishly looked out. The sidewalk tables were empty and there was a menacing feel to the street. Shadows were moving to the right. And to the left, coming up the street toward the café was the taxi. I turned back to the staring phone lady and waved. She hesitantly waved, and I hustled out the door.

The taxi was 50 feet away and I did not know if I would be caught on the way. I quick-walked, holding my bag in one hand to swing at any attacker, and made it to the taxi. I got in the back and locked the door.

I told the driver the name of the hotel but he'd never heard of it, so I gave him the hotel's card – thank God I had it with me – and he recognized the street name. He turned off the overhead light and started to drive.

And there in the middle of the street, menacingly lit up by the headlights, were the gorillas. They *had* been waiting for me.

But it didn't matter anymore, because being Roman, the taxi driver continued driving straight at them and leaned on his horn.

Seeing that the car wasn't going to stop, the gorillas cleared out of the way and as we passed them I tried not to look, but still saw one of them grimace at me and draw his finger across his throat.

We pulled out into traffic and I leaned back in the seat, breathing heavy and wondering if this altruism business was really all it was cracked up to be.

The resume
Germany, 2004
This story first appeared in Applecart Magazine

I always figured what I needed to learn was somewhere beyond the Pennsylvania state line, so when I finished university, I packed up the car and drove out to fabulous LA. There, I had my heart broken, my car stolen, and basically lived in borderline poverty for months.

When I'd had enough of *that*, I drove my new, overstuffed Geo Metro through the Southwest and ended up in Missouri, where I applied to graduate school. I didn't get accepted, and I ended up moving back to PA. Despite the disappointment of getting turned down for grad school, it ended up being a great time for me – I worked five part-time jobs that I thoroughly enjoyed, including bartender, fitness instructor and freelance writer, *and* I lived in my grandparent's house free of charge.

There was a lot of history in that house; my father had grown up there, my grandfather had died there 15 years before, and I had spent a lot of time there with my grandmother since then.

At that point, however, gramma was in a nursing home, and the house had been unoccupied until two of my friends successfully petitioned my father to live there. And since *they* were paying rent, *they* got the upstairs rooms and when I moved in I got the spidery basement study that my grandfather had built for himself years before.

His study was actually a self-contained apartment, complete with a high four-poster bed and an adjoining bathroom. The centerpiece of the cramped 10x8 ft. space was granpa's sturdy roll top desk, inside of which remained a trove of files.

Moving into grandpa's space proved to be a wondrous experience in discovery. Since he'd died when I was 12, I hadn't really had much time to get to know him, but living in his space allowed me to understand him better.

When I had the time, I rooted through the files in his desk looking for gold; journals, old letters – whatever. Unfortunately, I mostly found old financial documents, occasional business letters, and household appliance manuals dating from the 1950s.

I thought I'd hit pay dirt when I came across the journal he'd kept during a solitary trip to our family's mountain cabin. I opened it with great interest and read the first entry:

Date: September 28, 1978
Time: 6:23 p.m.
Temperature: 64 F
Wind: SW
Sky: Cumulous clouds
Barometer: 30.2, rising
Distance driven: 154 miles
Gas mileage: 12.9 mpg

And then the entry: "Good day for driving. Not much traffic. Upon arrival, mouse in kitchen trap. Creek running low. Neighbors not here."

That was the whole entry. Truthfully, I had been expecting a lot more – emotional insights about my grandfather the wise old man, or maybe timeless thoughts I could cherish and pass on to my children. I sure didn't get that. But I suppose the main thing I was after was information about my grandpa, and I certainly learned about his character from reading those laconic entries.

Grandpa's old travel journal wasn't the only interesting thing that I discovered in the old roll top – I also found hundreds of old black and white pictures in which I recognized some of the people, but never the places. So I brought them along with me when I visited Gramma in the nursing home.

It turned out that Gramma hadn't seen those photos in years, and we had great conversations based on them – she would talk for hours about her past, and a light would come into her normally vacuous eyes, something wonderful to see. When I'd be leaving after a visit, she'd always encourage me to bring in more photos, and I always told her I had another batch so she'd have something to look forward to. In a very real sense, I was helping her reclaim her memories, and it was a rewarding experience.

But by far the best discovery I made in that roll top desk was the resume that my grandfather had compiled sometime during his career. It detailed all of the jobs he'd held, his education, hobbies, interests, and objectives. It covered two pages, was single-space typed, and took me over 15 minutes to read through. It was fascinating reading, and I enjoyed it immensely.

By and by, there came a long holiday weekend that I spent out at my parent's house. I brought the resume with me, and at about 7 p.m. I gave it to dad.

He had never seen the document and was surprised to discover that his father even had a resume. He was immediately engrossed by it.

I was meeting some friends that night, so I headed out the door. When I returned at 1 a.m., the resume lay open at my father's spot at the kitchen table; I pictured it as the last thing he had read before going to sleep. And when I shuffled into the kitchen late the next morning, my father was again reading the resume, stopping occasionally to look out the window.

(Don't) Trust your government
Germany, 2004

This story first appeared on hackwriters.com

I was looking through a college Social Psychology textbook the other day, reading about time and Circadian Principles when I happened upon the following sentence: "In 1876, the wind-up clock was invented in Connecticut, and life was never the same again."

That sentence and its subsequent claims of Yankee ingenuity disturbed me for some reason. I re-read it three or four times, and then finally realized what it was that troubled me – I just couldn't believe that the wind-up watch was so recently invented.

So I reached for my New York Public Library Desk Reference book (NYLDR), a comprehensive reference book filled with the most random of facts, and turned to the list of important scientific inventions to check when the clock was discovered. Sure enough, according to the NYLDR, the mechanical clock was invented in 1360 by Henri de Vick of Württemburg for King Charles the V of France. Later, the portable clock (popularly known as the Nürnberg Egg) was invented by the German Peter Henlein around 1500. Even back then they used coiled springs that had to be wound up. Indeed, a little research on the Internet reveals that the first reported person to actually wear a watch on the wrist was the French mathematician and philosopher, Blaise Pascal, who lived from 1623-1662.

So why was this Social Psychology textbook telling me that the wind-up clock was invented in 1876? I read the textbook again and there were no references to Henri de Vick, Peter Henlein or Blaise Pascal. Instead, credit for inventing the portable watch was given to the Unknown Yankee American.

One may feel I'm splitting hairs here, but shouldn't credit be given where credit is due? I mean, if a Frenchman invented the watch, why shouldn't an American textbook contain that information?

One may posit ignorance, or even claim the textbook's author employed lackadaisical research methods, but a more conspiratorial answer is also possible: crediting the French for inventing the watch would grant a certain amount of legitimacy to an outside system, and that's not what the American educational system is all about. No, we don't inherit inventions from Old Europe – we invent them ourselves and claim first place.

The flag thing

Propaganda is a powerful word that evokes dark, disquieting images. Perhaps we picture Nazi Germany or some other totalitarian regime of the worst sort – public address systems spewing rot throughout the town, posters everywhere espousing the system, fear of dissent.

But how about this for a startling premise: the American government, with the aid of its educational system, engages in propaganda every day.

Which will likely sound preposterous until you read the following. Think back to your school days – every morning it was the same thing, wasn't it? You had to stand, hand over your heart, and recite the Pledge of Allegiance. I haven't had to say it for over 20 years, but I still remember it word for word, as I'm sure you do.

"I pledge allegiance to the flag of the United States of America, and to the republic for which it stands, one nation under God, indivisible, with liberty and justice for all."

The words from the pledge are relatively benign (even though the word "indivisible" also describes China's policy towards Hong Kong, Taiwan and Tibet.) and after all, who isn't for liberty and justice?

But what the pledge *says* is not what I wish to draw attention to. The crux of the matter is that young Americans are required to say the pledge every school day of their lives – which, even taking skipped days into account, adds up to over 2,000 times.

The question is, what purpose does reciting the pledge serve? We're already American, are we not, so why do we have to restate our loyalties every day?

And while I'm at it, what about the singing of the National Anthem before every American sporting event that takes place? What purpose does this serve?

Could it be to reinforce patriotism? Bring about loyalty? Propagate American values?

You bet.

And forgive me for pointing it out, but propaganda and propagate share a direct relation.

Thinking outside the box

Most U.S. citizens have relatively little knowledge of what goes on in the rest of the world. In point of fact, the typical American's worldview is restricted due to the limited amount of international information to which they are exposed. The easiest way to describe this rather straightforward idea is to present an information-flow theory I was exposed to while studying mass communications.

The main hypothesis posits that a nation of high rank (i.e., possessing economic, political, or military power) generates much more information than a nation of lower rank. Because of the higher amount of information generated within the higher-ranking country, A) the population of that country will have a great deal of domestic information to deal with, and B) a significant amount of this information will be sent abroad.

Conversely, information produced by the aforementioned lower-ranking country will have a more difficult time entering the information market of the higher-ranking country because the population of the higher-ranking country, A) have adequate information from their own country to deal with, and B) lack the motivation to attend foreign media due to the foreign country's lower status and remoteness.

The practical side of this theory is that U.S. citizens receive a huge amount of information every day that is generated within the U.S., and information generated outside of the U.S. is seen as secondary in importance. "Around the World in 80 Seconds", boasts the newscast of a major American television network, as if this amount of time is adequate to cover the nuances of international affairs.

That Americans lack news and information from the world at large is no secret to people who live outside of the States. That many American tourists appear uninterested in the world because of this is also no secret. However, to Americans living inside of the U.S., this notion may seem completely unfounded and be quite insulting.

Notwithstanding how domestic Americans view this widely-accepted idea, I have come to see it as fundamentally true and was myself shocked to discover I was once under its sway as well.

In any case, my knowledge of the above theory has led me to the following suspicion, true or not: recent American foreign policy is nothing more than a series of calculated "screw-you's" directed at other countries, because the White House not only knows about, but simply LOVES how American media drowns out coverage of events that occur outside of the United States, thereby keeping its populace in the dark about its less savory actions abroad.

Americans are not dumb – far from it – but in many cases we are grossly uninformed about the world and the actions of our government in it.

Homeland (in-) security

The Homeland Security website tells us that the world is a changed place since Sept. 11, stating that the U.S. is at risk of terrorist attacks and will remain so for the foreseeable future. And so we have the Homeland Security Advisory System, which actually tells us how to behave under certain conditions. Code Yellow: We should be guarded and suspicious of people, especially strangers.

The explicit message is, don't trust anyone, but trust us, your government, because we are here to protect you from those who hate our way of life, those who hate our freedoms, those who hate the United States of America.

In my opinion, the climate of fear that the government created in the wake of 9/11 is unhealthy and unnecessary. When one goes about their daily routine suspicious of others, on "Elevated Alert" status, the negative energy that is created leads to a population concerned with just one thing – survival. And according to Abraham Maslow's hierarchy of needs, when one is concerned merely with survival, one has precious little time to devote to the important things such as friends and family, morality, lack of prejudice, or even the clear acceptance of facts.

Since its inception, the Homeland Security Advisory System has never been on Green, or Low Alert. In fact, as I write, it stands at Yellow, or Elevated Alert. We are under significant threat. Don't forget that.

And don't forget what Hermann Göring, a Nazi Germany politician and military leader said at the Nuremberg Trials, either: "Of course the common people don't want war, but after all, it is the leaders of a country who determine the policy, and it is always a simple matter to drag people along whether it is a democracy, a fascist dictatorship, or a parliament, or a communist dictatorship. Voice or no voice, the people can always be brought to the bidding of the leaders. That is easy. All you have to do is to tell them they are being attacked, and denounce the pacifists for lack of patriotism and exposing the country to danger. It works the same in every country."

No pride in prejudice
Germany, 2003
This story first appeared in Clever Magazine

I was living in Berlin when the World Trade Centers were smashed into by jet planes. During the following months, my wife Jarmila and I watched television relentlessly: press briefings by White House officials, footage of the airplanes hitting the buildings, cleanup efforts, victims names. And of course we learned about the Taliban and the al-Qaeda network.

It was a difficult time for us as we attempted to find a middle ground between the sense of vengeance that I as an American felt, and the level-headed approach that my Czech wife took.

My parents, who live in western Pennsylvania, were very concerned about their son and daughter-in-law living in Germany, especially after it was found that some of the terrorists lived in Cologne and Hamburg. So our weekly
Sunday conversations turned into twice-weekly conversations, and the cost didn't much matter.

It was during one of those conversations that my father related the following story to me: as part of having his own business, dad has to visit various clients and one day while on the road he stopped in at a fast food restaurant. He got his order, sat in a booth and was eating when a little while later, two Arabic-looking men sat nearby and started to eat their own meals. Dad didn't feel scared or angry, he said, but he did notice them right away.

A few minutes after these men sat down, two large men wearing hip holsters came into the restaurant – hip holsters that were full of big handguns. The men walked directly to the Arabic men and sat down at the table beside them. They didn't come in to eat – they just sat and stared at the Arabic men. Naturally, the unarmed men became alarmed and left.

My father presented the story as a humorous anecdote that perhaps captured the feeling of people in the States during that time. But far from finding it funny, I saw it as a dangerous episode that not only highlighted the dangers of legalized guns, but the breakdown of a supposedly civil and democratic society. Whatever happened to "innocent until proven guilty?"

Still, I cannot claim that I myself was without prejudice. Indeed, after the beginning of the military reprisal against the Taliban, scarcely a day went by when I was able to avoid the media telling me of the evils of the Islamic religion and the backward people who practice it. Unfortunately I am not completely immune to such messages and were it not for my clear-thinking wife, I fear I would have been more affected than I actually was.

Moreover, my sense of security was threatened when the State Department issued multiple warnings of impending danger to Americans living abroad. That the American and British embassies in Berlin were barricaded and lined with tanks and soldiers did nothing to assuage my concerns, and I admit that I was a leery American living in a foreign city during a time of international crisis.

Why would you live there?
So it was with trepidation that we approached our move to the Neuköln (New Cologne) district of Berlin. You won't find much information about Neuköln in the travel books aside from blurbs on the incredible size of some of the tenement buildings or that it is a district to avoid. In fact, when you mention to Berliners that you live in Neuköln, their reaction is either unfavorable or of polite but unmistakable surprise. Simply put, Neuköln is not a beautiful district.

There are several things about Neuköln that give it its distinct feel: first is its population density, which is the highest of all Berlin districts. Secondly, Neuköln has the highest concentration of foreigners of all the Berlin districts – partially related to the import of *Gästearbeiter* (guest workers) from Turkey, who helped rebuild Germany after WWII. Thirdly, Neuköln has the highest unemployment rate of any district in all of Germany.

These factors all contribute to the gritty feel of Neuköln, and made my wife and I question the wisdom of moving there, especially given the political climate of the time.

However, we were offered a living deal that was too good to pass up: our friend had scored himself a visiting scholar position in America for six months and was looking for someone to move into his family's flat. The apartment was huge by European standards, about 110 square meters, and it was fully-furnished and equipped. So even though we were moving into the rough part of town, we would have a fine flat in which to live and work.

Circumstances, then, brought us to Neuköln.

Direct observation

I was more concerned than my wife was about living in an area highly populated by people of middle Eastern descent. After all, *I* was the American who had been listening to the whispers of danger and the evil of the Arabic-speaking population for months.

Thus, on our first Sunday in Neuköln, my wife had a difficult time convincing me to go for a walk, as had been our Sunday custom in our previous neighborhood. She wanted to check out the nearby park, and thought that it wouldn't be too crowded on such a cold and rainy January day. I relented out of sheer curiosity.

As it turned out, our first walk through the park brought us face-to-face with no less than six brown- and black-skinned drug dealers. What's more, they were highly organized, with sentries at every entrance to the park. Now, ten years ago as a single man I wouldn't have been fazed, but as a man walking with his wife, I was extremely anxious being surrounded by them in a deserted park in the middle of Neuköln. This ended our traditional Sunday walks.

That very same night we were horribly awakened at 2 a.m. by the sounds of our neighbors having an intense fight. I had seen the man in passing when I was moving in: he hadn't returned my greeting and he was of Middle Eastern descent. From the cries and screams that we heard, we could tell that there was a wife and a daughter in the way of the man's anger. The melee ended just as my wife was picking up the phone to call the police, and we had a lot of trouble getting back to sleep.

Welcome to Neuköln!

Acclimation

The following weeks were easier to bear and we didn't have any more overly negative experiences. However, we were keeping a close eye on our surroundings, and what we saw was both interesting and thought-provoking: all the computers in our neighborhood computer store bore Arabic language screen-savers; there were thousands of heretofore unknown products available in the stores; the fruit and vegetable sellers would loudly hawk in Arabic at the passerby; there were dozens of exclusively male "social clubs" from a myriad of countries.

Indeed, when one of us would leave the flat, we would invariably return with a new and often strange experience to relate over dinner, and our discussions sometimes lasted for hours.

One of the first topics my wife brought up was the aggressive manner of the men in Neuköln. For example, while walking down the street, she had someone walk straight at her and place his face into her line of vision in an attempt to get her attention. Another situation saw a German man put his outstretched fist into her face.

And yet, the men never touched her. So while she sometimes felt uncomfortable, she didn't feel (directly) physically threatened. After awhile she became accustomed to avoiding the looks and stares, but there was always a feeling of tension and wariness when she walked alone. As she would say, "It was sometimes unpleasant walking there."

One of the things that I myself noticed was that an lot of women in the district walk two steps behind their man. As a topic of discussion, I suggested that it was a bit unfair that the man and woman could not walk side-by-side.

This brought about a whole discussion on women's rights, which included the fact that many Muslim women are denied schooling and therefore any possibility to work outside of the home; this struck a strong chord with my wife, who, through diligent study, has been able to leave behind the limited opportunities of small village life and move into the international marketplace. On the other hand, we also spoke about the many benefits that the Muslim family unit must enjoy from having a stay-at-home mother.

Acceptance

When we moved to Neuköln, I admit that I was prejudiced against Arabic-speaking people. Indeed, I was against them as a concept; they had destroyed the World Trade Centers and were a threat to Americans everywhere.

However, as time wore on, my wife and I began to accept that even though we don't agree with some of the practices and attitudes that we observed in Neuköln, the people who apply them have every right in the world to live as they choose. And that's the point, really; the freedom to choose.

The problem, however, is that people afflicted by dogma or prejudice of any kind are denied choice by a narrow range of thought. This not only goes for prejudice against racial groups or religious beliefs, but also for blindly patriotic dogma or fundamentalist conservative dogma as well.

At any rate, I am glad to say that after being exposed to the Turks and other people from Arabic-speaking countries in Berlin-Neuköln, I learned through direct observation that I am not prejudiced against them as a whole: I simply disagree with some of the things that they believe and practice (just as they likely disagree with some of mine).

But I arrived at this opinion only after long discussions about the things that my wife and I bore witness to; discussions which confronted our own values and beliefs as we attempted to understand what others believe and value themselves.

If only more of us could do the same.

How Nice
Germany, 2004

Our first taste of French hospitality came at the Nice airport information desk, where we waited for the youngish clerk to finish his phone call. After hanging up, he raised his eyebrows at us.

"*Bon jour*," I said, "*Parlez vous Anglais?*"

"*Oui.*"

"Great. Where can we get the bus into town? Is there-"

He held his hand up to stop me and then picked up the ringing phone. Jarmila and I traded glances.

A minute later, still on the phone, the clerk seemed to remember us and unfolded a map, made an "x" and traced a bus route. Then he pointed to the nearest exit and turned back to his conversation.

"Nice fella," I said to Jarmila.

"Mmm."

Wheeling our luggage behind us, we eventually found our bus, purchased tickets from the driver, and stood over our bags as we rode into town. We had searched for and found reasonably-priced accommodations on the web, but it was booked out. Not to worry, wrote the booking service by e-mail, there's a nearby hotel in your price range that you will have accepted if you don't indicate otherwise in the next hour.

Since we got this email a day later, the Hotel Lodarno it was.

From behind his mahogany counter, a deeply-tanned young man welcomed us and bade us sign our room confirmation before giving us our room key. We gratefully took it, tired from the long day of travel, and took the tiny elevator to the 2nd floor. We heaved and trundled out into the dark hallway and found our room directly across from the elevator.

I opened the door for Jarmila and she sniffed the air apprehensively. Walking in behind her, I saw that the room was small, dark, and filled with scratched second-hand furniture one might find at a weekend cabin.

"Hey, there's a balcony," I said with artificial enthusiasm.

I gestured toward the floor-length windows, which had a waist-high bar across them. Opening one window and looking out, we were treated to a view of the dreary inner courtyard. Below, a weatherbeaten couch and sundry old furniture littered the ground.

Jarmila looked at me with her arms crossed.

"Should I talk to him," I asked.

"No…"

"Let's test the bed. If it's bad, I'll go down."

We lay on the bed side-by-side, our feet on the floor, and looked up at the ceiling. Directly above us lived a colony of black and green mold that stretched across the room.

Jarmila hopped up and said, "That's unbelievable! How could they offer such a room for €85 per night?"

I started laughing and got up. "And who knows what's growing *on* the bed."

We left our bags in the room and went down to the reception desk. The young man was at the computer pretending to work. He looked up when we approached, however.

"Oui?"

"The room you gave us has mold on the ceiling. Do you have any other rooms?"

Without looking, he reached behind himself, grabbed another key, and handed it to me.

"Maybe this one. You can choose."

"Thanks."

The new room was on the same floor as the first, but was bright and clean, had new furniture, a sparkling bathroom, a balcony with a view of the public square and zero visible mold.

After moving our baggage, I took the old key to the reception desk and pointedly didn't thank the kid.

We were on the promenade Saturday morning at the crack of 10, carrying our picnic lunch in a plastic bag. The beach was far rockier than we would've thought, and since this was to be our big day in the sun, we inquired with a shoreline restaurant that provided cushiony lounge chairs next to the breakers.

The waiter told us a chair cost €10 each, then told us we couldn't stay because we had our own food.

"So if I buy food from you, the beach chair is free," I said.

"No. You must still pay."

"Can we rent a chair and just put our food away?"

"No. You must come back when the food is gone."

As Jarmila and I frowned at each other, the waiter turned away.

Further along the shore, we found a quiet spot and spread the blanket we'd smuggled from the hotel. We organized ourselves and sat cross-legged facing the water, listening to the waves; as they receded, the water loudly clacked the smaller rocks together.

Time slowed and the tension we'd brought with us was melted by the hot sun, blown by the sea breeze, and washed away by the impossibly blue waters of the Mediterranean. We swam, joining with the waves and choking on the salty water that sometimes sneaked up on us. We marveled at the jets coming in for landing, making their hard bank left just offshore and very low over the water in front of us.

The sun dried and drained us, and we read and napped our day away.

We stayed for the sunset before succumbing to the windy chill of the evening, and once back in the room, we showered and went to bed early.

We both felt bouncy on Sunday morning, despite the fact we were leaving that day. We went downstairs for breakfast, old hands by day two, and soon after the clerk asked if we wanted coffee or tea. Moments later he brought us the simple breakfast tray with a section of baguette, two croissants, and hot drinks.

Chatty about how the sea had energized us, we went up to our room and packed. It wasn't the depressing activity it could have been. Rather, we were optimistic and funny, and I wasn't even worried about flying later that day.

After taking a last look around, we trundled down to the reception desk.

"How would you like to pay for your breakfasts," asked the dark-haired clerk.

I blinked at him.

"It wasn't included in the price?"

"Non."

Jarmila looked at him coldly.

"Why didn't you tell us it wasn't included on the first day? You only asked if we wanted coffee or tea..."

"I'm very sorry... but I tell you. Since is a problem, I charge you only half, yes?"

"Uh-huh... and how much is that?"

He pretended to be figuring numbers on his pad before he said, "50 Euro."

"What?! It was just coffee and bread!"

"Ok, ok. Forty."

I looked at him without expression and said, "Thirty."

He looked at me with narrowed eyes and said, "Thirty-five."

I shook my head.

"Ok, ok," he said. "Thirty. But in cash."

As I paid, Jarmila asked about storing our bags for a few hours, and the clerk pointed to a room behind us. "Yes, you can store them there. Just a moment, I'll open it."

He came around the front desk, walked over and opened the door. It was dark and there was room for only one person, so Jarmila maneuvered our bags into position and closed the door.

"See you soon," said the clerk, smiling.

After sitting along the promenade and watching the beach for an hour, we walked into the Old Town to buy gifts. On the walk back through the close streets, we bought a roasted chicken and headed back to the promenade to eat with a view. Passers-by stared as we ate with our fingers and threw scraps to the hovering seagulls.

Fulfilled and smiling, we walked back to the hotel to collect our bags. The sea was still in us, making everything seem just a touch irrelevant.

When we entered the hotel, the reception desk was empty and we walked back to the lobby toilets. I returned first, and went into the baggage room.

I wheeled Jarmila's bag over to the reception desk, put my backpack on top of it, and rang the bell on the counter.

A moment later, a grey-haired man I'd not met popped his head out of an office next to the luggage room and said, "Yes?"

At the same moment, a carefree Jarmila came around the corner to hear me tell the man, "My bag is gone."

Jarmila stopped short. "What?"

The grey-haired man stepped out of his office and said, "Yes," again.

Jarmila went into the unlocked room to make sure it wasn't there. She came out shaking her head. "Its gone. We stored two bags and one is gone."

The man walked behind the reception desk and placed his hands wide on the counter.

"I'm very sorry."

Jarmila and I looked at each other, then back to him.

He shook his head sadly. "I'm very sorry."

"Uh-huh. Where is the boy who was working before? The dark boy?"

"Mark? Gone."

"Will he come back today?"

"No, but I call him."

He started shuffling papers, looking for Mark's number. Jarmila was beside herself.

"I can't believe someone stole your bag! And look at the door – it was unlocked the whole time – no wonder people's bags are stolen here."

The grey-haired man looked up from his papers. "Madame, bags are not stolen from this hotel. Perhaps it was a mistake."

Jarmila's eyes grew. "The mistake was staying here in-"

"Sweety," I interrupted, "getting worked up won't help us. Maybe Mark knows something."

Jarmila took a deep breath, smoothing her hair back with both hands. "Ok, if it was a mistake, we need the addresses from the bags in the closet…"

"Good idea." I asked for a pen and paper.

The man gave us these and Jarmila went to get the addresses. I stood there as the man called Mark. The part of the French conversation I understood was that Mark had no idea about the baggage, that maybe it was a mistake.

After he hung up the phone, the man put his hands wide on the counter again. "I'm very sorry. But Mark… he said several guests collected their bags from the room today."

"What if they took mine by mistake?"

"Then… I will send it."

"You'll send my bag to me?"

"Yes, of course. Just give me your address."

Jarmila returned and I used a piece of the paper. As I wrote down our address, Jarmila said, "And what if someone stole it?"

"Madam. There is no thievery at this hotel." He pulled the bottom of his right eye down with his index finger, meaning he was telling the truth – just look in his eyes.

"Yes, well," she responded. "Our bag is gone. It is *possible* it was stolen. What if it *was* stolen?"

He looked at us blankly. "Send me a list of your things."

"And…"

He hesitated and then said, "I will pay."

"You'll pay us for the stolen bag?"

"*If* it was stolen. But we wait for to see if it returned. Then you email me the list."

"Ok. And what was your name?"

"Jean-Yves. I am the manager. I get you my card." He walked back into his office and Jarmila and I looked all around for my bag. It wasn't anywhere.

I shrugged my shoulders and said, "Maybe it'll turn up."

"I can't grasp that it's gone," she said.

I thought about the lost perfume we'd bought for our mothers and my favorite hooded sweat-shirt I'd had for ten years. My stomach lurched and I shook my head.

I shrugged. "Maybe it's not."

Jean-Yves bustled back out with his card and handed it to us.

"I'm very sorry," he repeated, with all the sympathy of someone who hasn't lost their belongings.

On the bus to the airport, standing close to Jarmila, I said, "You know we'll never see any money for that bag, right?"

"Don't say that," she said. "I can't think about it."

"At least our passports and money weren't in it."

Jarmila's eyes lit up. "Hey! Maybe the bag is at the airport. Maybe someone took it by mistake and then at check-in realized it wasn't theirs and took it to the lost and found!"

"If they didn't recognize it at the hotel, why would they recognize it at the airport?"

She glared at me. "Can't you at least try?"

I breathed deep. "I think that dark kid stole it."

We arrived at the airport less than an hour before the plane was to leave and checked in. We explained our dilemma to the check-in lady and she suggested we try the lost and found, which was downstairs.

"But hurry! You have only 15 minutes before boarding!"

We power-walked downstairs and to the far end of the building, dodging people and luggage the whole way, but couldn't find the sign she'd described.

At the nearby Information Desk, the woman was on the phone. As we stood in front of her impatiently, she did her best to ignore us until Jarmila asked her where the lost and found was, and the woman took the receiver away from her mouth. She pointed in the direction we'd come from and told us to go to a second Information Desk.

The place we were after was behind a glass barrier, and a security guard, chatting up some lady colleague, stood apathetically by, watching us struggle with the needlessly complex door-opening procedure. Finally he pointed to a hidden button behind us, nowhere near where a door-opener would be, and we rushed in to the baggage claim office.

A representative walked over to us and we explained our situation in harried English. The look on his face indicated he understood maybe two words, but he still led us back to a room filled with unclaimed baggage.

Mine wasn't there.

We hustled back up to the security check-in, absolutely sure we'd miss our flight, and were about to scan my backpack when Jarmila remembered the Swiss-Army knife we'd used to cut the chicken for lunch. It was still in my rucksack. My father gave me that knife when I'd first come to Europe.

I snatched my bag from the x-ray machine, prompting suspicious looks from the security personnel, and barged my way back through the waiting line and over to the check-in lady we'd originally spoken to. We told her about the knife and she said I could either check in my backpack with the knife inside, or leave the knife in Nice.

Since I was already leaving more in Nice than I wanted to, I rifled the bag for things I might need if it too was stolen or lost, and then hustled back to security at the woman's urgings.

We made it through without incident, but our gate was physically closed, and we could see some of the cabin crew walking down toward the plane. We pounded on the glass doors until they turned around and saw us gesturing madly to be let in. One of the women, a short blonde woman in her late 40s, came running back. She opened the door and said, "You're lucky I'm in a good mood today."

We made our way onto the plane, got stared at by a cabin full of seated passengers, and eventually collapsed, sweating, into our seats in the very last row.

An airplane, three trains and a taxi later, we arrived home at midnight.

The next day we called one of the phone numbers Jarmila had collected from the baggage storage room in the hotel. An English lady answered and very politely listened to our story, but simply couldn't fathom that her bag was in the storage room in the Hotel Lodarno when it had been stolen from that same establishment five months previously.

Eyes of blue
Germany, 2004

My first summer job was to dismember things. I started by hacking and removing trees with a modified weed-whacker that had a saw blade instead of nylon string. Later, when I had acquired a bit more hacking experience, I was promoted to the garden tractor that we used to reclaim overgrown fields. Toward the end of the season, I made the big time – I was entrusted with a farm tractor that pulled the gang-mowers (which wreaked absolute *havoc* on snakes).

But this story has nothing to do with the sweat and blood and sap that was spilled that summer. It's actually about the lady that ran the lunch counter for the golf course I dismembered things for. See, about once per week that summer I would eat lunch in the clubhouse diner. The woman behind the counter, Marlene, was red-haired, pleasant and somewhere in her 50s. We would shoot the breeze while she cooked or I ate.

About midway through the summer, after we had exhausted our supply of complaints about the boss, she asked where I was from, and I told her Chippewa Township.

She looked at me hard and said, "But your father, I bet he's from Hopewell."

"Yeah, he is, and my grandmother still lives there."

She had a *Eureka* look in her eyes and said, "I knew it! You're a Curtiss boy, aren't you?"

"Yeah – how'd you know?"

"Your eyes. Your father has the same beautiful blue eyes."

I swallowed a mouthful and blinked.

"Oh, that Jerry Curtiss," she sighed, and looked faraway before returning to the diner.

"All the girls loved him in high school, you know. He was a year ahead of me, and me and my girlfriends all had the biggest crushes on him. He had the most beautiful blue eyes you ever saw. Are they still so blue?"

"Uh… I guess."

"Oh, he was so *dreamy*," she gushed. "What a handsome boy he was."

I scarfed down my sandwich and was, for the first time ever, looking forward to getting back to work.

"How much do I owe you?" I asked her.

"Oh, today it's on me, honey. But you tell your father that Marlene Hendrick said hello, willya?"

"Ok, I will," I said, and hustled out. I was halfway out the door when she called after me.

"And don't go telling him about the crush I had on him, ok, honey?"

"Ok," I said.

But you know, sometimes secrets are just too good to keep.

Fiction

Report this
Spain, 2008

An anecdote, huh? Well, I could tell you about the dog, I guess. Basically I didn't see it coming and probably couldn't have stopped it anyway. But luckily – if you wanna look at it like that – when the bastard sank its teeth into my calf I dropped my grabbers and I guess the sound of the metal hittin' the sidewalk is what scared it enough to let go. I reflexively tried to clutch at my calf, you know, but I only managed to dump the sausages and some of the bread on the pavement. This is obviously what the freakin' dog was after and I tried to kick at him and not let him have the meat, but he got two of them before I was able to chase him off. Anyway, I un-buckled and placed the cooker down, wondering how I was gonna get the thing back home if not on my back, and checked my leg. At least there was no blood, though he did break the skin. And you know, a crowd of about 20 people gathered, but none made a frickin' move to help. That's what it's like on the street, you know? You can't expect nuthin'. You turn your back for a second and some jerk steals your bag or your shoes or your bike or whatever. Believe me, I seen it. Just last week some Pedro on a scooter knocked a lady down, jumped off the scooter, grabbed her bag, and took off. No plates on the scooter, of course. And there's me standing nearby with a frickin' propane tank strapped on my back, waddlin' over tryin' to help. I did manage to squirt the guy with ketchup as he made his getaway and they were able to track him down because of it, which is great and all, but then I had to give a statement down at the station during my peak selling hours. Which is what you get for caring, you know? You get inconvenienced. I mean yeah, we all seem nice and sociable, but we're just concerned about appearances, really. We want to appear nice and I guess mostly we are until something screwy happens. For example, when you show your white or black-skinned mug and speak your pidgin Spanish here, you get *that look*, and things go frosty. They're even worse to the South Americans – which is stupid, cuz as far as immigrants go, the Latin Americans have everything Spain could want – hard-working, Spanish-speaking and they look pretty much the same, you know? But they're still dis-criminated against. Like all foreigners, I guess. But I can't bitch too much… hold on a minute.

<speaks to a customer in Spanish>

Before I forget, I wanna mention that I had to hire a buddy to come around and top up my sau-sage filler every night. The sausage filler, in case you want to include that in the article, is a long tube that feeds the meat paste into the sausage casings, which I tie off and cut before making another one. The whole process takes about three seconds. I don't like to do it in front of the customers, but sometimes I have to.

What's that? Oh, I guess what I like is the talking – I gotta amuse myself somehow, and havin' a grill on my lap for 8 hours a day just don't cut it, you know what I'm sayin'? So I try to engage my clients. The younger ones, I ask them about Spanish music and concerts comin' to town. The tourists, I bust out my German or English and ask 'em if they like the heat. The Spanish, I stick to the local stuff like the new metro, or ask them why the hell my neighbor insists on makin' Gazpacho at 1 in the morning. I shit you not – really happened. With the repeat customers, the older ones, I talk politics to get 'em fired up. Why is the ETA still operating, the March 11 bombings, that kinda stuff. Funny thing about March 11 – the supplier of the dynamite was a

Spanish guy who was an ex-miner. Think of that – a Spanish guy cooperating with foreign ter-
rorists. Did you know that most of the Spanish think it was the government that brought about
March 11 by being in Iraq in the first place? And I agree… because you don't see – I don't know
– *Mexican* commuter trains blasted all to hell. You don't see hijackings in Switzerland.

Miss home? Nah. Speaking of that, I always get Americans askin' what made me come here
and peddle the sausages, and you know what I tell 'em? The weather. All the sun here is fantastic, though in the summer I sweat like a damn ox, especially with the cooker puttin' out all that
heat. But you know, the weather ain't really the reason. The real reason is Bush. I got sick of
hearin' his voice every day. That fake-cowboy Bible-thumpin' schtick he's got going may fool
other people, but I ain't buyin' it, you know what I'm sayin'?

Oh, you bet you can. It's an education watching people all day. I guess my least favorite thing
is the Spanish social distance, which is a lot smaller than in America. Here, people cut you off
left and right, and if there's a convergence of folks, the jostling is amazing. I worked Semana
Santa last year and couldn't believe the people and their bumping. They actually seemed to expect *me* to get out of *their* way, like I'm so frickin' light on my feet. I've also learned to be a
better server as well. At first, I had the location of the bread and the condiments all mixed up, but
now – wait, lemme finish – now I got a system. First the money. Then I start with a napkin and
the bread on the left – pre-sliced during slow times – and then the brat, then the onions and-

Whatsat? The worst? Well, the bathroom issue is tough. You can't just go when and where
you want, you know what I'm sayin'? But the thing I hate most is the accordion players. There's
a few who are good, but the ones who are still learnin' hit all the wrong notes and got that silly
grin they reserve for any tourist who pays attention to them. One actually went electric and has a
frickin' amplifier that belts out his gypsy nonsense. Now let me just say before one of 'em lays a
curse on me that I got no problem with the gypsies – they gotta make a living like anyone else,
but when they stick that stupid shrub of Myrrh in your face and then demand money, I mean, it's
just a scam. And if you take the shrub but don't give money, boy, they'll go all Harpy on you
and I seen one lady pay 10, then hand over another 20 just to get outta the team-up the gypsies
had going on. They're a nasty bunch, man. But the accordion-players, at least they got a skill. I
mean, I don't like the music, but I can see it ain't easy to play. The Myrrh scam is something
else, though – it's all confrontation and if you play it wrong they'll lay a curse on you, and I
don't care who you are, a gypsy curse ain't what you're after.

See, I really don't know… as long as I can, I guess. The money isn't all that hot, but my license
runs out in 2010, so if people keep buying the sausages, I guess I'll see what happens then. I'm
thinking of going down to the beach for the summer and selling down there, but I'm afraid I'd
get lazy and just lay around all day and slobber over the ladies.

Oh yeah, no problem. Happy to help. You'll let me know when it gets printed, right? Hey, you
want to try one? I'll only charge you double – ha! Just kiddin'. But really, you want one? Come
on, without the onions it won't hurt your breath. Really no? Now you see that – I spend a half
hour answering your questions and you won't even buy a freakin' sausage… Hey, you know
what? Off the record, I made all that crap up. Whaddya think of that? Now waddya gonna do for
your little article? You shoulda just bought one, Pedro. Shoulda just bought one. Now get the
hell outta here before I squirt you with the ketchup… Damn scribbler…

Węgierska Górka
Spain, 2008

The crunching of gravel brought the neighbor's sheep out of their shaded siesta spots and over to the fence, and Frank pet the ones that would let him. Further on, the path turned into two dirt tracks with brown grass growing in the middle, and all around were mountain fields covered with purple wildflowers and long tawny grass gone to seed. Frank saw the rocky tributary of the Sowa River coming out of the forested mountains far ahead of him, winding itself down into the valley to his right and eventually through Węgierska Górka. There, he frequently saw people swimming in the river below the dam; a nearby snack Imbiss sold ice cream and beer flavored with sweet syrup.

He made his way upwards, the overgrown grass tickling his exposed legs, until he came to an intersecting cart path. A line of beech trees stretched out in front of him, forming a border between two fields; on the left was a field of brilliant yellow canola flowers, the other was filled with wheat – its seeded stems bearing physical testament to the sporadic breeze.

Frank stood in the patchy shade for a moment. The hottest part of the day was just beginning, and he looked down at the town in the valley and breathed in the view. On the far side of Węgierska Górka were high, pine-forested mountains that strode imperiously above the town's three abandoned smokestacks.

After a moment of nervous meditation, Frank turned left onto the overgrown cart path. It graded slightly downward and was still a ten-minute walk to the next village, the name of which he couldn't pronounce. The day before, the owners of the Penzion had sent Frank and the other English teachers over to visit the caretaker of a nearby WWII bunker. The caretaker, a man, had walked them through the well-kept village to the edge of town where the football pitch was. Next to that was the small bunker.

The bunker's history gave way to the man's personal survival story, and he told the group how horrible and brutal The War was, and the terrible things that went along with it. The man said he had lived through government regimes so repressive that they, being Americans, could not understand it.

In truth, there were only two Americans, Frank and Terry, among the four of them. Of the others, one was a Ukrainian girl of 20 who acted as translator, the other was a gentle youth from English-speaking Canada.

During the war, the man said, he had been taken prisoner because all the able-bodied men in that region were either killed on the spot or taken captive. The man told them that he was one of the lucky ones because he had survived and could now tell them about his experiences. He told them they should be happy they were from the United States and they should truly appreciate the freedoms they now had around them in Europe as well, because war is the worst thing imaginable.

His words both fascinated and repelled the young group, who shifted uncomfortably when the Ukrainian girl related the more detailed aspects of his experiences. But the story that clinched his lecture was this one: after the man was captured by the German army he was taken to Auschwitz by train.

When Frank interrupted to ask what it was like at Auschwitz, the man looked him in the eyes and shook his head. When, after a long stare, the man finally spoke, Frank didn't understand the

There was a ruckus of dogs and the chickens they kept for eggs. The man appeared from the chicken coop, crossed the yard and came to the gate smiling. Frank smiled back.

---

words, but he felt the disdain the man was radiating unto him. The Ukrainian girl translated: "He said, 'It is impossible to say how it was exactly, it was so… uh… horrible.' He also said you are unwelcome to ask any more questions. Sorry."

Still glaring at Frank, the man resumed the story: one winter day in the camp, many prisoners were placed into a line. It moved slowly and nobody knew what was waiting for them at the end of it. There were periodic gunshots. After hours of standing in the cold, the man was close enough to the front that he could see a large contingent of guards. They were sending people off to the right or the left. Many of them were crying. There was a pile of dead bodies. As the line crept on, he could hear that they were sending many to the gas chambers. They weren't being secretive about the fact that many of them were going there, and the man was frightened beyond imagination.

When he arrived at the head of the line, he found himself face to face with the notorious Camp Commandant Rudolf Höss, who examined him for a long, terrifying moment before sending him off to the right. That meant he was allowed to work. He cried with relief as he shuffled away, but the cruelty he had seen in Höss' eyes would never leave him. Höss's decision to send him to work had spared his life, he said, and while he hated Höss more than anything, he was extremely grateful not to have been sent to the gas chambers. It was during this part of the story that the man began to cry. The Canadian boy, also crying, hugged him.

When the man tired of speaking, they all walked back to his house, where he introduced them to his daughter. The girl, Lydia, was studying at the university in Warsaw and spoke English. She was very pretty in a wholesome way, and shy. She translated, through her father, that the whole group was welcome anytime.

It was the daughter who Frank, his stomach tumbling over itself, was now walking over to visit. When he arrived at the man's house, Frank took a deep breath and rang the bell at the front gate. There was a ruckus of dogs and the chickens they kept for eggs. The man appeared from the chicken coop, crossed the yard and came to the gate smiling. Frank smiled back.

As the man opened the front gate and realized that Frank was alone, however, his cocked his head slightly. And when Frank asked for his daughter, the man's smile slackened. He drew himself up and crossed his arms, narrowing his eyes in the process. No longer the welcoming host, he had become the protective father right in front of Frank's eyes, and that the man come calling was the foreigner who asked stupid questions didn't seem to be to Frank's benefit.

The man sized Frank up for a moment before calling over his shoulder, "Lydia!" His eyes never left Frank's.

When Lydia came out of the house and saw Frank, the sweaty frown that she had been wearing was replaced by a wide smile. She walked over to them and spoke Polish to her father, who shook his head. The father stood between Frank, who hadn't been invited into the yard, and Lydia, who was sweating heavily and wearing a soiled white apron over her blue housedress.

"Hello… er… Fred, yes?"

"Close… it's Frank. You look busy – should I come back later?"

"No, no. I am only prepare lunch," Lydia said. "I would invite you in, but my papa, he say no."

"Then… maybe we could go for a walk?"

She hesitated, then said, "I must ask."

Lydia's father was clearly unimpressed by the situation. Again, Frank may not have understood the words that papa used, but his open scowl, his raised voice and his dismissive gestures didn't bode well.

But Lydia stood up to him, leaving Frank to embarrassingly witness a family feud in a foreign language. Frank thought for certain that Lydia was going to tell him no, she couldn't go, but then she started untying her apron.

"I must return in half hour," she said, smiling.

They left the man standing at his front gate, holding Lydia's apron and watching them walk away. After a few steps, Lydia looked back and shooed him into the yard, but he didn't budge.

A little further down the hill, Lydia and Frank's hands accidentally brushed together and Frank flinched, withdrawing his hand in surprise.

Lydia laughed easily and said, "What's wrong?"

"Nothing. I… just thought your father threw a rock at me or something."

Lydia laughed again and soon they turned the corner and were out of her father's sight. A moment later she said, "So how long you stay in Poland?"

"For the summer. I'm teaching English at the summer camp."

"And why in Poland?"

"Why not? It's a lovely country."

She wrinkled her nose. "Some places are not so nice."

As they walked past a row of houses that lined the village's main thoroughfare, an older man with a gray neck-beard leaned out of his window. He waved and spoke in a raspy voice to Lydia. Lydia let out a sigh and replied curtly. The man spoke again and Lydia shook her head quickly. Lydia turned to Frank and smiled.

"My father, he call this man and tell him to watch me."

"Really?"

"Yes – probably because you are American playboy," she replied matter-of-factly.

It was Frank's turn to laugh. "Tell him I'm Australian. Maybe that will help."

She giggled and turned back to the man. This did seem to lighten his mood, but then Frank was forced to make up answers to the man's questions about Australia: Yes, they eat lots of kangaroo. Yes, of course Aborigines go around naked in the cities. Eventually Lydia stopped translating and told the man they had to go.

The man insisted on shaking hands through the window, so Frank walked over and shook. The man looked deep into Frank's eyes and spoke.

"What is he saying?"

"He said it was nice to meet you."

"Please tell him it was nice to meet him as well."

Lydia spoke to the man, who hadn't let go of Frank's hand, and the man nodded solemnly. Finally he released Frank's hand and patted him on the shoulder. Not knowing how to respond, Frank patted him back.

"Ok, we go," said Lydia.

After they had walked down the street a bit, Lydia turned to see if the man was still watching. He was. "The people here," she said, "they are very nose. They always watch you and talk on you."

Frank giggled. "Yes, nosey people are difficult."

"Oh yes... nosey people! Not 'nose people'. Ha!"

"But Lydia, you speak well – where did you learn English?"

"In Warsaw. I go to university there."

"Huh. Do you like Warsaw?"

"Very much. Here I'm only worker for mama and papa. There, I am in... inde... I am for my own."

"Yes, I can understand that. And when will you graduate?"

"In two years. But next year I will study in UK."

"Good for you!"

"Yes. I feel forward about this... but what about you – how long will you to be in Węgierska Górka?"

"Until August."

"Oh, this is a pity... I return first from summer classes in September. They start next week." Frank's house of cards came tumbling down. "Yes... that is a pity."

"But why don't you come visit me," she asked with a cocked eyebrow. "Warsaw is a really town and no nosey people there!"

Frank laughed at her joke. "I wish I could, but I don't have any holiday." He was embarrassed to say he had no money for such a trip.

Lydia nodded her head and said wistfully, "Yes, it's pity..."

Ten steps later she asked, "So, we go to the river?"

"Sure."

They turned onto a narrow path that led through a wood, and because he was watching Lydia in her housedress and not the path, Frank's leg brushed against a plant that immediately began to burn his skin. He blurted out, "Jezus! Lydia, I touched this plant here and it's burning like crazy! What is that?!"

She came back to him. "Oh, it is only pokrzywa. Very healthy. You don't have in America?"

"No! Shit! When will it stop burning!?"

Lydia looked unconcerned. "Oh, in a few minutes."

Frank looked at her blankly. "This is the Polish jungle, isn't it?"

Lydia laughed again and said, "Oh, come on!"

Frank kept his eyes on the path to avoid more pokrzywa and so heard but didn't see the river gurgling and splashing ahead of them as they walked through the wood. When they reached the bank, they walked upriver in silence.

"Because I don't want you get sick by swimming," Lydia said, she pointed to how the Sowa River, which flows from the mountains and down through the town of Węgierska Górka, becomes polluted by the open sewer pipe that runs into it.

Democracy
Spain, 2008

A mid-February evening on the Berlin underground. A smattering of commuters in their seats, mostly reading. Others listening to whatever. Overall, it was quiet, civil. We pulled into a station, stopped. No one made a move to exit. Then a door opened up an in he stepped.

The first thing I noticed? The guitar hanging on his back was missing a string. The man himself was short, pudgy. A bird's nest of black hair hung over the collar of his peeling, black leather jacket. His beard didn't hide the red in his cheeks – a red so deep one might think he was drunk. Maybe he was. Certainly he wasn't in a proper state of mind, because he walked to the very center of the car, swung his guitar around and began to yell, in a high-pitched Scottish accent:

"Ohhh... they say it's a dem-OC-RACY... dem-OC-RACY.... a dem-OC-RACY....."

Having grabbed our attention by the throat, this man began to rant about the oppressive fascism that rules the world. Myself, I was fascinated with the guy, looking him in the eyes and being quite amused. He would look at me hard for a few seconds before scanning over the rest of the car to see what kind of reception they were giving him. It wasn't much – they were avoiding eye contact at all costs. *Just act like he's not there...*

In between his rants, every so often the guy would strum the guitar and sing bits of the Beatles' song Helter Skelter. Being a music fan, this was the part that I enjoyed – and you know, he wasn't that bad. After one particularly throaty chorus, though, the fellow let loose with this eyebrow-raising gem: "How can people say it's a dem-OC-RACY when Charles MAN-son has been in jail for 40 years without a fair trial? FORTY YEARS and no fair TRIAL!!"

And then he began jamming.

The entire car was sitting in stunned silence, trying at all costs to avoid eye contact with this... artist. Eyes continuously scanning for contact, the man seemed desperate to shoot his hate into someone; he even managed to re-shape my amusement into a sort of concern.

We arrived at the next station and only after the doors opened and closed again did it occur to me I should have gotten out of the car: I mean, here I was in a situation one reads about: Deranged Man Tommy Guns 50 on Berlin Subway.

Cue the man screaming: "And what about Rudolph Hess, what did he ever do? He was a hero of YOUR dirty country and you allowed him to be arrested! This whole country is just completely fucked up! And so are all you cowards!!"

No one looking his way now - just ignoring him. *Just ignore him and he'll go away.*

And then he ripped open his jacket and yelled, "Goddam it! Who's the fucker in charge of heating this place?! He should be killed! Killed!!"

Confession: I had thought he was going to pull out a gun, and I wondered what I would do if he started spraying bullets into us.

We neared the next station, the always-deserted Klosterstraase, and I decided I was getting off the car if this guy stayed with us. But then, as soon as the doors opened, the guy darted onto the platform. A second later the walls echoed his hair-raising scream of "MOTHERFUCKER!!"

In unison, the passengers relaxed and let out a collective sigh of relief. Some turned to their neighbors with a look and a shake of the head. Myself, I realized that I was gripping the bar far too tightly.

As the train pulled away from the station, I tried to locate the guy on the platform but couldn't see him. I reckoned he was pissing on the ticket machine or something, but then a few seconds later I spotted him through the glass door that led to the compartment ahead of us.

He was in that car now, yelling at the top of his motherfucking lungs.

Just enough to be dangerous
Germany, 2004
This story first appeared in here magazine

The men, hunkered down in the corner with their cups of coffee, eyed the new customer suspiciously. The bakery was a small neighborhood business, and the two of them didn't particularly like newcomers. They had been coming to the bakery for over three years during the wintertime, and the woman who worked the counter always gave them free coffee to get them going in the morning. They were of the official 20% unemployed in the *Sachsen-Anhalt Bundesstadt* of *Deutschland,* one of the former East German states. Nowadays in these parts, the fall of The Wall was seen as more bad than good.

The new customer, 30ish and just shy of stocky, looked at the baked goods, especially the wide variety of cakes that were fresh and savory. He felt the eyes of the lean, wiry men on him but ignored it. Instead, he gave the woman a *"Guten Tag"* and continued looking at the *Pannenkuchen.*

The men's suspicions were piqued and they leaned toward the counter to hear better. The accent was definitely not *Sachsen.* They suspected it wasn't even German. They looked at each other in confirmation and then back at the new customer. This time, the new customer regarded them calmly. They glowered back at him.

Frank looked back at the woman behind the counter. She hadn't returned his greeting. *"Eine Stadt Brot, bitte,"* said Frank. "A city bread, please." He thought he might have made a grammar mistake in ordering, but didn't know what it was.

The woman reached up on the rack behind her and took down one of the dense, round loaves. She placed it in a paper bag and said, "1.99 Euro." Like all Germans, she pronounced the "Euro" like *Oylo.* Oddly, she didn't include the word *"bitte,"* "please," at the end of the sentence, which is customary for shopkeepers in all of Germany.

Meanwhile, the grammar mistakes and the sporty attire had convinced the men that the newcomer was American. And even though they were too young to be of the generation that was greatly affected by the reduction and rebuilding of their society during the Second World War, they still harbored misgivings about *Amerikaner.* They stood up, gulped down their coffee and placed their cups on the counter, never taking their eyes off the newcomer.

Frank felt their suspicion. He had always been astute at body language, but since coming to Europe a few years before, he had become even better. He placed his money on the counter in the plastic money tray, which was between himself and the men. The woman placed his penny in change not in the money tray, but on the glass countertop close to the men. She again failed to say *"Bitte."*

Frank looked at her as he put his gloves on. *"Deine,"* he said.

It would have been better to use *"Ihren,"* the proper and polite form of saying "Yours" when addressing strangers, but he wasn't about to be rude politely.

He picked up the bread from the counter and looked at the men who were now turned and facing him from the corner.

The man on the left spoke in German. "You're American, aren't you?"

"Nein, Ich bin Tsechische." "No, I'm Czech," he lied.

"You sound American."

"Meine Frau ist Amerikanishe."

> He thought they were going to come at him at any second and he had never fought two men before. He thought about the Swiss Army knife in his pocket, and how he might hold it in his fist to make it harder, like holding a roll of quarters.

They narrowed their eyes in disbelief.

"Your president is an ass, and he is making a mess of the world. Why does he want to make war? There is no sense in fighting; there is never any sense in fighting."

The shopkeeper looked nervously at the newcomer. She agreed with her compatriot, but didn't like his tough talk. She had seen the two men fight before - over nothing - and she didn't want it happening in her store.

Frank, meanwhile, had only understood the words "president, war, and fighting." He thought the men were saying that they wanted to fight, and he felt himself tense up. Ok, he thought to himself, first talk like a diplomat, then talk tough. If that fails, fight hard. That system had gotten him out of many fights before.

The Germans didn't look tough to Frank. They were medium-sized, and had looks of uncertainty and questioning on their faces.

Frank searched his brain for any German that might be of use and found only "That's not my problem."

"It is *so* your problem, it's all of our problem, and when the fighting starts, it will be even worse for you, being married to an American."

Frank understood the man to say, "It's your problem, and we're going to fight and it will be bad for you and your American wife."

He had heard enough. He put down the bread and faced them. He thought they were going to come at him at any second and he had never fought two men before. He thought about the Swiss Army knife in his pocket, and how he might hold it in his fist to make it harder, like holding a roll of quarters. But for now, he put up his hands and said, "I don't want to fight you."

The men blinked at him and said, "Who said anything about fighting? We are talking about war! War and your president! We don't want to fight, and we don't want your president to fight!"

Frank blinked at the man. He understood all of the last sentence. The men didn't want to fight. He looked at the shopkeeper. She looked back at him anxiously. He looked back at the men and noticed they hadn't stepped towards him as he'd thought they had. They were still in the corner. He stood there for a moment not knowing what to do.

Just then the door opened, ringing the chimes that hung over it. Frank looked over his shoulder at the door and saw a young girl and her mother coming in. He turned back and looked at the men, then picked up his bread. He stood aside for the mother and young girl, and walked out the door.

Even though he lived right across the street, he walked around the block to make sure he wasn't followed.

Soon enough
Spain, 2008

"We go to mushroom. Don't you want to come with us?"

The mother-in-law. Does not mean mushroom in a Timothy-Leary-Summer-of-Love kind of way. More of a we'll-eat-everything-we-gather kind of way.

Ask her, "Where will you go?"

"Above somewhere."

The wife is occupied by household chores deemed too womanly for me to help with, so off we go into the wilds of Bohemia. Mother-in-law – mummy – rides shotgun. Her boyfriend drives. Me cramped in back.

We pull off the country road and onto a dirt lane. Mid-summer wheat ruffles golden under the overcast sky, the tight-lipped boyfriend wrestling with the wheel of the old Skoda. Pine forest up ahead. Ruts from the tractors and the wagons, mummy lashing him with driving instruction.

A pleasure to get out of the car. The smells of deep forest blow, exaggerated by the moist air. Rain any minute, seems like.

"Where you go?"

The boyfriend.

"Oh, just around. Then back home."

Mummy closes the hatch and arranges her mushrooming basket on the crook of her arm.

"Aren't you afraid?"

I blink. "Of what?"

She looks at me for a long moment, opens her mouth as if to speak. Closes it. Then… "This is that forest."

My mind races through the story of legendary Hussite marauders.

"But it's daylight."

"True."

"So no problem… see you at home."

"Fine. Ahoy."

A weight lifts as the distance grows between us. The high grass brushes against my calves until I find a narrow game trail and move into the forest proper.

Czech forests: bright, with grassy floors one can walk through without having to blaze trails. Youthful Birches and frenetic, aptly named Quaking Aspens. Ancient Oaks. Needled trees bare until the canopy. Stands of young pines so dense it's twilight all day. In brighter areas, birdsong. Darker spots, breathing. Broken sticks underfoot.

Spot a robust piece of deadwood and strip its protuberances. Bang it against a tree to test its resilience. Not much of a walking stick – more of a baseball bat. Pick up some pinecones and smash them into oblivion.

Emerge from the dark twilight of the closely-growing pines. There's distant thunder.

Find the path that Mummy described. Hasn't been used this year, looks like. Use the stick to fend off stinging nettles, but some make it past, burn the legs.

Mummy's question poses itself again as the forest draws ever closer.

Twilight in all the forest now, first drops. Pips and paps somehow comforting, though the birdsong has died away.

Hair on my neck stands up and a second later I'm thrown backwards by an explosion going off in my face. Awful heat. A concussion like I've never felt. I'm on my back, don't know where I am. Heart goes all weird and can't find its rhythm. Can't breathe right. Look up into the dark sky, rain falling in my eyes. Cover them with my hand and try to straighten my twisted body. The trees look like tall friends, gathered round to check up on me. They blur and go black.

A distant moan wakes me. Feel my eyes moving beneath the lids. Open one to blinding white pain. Close it. Slowly open both a minute later. The sky darker.

Reach my arms straight up. Open and close the hands, then lay them over my chest. Move the neck. Weeds all around me. Struggle to sit up. Another lightning strike nearby, followed quickly by thunder. Rain has stopped. The forest has a heavy, close feel. Ten feet away, charred earth. A newly-fallen tree, shattered near the stump. The thunder bangs on, shaking the ground. My hands, legs register the thudding of it.

Neck hairs straight up again. Hope the lightning hasn't returned. Nothing to do if it does.

Then a faraway thudding... clomping? Rhythm introduced, fades. Introduced again. Louder now, loud enough to alarm. Struggle to stand up, can't.

A glimpse of movement in the trees, but it can't be. Too thickly forested for riding. Then another glimpse. Two, three of them. Five. A group of ten, loosely ranked. Smoothly galloping, spectral on their steeds. Fully armed, urgent in their speed, the legendary band of Hussites crashes through the forest, oblivious of me.

Thudding continues long after they disappear into the forest again. Too thunderstruck to hear the solitary horse approach. Finally sense it when it's close enough to nudge at me.

Complete freak out. Horse starts backward. Flounder, can't stand up. Finally give up trying, gape at the horse. White steed, achingly beautiful. A type of understanding in its deep, glowing eyes. Comes closer, nudges at me with actual physicality. Snorts on me, hot and cadaverous.

Pat its nose and it kneels down to me. Don't know what to do. Finally grab onto the neck and mane. It straightens up, pulling me with it. Glad to find myself standing. Pain seems to vanish.

Don't know what's next, but the horse has a calming effect. Stand there a long time before it begins to walk. Go along with it, holding on for balance.

When it dawns on me where we're going, a weight falls off of my shoulders. I smile, find myself looking forward to finally, truly being home.

Then I remember the wife. Stop in my tracks. The horse continues on a few steps, out of my grasp. Leaves me standing unsteadily. It turns to look at me.

Moments pass... then I finally decide to let it go without me. Wave it off, make my way back to the body.

Not ready yet.

Will be, soon enough.

Change me
Spain, 2007
This story first appeared in the Sept. 2007 edition of INTHEFRAY

The Spanish I acquired at university had not prepared me for the real-life, stuck on fast-forward, mumbling, foul-mouthed Spanish speakers that I came across in Seville. I was continuously confused, couldn't seem to understand numbers at the checkout lines, and eventually I just put on my headphones as a sort of defense against unwanted verbal advances.

But I'll tell you what: the city is lovely during December. Most of the narrow streets in the town center are draped in lighting, and I'm not talking schmaltzy, blinking, trailer-trash numbers, either. These are mostly uniformly white strands, their elegance adding to the city's already over-the-top beauty.

And the streets are simply packed in the evenings – everyone just finishing up work, kids running around, street musicians competing for the attention of passersby. The stores are also packed with holiday shoppers, but the wares they have for sale are nothing like what the street vendors are peddling.

Largely South American, the vendor's routine seems similar to most illegal street sellers: spread a huge blanket on the sidewalk and arrange the goodies over it in a way that facilitates a hasty, gather-it-up getaway should the police come around. Most of the vendors, who often display their goods in packs of six or seven, sell rainbow-colored knitted caps and scarves, leather belts and bags, and other hand-made crafts. But I saw one fellow the other day who had an absolute gem of a thing. It was a foot-high stuffed cow standing upright on a fairly stable set of hind legs, and once turned on, the upper body simply thrashed in every direction. The action of the upper portion led the legs to waddle here and there, and the effect of 20 of the cows doing this in concert just captivated me.

I had been shopping for gifts for my family when I came across the cow vendor, and after being reeled in by the sight of them, I wondered who in my family might enjoy one. My first thought was my brother's two dogs, but then I thought they might be too freaked out by it. The second thought was my nephew, who is three years-old (but will argue with anyone that he's actually six). Picturing him enjoying the toy, I stood at a safe distance from the vendor and watched the things thrashing about on the blanket.

Standing there also gave me a chance to get a better look at the man who was selling the cows. A short fellow, he looked to be in his 30s, with a shock of straight, combed-over black hair. He wore a lined flannel shirt over jeans and running shoes, and though he had a pleasant-looking face, his eyes were nervous and constantly scanning the crowds. I must have looked suspicious to him standing across the pedestrian way, because his eyes kept returning to mine. Eventually, more to stop him from eyeing me than from a real desire to buy, I went over and asked him how much one of the thrashing cows cost.

"10 Euros," he said.

I had thought double that, and right then I decided to get one for the dogs after all.

"Ok," I said, "I'll take two."

The guy gave me a big smile and took two of the stationary, plastic-bagged cows from the back row and handed them to me.

"Batteries included," he said.

"What service," I responded, and smiled.

I wondered that the man would leave his wares just lying there – someone might steal one and run away while he was gone. But then I realized I probably wouldn't let anyone do that. They had somehow become my temporary responsibility.

I took 50 Euros from my pocket and handed it over. His face sort of changed as I held out the bill, and he fished around in his pockets before asking if I had something smaller.

I didn't. I had been paying by credit card all day. He looked around for a second and then suggested that I go into a bar – he pointed at one behind me – and ask for change. I turned around and looked. There was a side street that led off of the main shopping avenue, and maybe 50 feet down was a busy pub. The plastic garden furniture placed out in front was completely occupied and surrounded by napkins and other trash lying on the ground. I nodded and told him I'd be right back.

As I walked, I felt the weight of apprehension settle upon me – I wasn't sure how to ask for change. I racked my brain for the phrase and found an approximation before walking into the bar. First thing I noticed was that everyone had noticed me coming in and had seemingly turned to watch me. And no, it wasn't just my foreigner paranoia. It really was a case of the whole pub quieting down to check out the stranger. Probably 30 sets of eyes rested on me, but the most important set, the barman's, came nowhere close to mine. He studiously avoided eye contact for almost a full minute before I spoke up, asking him in Spanish to change me. *"Puede cambiar me?"*

He didn't lift his head from his task, but responded, "Into what?"

The people around me laughed, but I didn't understand the joke.

"Two 20s and a 10," I said.

He again said something I didn't catch; more laughter.

"I'm sorry," I responded. "I don't understand."

"I can't give change."

"Sorry?"

"I said, I can't give change."

"Oh. Well, thanks," I said. "That's very kind." I tried to say it ironically, but in a foreign language one can never tell.

"Nothing to thank," he responded.

I walked out, wondering how I had managed to find the only unfriendly place in Seville to ask for change. The strange interaction had completely deflated my will to speak, as well as my will to buy. I saw that the cow vendor was occupied with another customer, so I slipped into the crowd and walked down the street, already feeling relieved at leaving it behind. I had walked a good distance before the picture of my nephew enjoying the cow forced me to stop, then turn around. I weaved my way through the crowd and back to the man. As he saw me coming, he picked up the two cows he had chosen for me and said, "Ok?"

I shook my head and showed him the 50 again. He looked at me and said something I didn't understand, and as people tend to do when they don't understand, I nodded my head and agreed with him. He smiled then and placed the cows among the other cows, then reached out for the 50. I blinked in confusion as he did this, and he said, very slowly, that he was going to try to get change and that he would be right back. I said ok, and he smiled and took the money, then weaved across the pedestrians and into the bar.

As I stood there in front of the thrashing cows, distracted by their non-stop action, I wondered that the man would leave his wares just lying there – someone might steal one and run away while he was gone. But then I realized I probably wouldn't let anyone do that. They had somehow become my temporary responsibility. I even moved behind them to let the pedestrians have a better view, and this seemed to be the right move, because just a moment later two children, probably brother and sister, ran over and stood in front of the cows.

They were really beautiful kids, dressed in formal winter wear. The girl was in a tan, knee-high wool jacket, and thick stockings. Her ensemble was topped off by a matching ribbon in her hair. The boy was wearing the same jacket and brown slacks, and I couldn't help but smile at them as they jabbered away, pointing and giggling at the raucous cows.

Still smiling, I looked up at the parents, who looked like they might buy. They edged closer and asked me how much the cows were, and I told them 10 Euros. They smiled at each other and nodded, then tried to pull their kids away. There were protests, but the parents placated them and the man winked at me as they walked away to the right – I took his signal to mean that he would return to buy.

Buoyed by the positivity of the kids and thinking of how I could tell the man he had a customer, I was smiling and on the verge of a chuckle when I turned my head to the left and saw the two policemen coming towards me. They did not look nearly as fun-loving as the children had. My smile fled as they came up to me.

The big one looked me up and down and demanded something of me. I told him I didn't understand and he took a step towards me, as if making to grab me.

The second one said, in English, "Speak English?"

"Yes."

"Are these yours?"

"No!"

"Why are you standing over them?"

"I was just… just looking," I stammered.

"Whose are they?"

I shrugged, looking at the English speaker. Just then, over their shoulders, I saw the vendor emerge from the bar. He stopped short when he saw the police standing in front of me. I told the policeman I didn't know whose they were.

This brought out a grunt and they commenced to speak among themselves. As they did this, I looked back to the vendor and saw him hold up the money, crumble it, and throw it to the ground. Then he shrugged and ran like hell.

The Spanish-speaking policeman must have seen my attention shift over their shoulders, because a moment later, he yelled to his partner and pointed at the fleeing vendor. They both looked at me and yelled. I didn't understand the Spanish-speaker, but the English-speaker said, "Is that the owner?"

"I… I don't know."

I saw him hold up the money, crumble it, and throw it to the ground. Then he shrugged and ran like hell.

Despite my answer, the bigger one started running through the gathering crowd, but it was hard for him to get through. The English-speaker moved closer to me. "I want your identification."

"I don't have any. It's… in my hotel."

"Then tell me your name and your hotel name."

No idea where this came from, but out it popped: "My name is Michael Moore. I'm staying at the Holiday Inn."

The policeman wrote down my "name" and told me to go back to my hotel – they would come visit me shortly.

"Yes, sir."

Glaring at me meaningfully, he tucked his notepad into his jacket and then gathered up the cows with the sheet. He bound the resulting sack – which was thrashing everywhere with the cows inside – with a pipe tie that he'd fished out of his pocket, then fought his way through the crowd in the direction his partner had gone.

Facing the inquisitive crowd that had gathered, I suddenly felt sick to my stomach from the stress. It isn't often that one gets to experience another man's lot so completely. I puffed out my cheeks and made my way through the people and over to where the vendor had thrown the money. I had to search for awhile, but eventually I found a wadded-up bill and unfolded it. It was the 50.

The bastard wouldn't change him, either.

Bad trip, 2001
Germany, 2006

Instead of grabbing a bag of chips at the gas station and pushing on as I'd suggested, we pulled off the Autobahn and cruised into a poorly-lit village looking for a place to eat.

Mr. Munich was driving, Ms. Amsterdam was riding shotgun, and me and Mr. London were the smartasses in the backseat. We pulled into a small parking space in the middle of the dark village, and the second car, driven by Mr. Denmark, pulled in behind us.

"I'm going to investigate," said Mr. Munich as he got out of the car and slammed the door. I noted his Hugo Bossy style until he was across the street and then I commented, "He does seem like an investigator, doesn't he?"

Ms. Amsterdam was wrapped even tighter than Mr. Munich and didn't acknowledge the comment, but Mr. London picked up on it and said, "I hope he investigates a toilet."

Or maybe he'll discover a clue in there, I thought. After just 3 hours on the road, he'd already taken two major wrong turns.

I watched him knock on and then enter the front door of the stucco, two-story house without waiting for an answer.

"He just walked in the front door," said Mr. London.

I looked over at him in the half-light. He was a small kid, but more than made up for with his charisma.

"I bet he gets his ass kicked in there," he continued. "Hey! Maybe we can just leave him! After I piss, of course. Ms. Amsterdam, could you let me out?"

Just as she opened the door, Mr. Munich emerged from the house and walked over to the car behind us. Ms. Amsterdam closed her door and soon Mr. Munich got in and said, "We can eat here. I thought so."

Mr. London and I traded looks and head wiggles as Mr. Munich moved the car to the parking place. We soon piled out of the two cars, eight road-tripping international students all jabbering in English as we followed Mr. Munich up the musty stairway that was hidden behind the front door.

It was loud upstairs. Or rather, it was loud until the eight of us filed into the large room heavy with smoke and filled with long, rough wooden tables. That's when the inhabitants of the half-empty village beer hall stopped talking and looked at us like we were covered in manure. There was a long silence before Mr. Munich said something, and then we were pointed to a table in the corner.

A few minutes later the proprietor, a Gunter-looking type with rosy cheeks, came to the table carrying eight beers – four glass-handled mugs in each hand – and banged them down in front of us.

He said something to Mr. Munich, who shook his head and then translated for us. "He says there is no warm food. They were working in the garden today and are tired. We can only have *cold plates*." He pronounced "cold plates" as if he had been eating gazpacho for a week.

A round of groans went up from the table, with bespectacled Mr. Brussels and gangly Mr. Stockholm visibly angered. Mademoiselle France lit a cigarette and blew the smoke in my face, and through the haze I asked Mr. Munich, "Do they have anything vegetarian?"

A moment later he asked this of the proprietor, who responded with a loud guffaw and placed a stack of menus on the table. Mr. London and I had distanced ourselves from Mr. Munich, and at that point Mademoiselle France, who spoke German, was still being fussy about the lack of warm food, so we didn't have the benefit of either of their German knowledge when we were picking out our dish.

My version of German roulette ended poorly, as I was presented with a selection of five cold-cuts, including a very red (blood?) bologna and a type of jiggly, gelatin-based meat product. I ate the turkey but couldn't stomach the rest, which Mr. London and Mr. Brussels welcomed.

As I was watching my plate being divvied up, an older gentleman smoking a thin cigarette pulled up a chair and insinuated himself between me and Mr. London.

"You are from America, yes," he asked me.

"That's right. From Pennsylvania. My friend here is from England."

Mr. London smiled at him but was ignored.

"I have been to America," the newcomer said.

"Is that right?"

"Yes, I have been to Boston, New York, and San Francisco."

He took another puff and moved closer to me.

"And in San Francisco, I had the most amazing time."

He touched my arm to accentuate the word "amazing".

"We were clubbing with new people every night."

I took a drink of beer. "Sounds like fun."

"Oh, it was… but it is possible to have fun wherever you are, don't you think?"

"Sure is."

Mr. London gave me a look and just a second later the newcomer said, "So if you'd like to have some fun while you are here, why not to follow me?"

I blinked at him for a second and then he got up and strode down the hallway towards the toilet. I don't know why I watched him the whole way, but I did, and when he got to the door, he winked and beckoned me to follow.

"What are you waiting for, Mr. America? Go have some fun."

It was Mr. London.

"Did you see that," I asked him.

"You're just too hot for your own good."

"Oh, fuck you."

"Not me. That's for your letch uncle over there."

"Why can't that happen with a beautiful woman," I asked and stood up. I placed the newcomer's seat back at his table and then sat down again. Later, when the fellow came out of the bathroom, I did my best to ignore him, but it was hard with him staring into the back of my skull.

Finally we piled back into the cars, and while it was a relief not to be stared at any longer, it was no fun having to listen to Mr. London's continued joking at my expense. I pretended to fall asleep for awhile and I guess I eventually did because when I opened my eyes, we had arrived at the campsite.

We had thought that by arriving on Monday we would cleverly avoid the crowds, but apparently there was no good time to arrive at such a festival because it was just a complete mob scene. We cruised through the campground looking for empty spaces, but ended up near the entrance again. All that was left was a sandy patch next to the picnic area and the playground.

Setting up the tents took forever in the darkness, and none of us were drunk enough to ignore the fact that we were sleeping on the ground. The party raged all around us until 5ish, and then the children started up on the playground at 7ish. I was up by nine, a beer in hand and already fed as Mr. Denmark and Ms. Amsterdam brewed coffee, set up a big breakfast, and took their freakin' time about it.

In fact, of the eight of us, only those two insisted on showering; no one else cared to fight through the huge lines to obtain tokens for the showers, and then the huge lines for the showers themselves. But even worse than the shower situation was the toilet situation; there were no seats on the toilets and no paper, either. It felt more like a refugee camp than a camping site.

Finally at about 1 p.m. everyone was ready and we headed into Munich. We took the metro into the city center and – BAM – we emerged into Oktoberfest.

Only it was nothing like I had expected.

In front of us were thousands of people milling everywhere in a huge *amusement* park. There were spinning rides and roller-coasters and Ferris wheels off in the distance, and immediately in front of us were gaming booths with stuffed animals as prizes and cotton candy and so on.

Mr. Munich finally made a good suggestion – he thought we should go drink in one of the beer tents, which were set back in a row about 50 yards from the gaming stands. Actually, they weren't really tents, but more like monstrous pre-fabricated buildings, 15 of them in all we later learned. But at that point we could only see five of them because they were so large – each occupied roughly the footprint of a soccer field.

We entered the first tent through a low, paneled hallway lined with vendors peddling giant pretzels and grilled bratwursts, and were accosted with the competing aromas of open-pit barbecue and spilled beer. The low ceilings in the entryway restricted my view and by craning my neck I could just glimpse the action over and around the heads of those in front of me. I had only the smells and the sounds of revelers to let me know we had come to the right place.

Emerging into the beer hall proper, I suddenly felt tiny, because the ceiling rose three stories above to the exposed support beams. I could barely see the other end of the hall because of the dim lighting, lingering smoke and funk from the grills.

And in the middle of the tent, the festival was just raging. Thousands of people were partying with abandon. Through the yelling, singing, jumping mob we made our way to one of the few tables that could hold all eight of us.

I was excited at the vibe of the place and before the beers were even delivered, two Spanish kids came over to our table with black magic markers wanting to give us tattoos. I got them to write PEACE on one arm, and NIK on the other. Naturally only Mr. London thought it was funny. The others couldn't see the buffoonery of the scene just yet and an awkward silence hung over our table.

It was like that for the first two beers – Mr. London and me having a great time carrying on with anyone who happened by, and the rest of the group quietly chatting amongst themselves. At length the beers took hold and even Mr. Munich loosened up – "They party like Vikings here," he commented.

Indeed, people were wearing Viking helmets and Cat-in-the-Hat replicas and a lot of the men had taken off their shirts. The rowdier ones were pouring beer on each other and some of their women friends were flashing their breasts to anyone who asked properly.

But the beers were more expensive than I had counted on, and finding that I was suddenly broke, I decided to go out and hit a cash machine for a credit card advance. On my way out, the security guards told me that if I left the building I wouldn't be allowed back in, but I didn't care. I had talked my way into tighter security than that.

The crowds were still shoulder to shoulder, but I was feeling keyed-up and half-lit, so I began walking as fast as I could, anticipating openings in the crowd before they appeared, shooting

Feeling smug, I walked back into the main hall and had to do a double-take. No longer raucous or merry in any way, the tent was now filled with people staring and shaking their heads. Some were even crying.

through gaps that I saw and creating others with my shoulders and man, I felt like a big kid. Getting barked at by miffed slowpokes only reinforced the feeling.

Once I made it out of the main gate, the crowd dwindled to normal pedestrian traffic and I came across a cash machine fairly easily. I was walking back towards the party flush with cash and feeling chipper when I came to a small crowd gathered around the window of an appliance store.

They were watching some sort of action flick on the assorted televisions. Scenes of burning buildings interspersed with panicky talking heads filled the screens and I walked off thinking, *Man, get a life*.

Back at the beer tent, I walked up to the entrance and began to badger the doorman. He was standoffish and didn't talk much English, but I described his boss to him and told him that I had been given permission to use the telephone – yes, of course it was a capital-E emergency – and after about ten minutes of this, he finally let me in.

Feeling smug, I walked back into the main hall of the tent and had to do a double-take. No longer raucous or merry in any way, the tent was now filled with people staring at each other and shaking their heads. Some were even crying. The eerie silence of the tent was broken only by the public address system, which was carrying what seemed to be a live broadcast in German.

I walked up to one of the bars and ordered myself a beer. When I spoke to the woman, she looked at me strangely, then asked if I were American.

"Yeah…"

She began to cry and came out around the bar. "Very, very sorry," she said, and put her arms around me.

I hugged her awkwardly until she let me loose. Then she looked deep into my eyes and said sorry again.

Wiping her eyes with her apron, she went back around the bar, topped up my beer and handed it to me. When I tried to pay she waved me off, so I said a confused thank you and turned back to the crowd to locate my group.

They hadn't moved from the table, but were now sitting. As I approached, Mr. Munich came up to me and said, "It is terrible. I cannot imagine someone would do such a thing with planes."

"What are you talking about," I asked.

And then he told me.

I heard his words, but I couldn't really grasp the magnitude of it.

I looked around at my group of acquaintances, and half of the girls were crying. Mr. London had his head in his hands.

As I stood there wondering what to do, Mademoiselle France got up and gave me a teary-eyed kiss on the cheek before hugging me.

I hugged her back and said, "It's fine. Everything will be fine."

"But those people..."

I went on hugging her for awhile and then she sat down. Ms. Amsterdam turned to me.

"I don't understand this," she said.

"Me, neither."

We looked around the beer tent. The revelry was utterly gone, and in its place was a forced, unnatural quiet as everyone listened to the radio broadcast.

"What do we do now," she asked. "We just got here, but it seems strange to stay."

"I don't know," I said. "Why don't we ask the others?"

After several minutes of blank-faced answers, a consensus was reached; we would have one more beer in honor of the victims, then go back.

The waitresses had stopped coming round, so me and Mr. London went to collect the beers. When we returned and distributed them, everyone stood up and touched glasses.

I was asked to say something and actually managed to, but I remember that my words sounded like some bad play – a pathetic, forced contrivance. And that was the thing about our trip – previously inconceivable contrivances had popped into existence, making reality itself unrealistic, in the process killing off any sense of innocence that we may have had.

In the end, we did finish our beers and we did return to the campsite.

What we didn't know is that finding our way back would take a lot longer than we imagined.

In misery
Spain, 2008

I first met Wilma Waslewski at a committee meeting during my third month at Information Processing. There were over 30 people at the day-long Committee Action Retreat (CAR), the tables set with water, coffee and cookies for every two persons. Wilma was seated at the end of the main players' row.

It was my first committee meeting, and I instinctively gravitated to the group members who seemed to share my attitude; tickled to find myself serving on a committee to which I didn't have to contribute but which would regularly get me out of the office.

The task of the CAR that day was to determine a new layout for its free pamphlets, which were available at welfare offices across the state. The pamphlets hadn't been redesigned since the late 1990s and a change was in order. And apparently because they were all paper-pushers, it was assumed that the 30 CAR participants had the expertise to discuss graphic design.

The Cape Girardeau representative got the ball rolling by saying that the colors were all wrong. "We need something that makes people feel good, not some dark color that reminds them that they're… well… you know."

I glanced around at the other participants and found them thoughtfully nodding in agreement. There wasn't one person of color among us, which allowed Mr. Girardeau to get away with his remark.

Wilma was the next one to speak. "The colors are fine," she airily proclaimed, "but what we need to consider is the reading level of our audience. After all, most of them are only high school graduates, if that, and the text should be simple enough for them to understand."

I found myself speaking before thinking, something I tend towards. "That's a good point, uh… sorry, I can't see your name card properly… is it Willa?"

"Wilma," she said with a tight mouth.

"Right. Wilma." I gave her my Big Smile, to which she didn't respond.

"Anyway Wilma, it's a good point about the reading level of our audience. But judging from the pamphlets we have in front of us, the previous writer has already achieved the goal of simplicity. In fact, I've spotted a handful of mistakes in the "Fathers are for Fathering" pamphlet, and can only presume that the other ones could use some help, too."

There were light snickers from the shirker corner, but otherwise silence. The committee, which had been looking at me, looked over to Wilma, who was giving me the stink-eye.

"What's your name, son?"

"Elijah Counts."

"Well, Elijah, as *most* members of this board are aware, I wrote those pamphlets myself. And I doubt that there are any mistakes *you* could find."

More slight sniggers, and the heads turned back to me.

I caught the insult and said, "Well, you did a fine job of writing simplistically. And… if you really want me to point out the mistakes I can, but…"

"Please, Elijah," she said, "bring these 'mistakes' to our attention. It will please me to hear about them, especially after they've been accepted as correct since *you* were a teenager."

I cleared my throat at the second insult, swallowed and said, "All right, then."

…from then on, Wilma not only undertook a smear campaign against me, she also endeavored to bring me under her thumb. And as the Director's Administrative Assistant, she had considerable power to exert over an intern…

I stood up and walked around the tables, avoiding the corner where Wilma was sitting, and up to the white board behind the main players. The room was silent and I was glad I had worn a tie. Still, the Dogs Playing Cards design did nothing to establish credibility.

Jittery, I wrote the following sentence on the board: "Put a hand on your childs shoulder as you talk to him or her."

I turned to the group and said, "Shouldn't there be an apostrophe somewhere in there?"

Thoughtful nods. Raised eyebrows. Again the stink-eye from Wilma, who said, "That's hardly an important mistake."

"Ah, but a mistake nonetheless, Willa."

"It's *Wilma*."

"Of course. Sorry."

I underlined the possessive mistake with a red marker and wrote the next sentence underneath it: "Children who grow up with a fathers are two times less likely to experience behavioral problems."

I turned around. "A fathers? And also, two times less likely than what?"

Wilma jumped on me. "It's obvious that it refers to two times less likely than without a father!"

"Perhaps it is to us. But as you said, we're writing for a less sophisticated audience. We can't assume they understand everything."

I turned around and wrote another word on the board: assume.

"Because you know what happens when we assume, Wilma." Again with the Big Smile.

Wilma's eyes bulged and she was about to bluster at me when the chairman stepped in.

"Thank you, Elijah, Wilma. That should be enough. Let's move back to the layout issue, shall we?"

As I walked back to my seat, all eyes on the smartass, I felt a mixture of merriment and dread. I sat, kept my head up, and a short silence followed. Even out of the corner of my eyes, I could see that Wilma's face was red. People around me were muttering things like, "You're dead now," and, "I've wanted to do that for years," and the contradictions captured precisely how I felt.

The CAR eventually lurched forward and I emerged from the day unscathed. But from then on, Wilma not only undertook a smear campaign against me, she also endeavored to bring me under her thumb. And as the Director's Administrative Assistant, she had considerable power to exert over an intern, meaning it was only a matter of time before I was transferred over to her Child Wellness Division, ostensibly as a PR man.

Anxious and suffering from a lack of alcohol, I wrestled with sleep on Sunday night and woke up groggy Monday morning. The coffee only made me more nervous, so I kept my green, year-old Jeep well below the speed limit on my 30-minute commute to Jefferson City. It was my first day at Child Wellness and I felt sick to my stomach knowing that a new, shitty chapter of my life was about to begin.

After several wrong turns, I found my new building – a squat, brown bricked affair – and parked between a rusty pickup truck and a gold Oldsmobile. After I turned off the ignition, I white-knuckled the steering wheel and listened to the end of a jaunty song about freedom that I didn't know the words to. When it finished, I looked at myself in the mirror and said, "You just keep your head up."

As I walked towards the double-doors of the Child Wellness Building, my stomach knotted when I saw the fifty-something Wilma glaring at me from in front of the receptionist's desk. Noting her conservative dress suit, I forced a smile and walked through the doors.

"Good morning, Wilma."

Without a smile she said, "Welcome to Child Wellness, Elijah. Follow me."
Wilma power-walked her plump legs down a narrow, brown-carpeted hallway – on the right, with a parking lot view, were proper offices, while on the left was the cubicle shantytown. I caught up to Wilma just as she arrived at my new workspace. It was a generic cubicle near the bathroom, fully equipped with a disused computer.

"Here you are," she said. "Leave your things here and we'll go get you something to do."

"Something to do" turned out to be a huge backlog of data entry work that Wilma had lying around on her desk. It was mindlessly repetitive and the only saving grace was the iPod that I fetched from the Jeep at lunchtime.

During my first two weeks at Child Wellness, where I myself felt anything but well, Wilma put me through the intern equivalent of boot camp, even giving me work over the weekends. But during the third week of showing me how hard life could be I noticed a slight change in her behavior. Her vengeance apparently sated, she began to speak about the defunct division newsletter – she wanted to resurrect it and wanted me to start on it straightaway. To this end, she gave me a handful of ideas to research and set me loose.

My deadline was the following Tuesday and meeting it was no problem. But then Wilma left the newsletter sitting on her desk without reading it until Friday, the day it was to go out. After lunch, she "suggested" carrying two of the stories over to the next issue, and forgetting about the rest. I was naturally disappointed and went home with a feeling of discontent which lasted just into, but not through, the first beer.

The same scenario repeated itself for the next three weeks – I produced a newsletter and Wilma failed to read it for approval, saying she was just too busy to get to it.

I should have contented myself with at least being allowed to write for a change, because four weeks later when she finally did manage to review the newsletter on a Tuesday, I was thunderstruck at her corrections – the draft copy was redlined like a freshman paper, and not only for legitimate reasons.

For example, where I wrote, "The committee met last week in Rolla to discuss child wellness," Wilma wanted it changed to, "The committee met in Rolla last week to discuss child wellness." The corrections she demanded were 50% stylistic, and 50%, "Screw you, Elijah."

I considered all the corrections and in the end decided to ignore the "Screw you's." I gave her the corrected version at 4:30, quitting time being 5.

At 4:45, she huffed into my cubicle. "Elijah, you only made half of my corrections. Why?"

"Well, the ones that I didn't do seem to be a question of personal style, not a question of being correct or incorrect."

Wilma's eyes narrowed. "Elijah, the corrections are not a matter of *your* judgment, but of mine. You will make them EXACTLY as I tell you to. Is that clear?"

Though I tried very hard to make it sound as if I were saying "I hate your guts", what I actually said was, "Like the rainforests."

Wilma looked at me for a long second before asking, "What does that mean?"

"It means yes, it's clear. Can I give you the changes tomorrow?"

"No, I want them on my desk before you leave."

I breathed out of my nose like a bull and said, "Fine."

With that, she walked away. Distracted by my anger, it took me an hour to make the screw-you corrections and when I finally found myself walking across the parking lot, I was just ballistic. I got in the Jeep, took the can from the console, and put in a chew of Copenhagen. Looking down, I noticed a dusting of tobacco on my shirtfront and brushed it off. This left thick brown streaks everywhere.

I roared out of the parking lot in a rage.

Before even unpacking the groceries, I called my law school friend Katrine to unload on her.

She answered on the fourth ring and I started right in, "Man, The Big Wazoo made me stay late doing stupid newsletter corrections, which nixed my workout, and you know how crabby I am when I don't exercise."

"Pfhh. Don't I?" I heard her light a cigarette, her favorite Ani Difranco album playing relentlessly in the background.

I continued on. "She probably won't even post the thing… again. Anyway, instead of workin' out, I went shoppin' at-"

"I don't like how this is starting."

"Yeah, well, it gets worse. I pulled into the Val-You-Mart as a solid, contributing member of society and-"

"Yeah, you contribute... what, a whole 20 hours a week?"

"That was an exceptional week and you know it. I work-"

"You're *such* a shirker," she interrupted.

I took a deep breath. "Anyway… three crazy things happened to me. First, when I was at the salad bar, some lady leaned RIGHT across me, hair danglin' all over the salad I was preparing. So I go, 'Excuse me!' And she looked at me like *I* was the fungo for sayin' something! Not even a word of apology!"

"Was her hair long?"

"Not only long, it was like, pubic hair thick."

"Eww. Did she get any in your salad?"

"I have no idea, cuz I threw it down and walked off all salty. Oh yeah, another thing: they'd run out of carts, so I was hugging the groceries to my chest when I fumed up to the checkout line, right? Anyway, in front of me was some lady reading *Weekly News Enquirer* or some damn thing, and the headline – get this – was "SATAN ESCAPES FROM HELL.""

Giggling, Katrine asked, "How could he *escape* from H, E, double toothpicks?"

"No idea. So this lady put the paper back in the stand all wrong and it fell to the ground, right? I mean, it didn't just *fall* to the ground. It actually split apart into like 10 sections at my feet. And you know what she did? Looked away!"

"What?"

"Yeah, she looked at it like it was an SEP."

"An essy-what?"

"Somebody Else's Problem? Douglas Adams?"

"I never read him."

"Anyways, Jasper lady looks at it like it's an SEP, and a couple seconds later the checkout lady sees the paper on the ground in front of me and tells me to pick it up. No please, no nothing. Just an order: 'Pick it up.'"

"*No way!*"

"Really! And the Jasper in front of me didn't say a word, just happy to blame shift."

"Wh… what did you do?"

"Man, it was just too much. I looked at the clerk for a second – my hands were still full, right, there's no way I could pick anything up – and then I aped-out and started shufflin' my feet and rippin' the hell out of the paper. "

"What?"

"Yeah. So after like five seconds, I stopped and looked up at the clerk, who was just agape – who wouldn't be – and I said, 'I'll pay ya for it, but I ain't pickin' it up.' And the Jasper in front of me who dropped the paper in the first place was also looking at me like *I* was the hooligan, when in fact it was *her* neglect that caused the whole situation."

"Uh… yeah. *And* the fact that you were all pissed off."

I sighed and said, "So the whole checkout scene was uncomfortable. I even had to bag my own groceries."

"Stop it! They didn't bag your groceries?"

"Surprised me, too. But when I walked out of the store, you know, I was already calm – just happy to be away from the whole scene. But then, as I was crossing over the strip mall's traffic lanes, I looked over to my right and this guy was doin' a fuckin' Dale Earnhardt, passing and weaving, and he just *barely* missed an oncoming car. Everyone screeched to a halt except him, and to frickin' boot, I literally had to run out of his way!"

"You're lucky he didn't hit you!"

"Dude, I was like a jackrabbit."

"Wait… you didn't get into a fight, did you?"

"No…. but this new idiot did park in my aisle, so I kinda went outta my way to walk by his car."

"That doesn't sound good."

"And I had my hate rays all ready for him, but man, when he opened up his car door he literally SLAMMED it into the car next to him! Forget my hate rays, my jaw just *dropped*. I could not *believe* this cat."

"Was he bigger than you?"

"Yeah, but in an Archie Bunker kind of way."

"And of course you confronted him."

"Mm. Not really."

"Whaddya mean, not really?"

"I kinda stalled around by the cart return while he went into the store, and then I walked over to his car and-"

"Did you write down his license plate number?"

"Uh... no."

"Wh... what did you do?"

"I keyed it."

"*What*?"

I breathed deep, a bit afraid to re-create the scene. "I keyed his car."

"For God's sake, Elijah! Where are your *morals*?"

"Yeah, funny you should ask. Because when I did it, it felt really great-"

"It felt '*really great*' to key someone's car. Is that what I'm hearing you say?"

There was a silence and then I said, "But after my vandal-glee wore off, I was wondering about how I acted – you know I'm not normally like that. I'm Mr. Benevolence for the most part."

"Oh, right! You're like-"

"But today, thank you, I was in a foul mood, and when I was driving home I couldn't help but wonder if someone were like, pullin' my strings."

"No, no. You have the freedom to do as you see fit, says REM."

"Yeah, ok, but I wonder if I was somehow compelled to be in a foul mood today for the sole purpose of meetin' that guy and teachin' him a lesson. I mean, maybe I was the patsy in some cosmic justice play…"

Katrin humphed. "A valid, if not flaky question. But I think that ultimately, *you chose* to key that guy's car. Just like you *chose* to get angry at the lady at the salad bar. It all comes back to how you react to external influences."

"Yeah, alright. But let me ask you this: do you think I was the enabler of punishment upon someone who needed it, or did I just sully myself?"

"Hmm." I heard her light another cigarette and take a drag.

"Well, that guy had it comin' to him, alright. But I think you're better than that. True, we all think about violence or lust, or whatever, but the real question is how we act upon those feelings. In the end, I think that guy probably isn't going to be happy where he ends up. It seems like he's making the wrong choices. But your choices don't seem all that swift, either."

I thought about it a second. "I just know I feel shitty when I think about keying that car."

"*Bravo*," she said. "And would you key someone else's car now?"

"Mmm. I guess not."

"You guess not. You just told me you feel dirty after keying that car. Do you feel dirty after you visit your Gramma?"

"What? *No...*"

"There's my boy! You kinda do know right from wrong after all."

Workers for the state government in Misery, as part of our generous compensation package, were given two paid hours off (Wilma only let me have one) on primary days in order to exercise our constitutional right. On my way to fulfill this right I exercised what should be another right and smoked a big fat joint.

Amused with myself for getting high before voting, and wearing my John Lennon prescription sunglasses, I pulled into the parking lot of my designated polling station – an elementary school nearby my apartment. It was twilight, and the polling seemed to have passed its peak. There were five or six cars in the parking lot.

As I opened the first series of doors that led to the school's foyer, I was struck by the strange, generic smell of the place – both clean and musty at the same time. I had gone to grade school in another state, but this school smelled exactly the same.

They must use the same cleaning agents, I thought, pleased to have such profound insights while high.

Entering the foyer of the school, I noticed the trophy case opposite me filled with abstract clay art projects, budding impressionist watercolor posters on the walls, and a mini-me water fountain. It was a pleasant atmosphere, and as I took it all in I smiled in nostalgic fondness.

At the tail end of my gazing, I dimly noticed some people. In front of me, behind their paper-strewn registration table were two smiling, gray, officious-looking ladies. To my left, there was a long table divided by high partitions. Capable of accommodating 8 people, four per side, the semi-private voting booth currently hosted a handful of voters.

Hiding my bloodshot eyes behind my sunglasses, I walked over to the woman on the left.

"Hello ladies," I said. "What's the system?"

"Hello young man," said the woman in front of me. The second woman also gave a warm hello, but her smile faded as she scrutinized me.

The woman in front of me said she needed a picture ID and I handed over my driver's license. She looked at the name and began scanning down a long register. Having a last name that begins with a "C" has always been a small source of pleasure – it means I'm always near the front of the alphabetical line, and procedures such as this take less time. I stood there grinning.

As the woman in front of me scanned the list, the woman on the right gushed, "I thought I recognized you! You're that young volunteer from the Presbyterian Church, aren't you?"

I snapped my head to face her and regarded her for a moment before I deadpanned, "No ma'am. I don't believe in God."

During the long pause after I said it, I slowly looked at her over the top of my glasses.

Her eyebrows shot up and her smile melted away. "Oh."

Distracted by movement on my left, I turned my head and noticed that the register lady was staring at me apprehensively, and, further left, two of the voters had Prairie-Dogged their heads over the partition to see who had just professed Disbelief.

I smiled my Big Smile at them and they quickly shrunk back down. Turning back to the register lady, I took the proffered ballot and my identification from the woman on the right (who was now quite standoffish) and walked over to vote.

Ralph Nader wasn't on the ballot, so I wrote him in. Not even 30 seconds after sitting down, I stood up and approached the now-wary ladies. I handed over my ballot, smiled my Big Smile at them, and said goodbye.

Their tight-lipped goodbye's hit me in the back as I made my way across the foyer.

Just before the doors I did a James Bond twist towards the partitioned table and busted all three of the Prairie Dogs who were staring at me. Startled, they all shrunk back down and I walked out of the polling station giggling, feeling like the funniest mofo around.

After Spring Break, Wilma seemed to lose interest in her intern plaything and realized that she just wasn't keen on publishing a weekly newsletter – she left me alone for weeks at a time. Meanwhile, Tanya, my previous boss from Information Processing, must have gotten wind of this because she decided she wanted me back to author a mentoring program (the irony of this did not escape me).

Still, The End of Wilma was queer. Tanya called me on a Tuesday morning and told me to come over to my new office. But Wilma was away for the day and it felt, well, *sneaky* to be leaving without telling my Nazi boss goodbye. And one thing I learned from Wilma was that you don't sneak around when high-strung Nazis are patrolling.

After hearing my worries, Tanya soothed me. "You don't have to worry about her anymore, Elijah. Just come on over and we'll get you settled back in."

So I erased my files, packed up my things, and giddily strode out of the Child Wellness building for the last time.

A full week later as I was skulking toward my napping spot in the Governor's Rose Garden, who did I see coming the other way but Wilma. She was talking with a suit I didn't recognize and I nervously considered turning heel, but screwed up my courage and continued on. We glanced at one another in passing, and so help me, Wilma *winked* at me.

Winked!

It shocked me so much it brought me to a standstill. I stared after them before I continued on to my spot, but was so disturbed that I wasn't able to nap. I just lay there looking at the clouds and wondering why Wilma of all people would wink at me. Nothing came to mind.

Back at the office, though, everything snapped into focus. She had sent me a blank email with an attachment. When I opened it up, I discovered an absolutely *glowing,* signed letter of recommendation. It was so nicely-worded that I had to read it twice to make sure it was really about *me.*

As I sat there shaking my head and wondering about the utter unpredictability of human nature, a snippet of conversation drifted my way.

It was my new boss Tanya, talking to a colleague about how expensive the new paint job on her husband's car was going to be – apparently some idiot had gone and keyed it.

Excerpts from the forthcoming novel
Every Thing Counts
(The Akashic Reader)

This excerpt, titled Sheboygan, Poland, was a finalist in the 2005 Glimmer Train Short-Story Award for New Writers.

As I ate breakfast while staring out the kitchen window, the phone rang. I let the answering machine take it and was startled to hear, "Hello, I'm calling from the American School of English – I was told Elijah Counts could be…"

I spit a mouthful of Cookie Crisp into the sink and ran over to the phone.

Taking a deep breath, I picked up the receiver. "Hello?"

The speaker continued: "…and if he could – Oh… uh… Hello. Can I speak to Elijah Counts?"

"That's me."

"Great, I'm glad I caught you! Elijah, I just got your online application, and I'm really happy you're interested in the job in Poland!"

I blinked.

"Elijah? Are you there?"

"…"

"Elijah?"

"Uh…sorry. D…did you say… *'Poland'?*"

I switched on the speakerphone and paced as Todd, the smooth recruiter from The American School, promised me three meals a day and a private room, with bathroom, for the whole summer in the resort town of Węgierska Górka, Poland, an hour south of Katowice.

There, I would spend a leisurely summer – beginning just three weeks hence – teaching children and teenagers English over four two-week intervals. A substantial bulk payment, in Polish Zloty, would come at the end of the summer.

"So, Elijah, are you interested?"

After a short pause I said, "You know, on a certain level I am. But I honestly never considered going to Poland, so you'll have to give me some time to think about it."

"Absolutely," he replied. "In the meantime, I'll send up the contract for you to look at. It's all on the up-and-up, I assure you."

What?

"Yeah, well, it better be," I blurted.

"Listen," he said, "I've been doing this for years and haven't had a teacher quit or be dissatisfied yet. In fact, I even have the phone numbers of some former teachers if you're interested in calling them."

"Great. I would, actually."

I wrote down the numbers and said, "Ok, I'll speak to them, think about it, and then call you in a few days."

"No, Elijah, I'll call you."

After I hung up the phone, I ran a hand through my hair. I was *sure* I had applied for a job in Rockville, Maryland. I went back to the website and sure enough, the job was listed for Rockville.

So how the hell did Poland come into play?

Calling the references Todd had provided did precious little to ease my misgivings: the numbers were all disconnected.

Not that it really mattered, I guess.

Through a gross miscalculation of distance that can aptly be described as my first screwup, I flew to Vienna, planning to hop a quick train up to Poland (See some of the continent, you know?).

Unfortunately, I hadn't considered a number of things: how taxing the red-eye from the U.S. would be; how I'd land at 6 a.m. local time and the train would be rush-hour crowded by the time I caught it; being exhausted, how little I would actually *care* about seeing the continent; and lastly, how far it really is from Vienna to Poland (looked close on the map, though).

In Vienna, I waited around Südbahnhof guarding my bags for three hours before, in my ignorance of the German language, I got on the train to Prague at noon (second screwup). I then rode for over two hours before being told by the conductor, primarily in sign language, that I was on the wrong train, going the wrong way. Poland was pretty much to the north and I was going west. My compartment mate, an attractive blonde girl, smiled at my agitation.

Frustrated, tired and confused, I got off at the next stop (third screwup), which was literally in the middle of nowhere, Czech Republic. There was no town surrounding the train station – just a decrepit concrete platform in the middle of a narrow, wooded valley. As the train pulled away, my compartment mate leaned out her window and waved. Disgusted, I waved back.

After more than an hour of pacing, chewing tobacco and cursing my stupidity in the early-summer sun, a train coming the other way "stopped" long enough for me to load my bags and hop aboard. I say "stopped" because the train actually crept ahead during the whole operation, and getting my last bag aboard required a duffel-carrying galumph that was worthy of any Highland Games event. I was juiced up when I finally got settled in, and after an eternity of stopping at every Czech village later, I put my head out the window and saw a large town in the distance.

Disembarking in Olomouc, I inquired at the station's information desk about a hotel. At first the Czech Information Officer appeared friendly, but when he heard me speak English, he turned completely surly and impatient. Wearing his official red hat and navy blue jacket, he was suddenly in a terrible mood when he came out from behind his desk. He hustled out the front entrance of the station, waving me to hurry as I trundled behind with my bags. He pointed in the direction of the biggest building in sight, then walked back into the station without a word.

The six-story building he'd indicated was well over a mile away and there were no taxis about.

By the time I dragged my ~~ass~~ bags into the hotel lobby (no wheels: screwup number four), I was a sweaty mess and had been propped up by the caffeine and nicotine for over 36 hours.

The desk person, who spoke a form of English, gypped me into one of the smallest, most expensive rooms in Central Europe, but at that point it didn't matter.

After I ferried my bags to the fourth floor (no elevator), I got my first taste of Central European hotel rooms – there was a sink with running water, but no phone, television or bathroom. I'd have to share the hopper with the rest of the floor.

It was stifling hot in the room and the ancient window was painted shut. I spitefully peed in the sink, stripped to my boxers and collapsed on the bed.

It was still daylight, but a dreamless sleep came quickly.

I awoke sometime after dark and blearily shuffled to the communal bathroom in my socks. This was yet another screwup because my first step inside was into a puddle of water. I retreated back to the room and peed in the sink again before laying back down, but anger, heat and conjecture ganged up to prevent me from sleeping. I tossed around until the first hint of dawn, then got up.

After finishing my ablutions – wearing shoes this time – I shuttled my duffel bags downstairs and as I nibbled at the meaty breakfast, had the clerk call me a taxi. No way I was gonna carry those mothers so far again.

From there on in – thank goodness – the trip came off without a hitch. I scored a direct train later that morning and was able to relax and enjoy the mountainous scenery of the Tatra Mountains without having to worry about any hustling switches or wrong turns.

Two beers kept me company until Katowice appeared outside of my window around 4 p.m., and I struggled with my bags through the station looking for the friendly face I had spoken to on the phone earlier. It must have been simple to pick me out – in addition to my bags, I was gawking at everything, from the trains to the vendors to the pigeons flying around inside the station's cavernous interior. Everything, and I mean from the shoes to the architecture, was so scintillating that I was overcurious and not paying attention to any one thing for more than a few seconds.

Then from out of the crowd, a middle-sized guy – early-30s, white undershirt – approached me and said, "Hi. Are you Elijah?"

"I am." I dropped my bags.

"Great. My name's Earnest. I'm the Assistant Director of The American School – the one you talked with this morning." He was sporting a buzz-cut and the thickest black-framed glasses I'd ever seen.

We shook hands and he said, "Can I help with one of your bags?"

"God, please! Take that one!"

I gave him the bag with my books, and he struggled with the weight of it. "Geez, whaddya got in here," he asked.

"Heavy, isn't it?"

After muttering something I didn't catch, he said, "Come on, we'll get you to the office."

Walking through the station, I felt as if the train were a time machine that had deposited me in the mid-1950's. The architecture was communist blocky, and the style of dress was so… well, *foreign*. There were the early Brady Bunchers, with high pants, pajama tops and leather buckle shoes. There were the sportsters, wearing what appeared to be the latest pirated brands of jogging suits.

> "By the way, Todd is no longer with the company."
> I blinked at him. "What? Why not?"
> "He was lying to prospective teachers."
> *Oh, lovely.*
> "What kinda lying?"
> "As far as we could tell, it was mostly about accommodation and work load."

And then there were the proper traditionalists; Babushkas and housedresses for the ladies and understated, earth-tone trousers and button down shirts (slightly soiled) for the men.

The smells were strong. Very on the two-days unshowered side. Very on the factory-nearby side.

We walked out of the main station entrance and crossed over a wide, concrete pedestrian bridge. As we walked, I ogled the dozens of vendors' goods on each side – they sold everything from socks to wallets, to bread to chocolate to tennis rackets. I fell behind immediately and Earnest had to come back to fetch me. He found me engaged with a crispy pretzel lady who was holding a bag of 10 and awaiting payment. I had my backpack on the ground and was rooting through it, my wallet hidden deep inside. Earnest hurriedly paid for the pretzels himself and said, "Come on, I gotta get back to work."

I looked up and thanked him.

As I was repacking my rucksack, he said, "Don't mention it. I'll just deduct it from your first paycheck."

I looked up again and said, "First paycheck? Todd said I'd get paid at the end of the summer."

"We can do it that way if you want. But mostly we pay in cash at the end of every month. By the way, Todd is no longer with the company."

I blinked at him. "What? Why not?"

"He was lying to prospective teachers."

Oh, lovely.

"What kinda lying?"

"As far as we could tell, it was mostly about accommodation and work load."

My concern must have been visible, because Earnest said, "Oh, don't worry. We'll work everything out. Anyway, do you have any Polish money now?"

"Yeah, about 200 Zloty."

He nodded. "That'll get you through. Do you have any change?"

"No."

"Well, I'll buy your ticket then. We'll take the tram over to the office."

"Great... thanks again."

We walked over to one of the tram stops and after a few minutes an ancient, roundish black and gray tram lumbered to a stop. We jostled to the doors amid the crowd, climbed up the high steps and then I guarded my bags while Earnest elbowed through to buy tickets from the driver. When he returned, he handed me a ticket and said, "Right. So when we get to the office, we'll take care of your paperwork and your drug test."

I looked at him a second too long through my rose-colored sunglasses.

"Drug test?"

"Yeah. All new teachers have to take one."

"Uh… ok." I tried to sound worry-free, but internally my house of cards was tumbling down. The send-off party hadn't been exactly legal.

Earnest looked at me for a long moment before he said, "No, I'm just kidding. There's no drug test. But I like to see the reaction of our new teachers when I tell them there is. Sometimes they confess to being huge dopers, and I can weed them out, so to speak, right away. Sometimes I can see them wondering whether or not they'll pass the test. *Your* reaction tells me you're not concerned about it, but my intuition tells me you're no stranger to drugs."

I weighed my words and came up with probably the coolest thing I've ever said under pressure: "It's not on my resume, but I've led a pretty experimental life. Still, I'd probably pass any test you care to give me."

He looked at me awhile and then grunted. "Well, you've already passed one."

After two days of acclimatization in Katowice (crazy sleeping patterns, vodka, cabbagey food) we made our way to the "resort" town of Węgierska Górka. To get there, we took a harrowing bus ride on the narrow, hilly country roads, and I made the mistake of sitting in the front seat so I could see everything. What I saw was that Polish roads were impossibly narrow, with no berms, and when two buses would pass one another I had to close my eyes and await the impact. It never came, but I never stopped expecting it.

Węgierska Górka came nowhere close to resembling the resort town that Todd, the American School recruiter, had promised. Yes, it was surrounded by pine mountains. Yes, there was a river. But the town itself consisted of an abandoned factory, a gas station, a down-trodden train station with most of the vowels missing from its name, a couple of food stores, and a Post Office.

In fact, the two primary topics of discussion for me, Trevor and Paul, the three summer English teachers, were the drawbacks of the Węgierska Gulag, as we took to calling it, and the misleading bullshit that Todd had spewed in order to get us there.

The smells of the first week: sweet mountain air; cut grass; fried food; hay, wet from livestock urine; smoky breath; unwashed people who eat a lot of fatty meats; suddenly overbearing cheap perfume; smoke from the garbage-burning neighbors; the acridity of a train's brakes; unwashed clothes, damp from the rain; Trevor's stinky boots.

The woman who ran the Pension where the summer camp was taking place agreed to do my laundry – for a fee – and by the end of the second week my coolest t-shirts had disappeared.

During a lunchtime in the third week, Trevor asked, "Elijah, why aren't you eating?"

"Uh… I don't have much of an appetite today."

"Can I have yours, then?"

I made a face at him and asked, "Are you sure you want it?"

"Oh Yeah! I'm always starvin' at this place. The portions are just too small."

"Alright, man. Here ya go."

I handed him my plate, and Paul and I watched uneasily as he scraped the sausage-based dish with tomatoes and cabbage onto his plate.

I wasn't eating because the lunch in front of us was hauntingly similar to what the ladies in the kitchen had served for dinner the previous night. Indeed, it was during *that* dinner that I happened to look through the server's window only to spot the head cook scraping leftover food from the dirty dishes back into the pot. Having seen me observe her, she quickly closed the shutters. Grimacing, I'd told both Paul and Trevor about what I had seen. Paul was as alarmed as I was, but Trevor didn't seem to care much.

At least, he didn't until about an hour after lunch that day when all skinny and clumsy 6 feet 3 inches of him lay in our shared bedroom complaining of intestinal cramps.

(One of the many lies Todd had told us teachers was that we'd have private rooms. Instead, our L-shaped room was big enough for three twin beds and a wardrobe, but not much else. And despite The American School's assurances to the parents of the English Camp participants, the teacher's room was the only room in the Pension that had a private, adjoining bathroom. Upon discovering this that first day, we squatted there and defied all attempts – some of them quite serious – to oust us.)

Anyway, the bathroom was coming in handy, as Trevor rushed between it and his bed for hours, until the next morning when he lay there moaning and unable to teach. Not that it mattered much, because most of the 30 campers had also acquired the same intestinal distress.

Toilets were scarce, accidents were plenty, and with most of the kids laid up, I spent the next couple of days writing letters.

Dear Dad,

Well, it's 8:15 in the morn and I'm waiting to get some food in my gut before starting the day. We take our meals at 08:30, 12:00, and 18:30 and really revolve around it. The meals are prepared by a group of Polish women and are very traditional, with lunch being the big meal of the day. Dinners are less substantial, but with lots of bread and tea or kava, so you get pretty filled up. I've eaten more here in the last three weeks than in the previous six months!

Polish words that I learned immediately:

piwo	=	*beer*
kawa	=	*coffee*
woda	=	*water*
proszę	=	*please*

Today's the last day of class for the 2ⁿᵈ session. Only two, two-week sessions left! It's now Friday and I'm going to Krakow for a couple days. I'll have a lot of time this weekend because Paul and me, who are teaching the older kids, have decided not to have class tomorrow. We're both about sick of the third guy that we live and teach with, so we thought getting out of "The Gulag" would be good for both of us. It will be the first time I've stayed in a private room for weeks and I'm really looking forward to it. (more later…)

(In a hotel in Krakow)

For the first time in recent memory, I have total privacy. I have a small room with a TV - there's only one channel, TVPoland, and it's currently showing the old Madonna movie "Who's that girl?" in Polish, with no English subtitles.

Problem: How do I convey to you what I am experiencing and why I love it so much?

There's a feeling here that I really enjoy and here it is: even though I am surrounded by people, I am largely unaffected by them. I don't know much about their government, their customs, their motivations, or their fears. Unless I want something from them, I am left alone.

In the U.S., I am inundated with such an overload of information: radio, TV, newspapers, Internet, people's conversations everywhere. My reality is created FOR ME. I am told what to think about, what opinions to have about what I think about, why I should think that way, and what I should accept as important.

But where I am now, I alone create my own reality. My reality is dictated by my surroundings and how I react to them. A Central European company wants to give me a job and I accept it. I leave the States. That's my current reality.

And I don't – at all – want to sound like a jerk here, but where I am now, the world stands before me and I can go almost anywhere, because jobs for ESL teachers abound.

No, by U.S. standards, the money isn't alluring. But because of the inherent travel and adventure, the whole package is really fine.

Hmm. Once again I find myself justifying my choices and path to you, and I don't want to do that. You'll probably never agree with me, and I want to tell you other stuff. I'm off, in four weeks, to Prague. I have solid job leads, offers if I choose, but I want to keep my options open for now.

I am seeing more than I ever thought possible – more customs and ways of life than I can fully ingest. Within this, I make my own rules, my own patterns, and my own way without question or constraint. I choose everything, and the freedom is nothing short of intoxicating. What could be finer than that?

Love to you and mom,
Elijah

Fifty-something Paul and I made our way to Krakow. The clackety train stopped at every Podunk station along the way, we had to make two switches, and it was late evening when we arrived. We found a decent hotel near the train station and checked into separate rooms and I can only assume that Paul was as happy as me to have some privacy. It was difficult living with three grown men in such a small space.

After stowing our things in the hotel, we met and then wrong-turned our way to the town center and finally found a seat at one of the wicker-chair cafes that line Krakow's gigantic, medieval town square. Drinking with the other tourists, for the first time all summer we actually felt like we were visiting Europe.

But we were still thinking about The Gulag.

Our main topic of conversation was Trevor. He was a Bohemian type, which I can sympathize with, but the problem was his odor. He showered like twice per week, and since he'd brought just one pair of shoes with him, a high pair of black Doc Martins, they smelled to high heaven. Paul had it worse than me, as the bed arrangement put his head near Trevor's feet. I could see the strain on Paul's face as his salt and pepper moustache twitched from the smell. We could only open the windows sporadically because of the smoke that filled the valley – the Poles burned everything, and often – and the stuffiness of the room was tangible.

Anyway, that first night in Krakow ended after many beers and we agreed to give each other a wide berth the next day, which I spent jogging and playing footbag. Later that evening I found a vegetarian restaurant and reveled in a meal that hadn't been fried. Afterwards, I drank beer and watched people on the square and it was nice not having to speak.

On the second morning we met for breakfast in the hotel, and Paul told me he wanted to see St. Mary's Church. I myself didn't really care to, so we agreed to meet for lunch at our place on the square.

After breakfast I walked the 30 minutes through the center over to the Wawel Castle complex overlooking the river. It was sunny and warm, and there were a lot of girls in mini-skirts; it had been awhile, so my leering was probably obvious. I found a bench and pretended to read, and I wasn't there more than five minutes when this sexy, sexy red-haired girl walked by.

She was wearing a knee-high skirt, a tight t-shirt and I was just smitten – so much so that I packed up and started following her at a safe distance. She had a really nice walk, long-strided and confident, and it was clear she enjoyed the looks all the men were giving her.

I followed her for about ten minutes, enjoying the sights and sounds of the tourist avenue, as well as the shimmy of her young bottom, until we reached the town square again. It was crowded, and as I negotiated through a large group of people, I lost the girl for a few seconds. When I emerged from the crowd, I scoured the area and finally spotted her going into St. Mary's church on the corner of the square. She was out of sight for maybe 10 seconds as I hustled over and went inside. My eyes took a moment to adjust to the filtered light and when things came into focus, all thoughts of the girl vanished.

The church was like nothing I had ever seen.

The walls were painted deep reds and blues, with intricate inlaid gold designs. The dozen or so marble columns stretched so high that they took my vision from the low, mundane sights I had been concentrating upon and I found myself gawking at the wondrous beauty of the vaulted ceiling, the inspiring stained glass, the enormous main altarpiece, and finally the enormous crucifix.

I was overcome, gripped even, by the cathedral's beauty – beauty that I had never even known existed! I stood there breathing heavy, a deep longing in my chest as I sighed, in awe of the serenity that I was in the middle of.

I stumbled over and sat in a pew to take it all in, and an interesting calm settled over me. I was tranquil and lucid as my mind started to empty itself. I felt like a whole new part of my brain had been unearthed – like a dream where you discover a new room in your house, there was a sense of deep familiarity. It was a profound experience, especially for someone who wasn't religious.

After a time, my reverie was disturbed by a trumpet playing, followed by the 12 o'clock tolling of the bells.

It was time to meet Paul.

"The answer's simple, Elijah. God knows which bait to use."

I looked at him a moment. "You're suggesting that God lured me with that girl for the express purpose of showing me the beauty of a church?"

Over a lunch that contained no cabbage or sausage, I told Paul about my church experience and how... mystical it had been. I told him I had always rejected religious teachings for a number of reasons, but had never been confronted by the actual grandeur of European cathedrals. I was not only impressed, I was agitated.

"The answer's simple, Elijah. God knows which bait to use."

I looked at him a moment. "You're suggesting that God lured me with that girl for the express purpose of showing me the beauty of a church?"

"What I'm saying is that this morning you outright rejected me when I asked you to come with to St. Mary's. But then you followed your pretty little girl there and ended up awestruck at the beauty of God's house here in Krakow. Now, I don't know if He lured you there or not, but it seems like an interesting coincidence."

"It's interesting, all right..." I took a bite of bread and then mumbled, "Hey, I see you reading the Bible in the mornings – how long have you done that?"

"Since I was in the Foreign Legion."

I raised my eyebrows at him and said, "Come again?"

"You heard me."

"You were in the Foreign Legion? You don't have to be French for that?"

"Hell, no. They take anyone. Might even take you. Point is, it was a real strange and difficult time for me and I took to readin' the good book back then."

"Where were you stationed?"

"Can't tell you that."

"Whaddya mean you can't tell me?"

"I had to sign a confidentiality agreement."

"Do all of the... uh... Legionnaires have to sign one?"

"Some of 'em."

"Which ones?"

"Can't tell you that."

I narrowed my eyes at him. "What can you tell me?"

"That it was a real strange and difficult time for me and I took to reading the good book back then."

"Dammit, Paul. I'm all curious now!"

"Sorry, but I can't tell you about it."

"Alright, alright, strange cat. So why do you read the Bible in the mornings?"

"There's a lot of good stuff in there. See, I recognize that I need help sometimes and since I've been alone most of my life, that's where I've turned."

"Have you found anything in there about boozin'?"

"Plenty."

"Because if this conversation is going where I think it is, I'm gonna need to be good and drunk before it's over."

"I'm not gonna try to convert ya, if that's what you mean."

"You don't have the power to convert me, Paul. Your ass isn't cute enough."

He laughed and then asked, "Can I tell you a couple of stories, though?"

"About the Foreign Legion?"

"No. About The Bible."

"Hold on a second…"

I flagged down the passing waitress and ordered some Polish vodka.

"Jesus," said Trevor. "What should we do with him?"

"PAUL!"

I was standing over him in the dark but he wasn't responding.

"PAUL!"

Again no response.

Moments before, Gosha, the head counselor, had come to our room in her pajamas. In a panic, she had spoken Polish before seeing our confusion and switching to English. She told us that Paul was laying in the empty field next to the Pension, so we got dressed and rushed out.

We came upon Paul lying fetal, dressed in cowboy boots, jeans and a denim shirt, and tried to pick him up straightaway. But out of nowhere, he flashed a worryingly large knife at us.

As we jumped back, Trevor yelled, "He's got a fucking knife!"

"Yell a bit louder, dingleberry!" I motioned to the Pension, where students were silhouetted in their open bedroom windows.

"Shit," he said. "Sorry."

I leaned closer and said, "Paul! What's wrong?"

No explanation was really necessary, because he simply reeked of puke and alcohol.

"We gotta get him up to the room," said Trevor.

"You wanna pick him up when he has that knife?"

We looked at each other, then I leaned over and commenced barking at him.

"Paul, gimme the knife. Give. Me. The. Knife."

No response.

"PAUL!"

Nada.

Trevor looked around and then walked over to a nearby bush, where he broke off a stout stick. He returned, somewhat giddily, back to the huddled mass of Paul and looked at me. I shrugged my amused complicity and then Trevor used the stick to poke Paul in the back. He did it hard, too.

The only response was me and Trevor breaking into a fit of giggles.

After a few seconds Trevor chortled, "I didn't know it until just now, but I've wanted to do that for a looooong time."

"Here, lemme try," I said.

"Just one more," said Trevor. This time Paul twitched after being poked, which motivated Trevor to sneak in another good one. It seemed to be working.

When I was able to control my giggles, I said, half-heartedly, "Paul, wake up."

No reply.

Trevor finally surrendered the stick and after a moment of consideration, I gently but firmly poked Paul right where the sun don't shine. Boy, did that do the trick. Paul's cheeks scrunched up, he mumbled what I can only assume was a vile threat and when I resumed the "Gimme the knife" mantra, he finally closed the knife and put it back into his pocket.

Trevor and I looked at each other. An armed Paul was not comforting after our little reindeer games.

While Trevor went to fetch a chair from the dining room, I got Paul to sit up. I had to hold him upright until Trevor returned, and then we lifted him onto the chair. We carried him through the field, stumbled up the gravel street to the Pension and finally made it, gasping, upstairs to our room. Along the way we'd crossed paths with the owner of the Pension, the camp director, and all three of the counselors. None of them seemed pleased.

We deposited Paul in front of our private toilet and he stayed there all night, serenading us with his heaving – dry and otherwise.

In the morning I very much wanted to ask Paul how it was that a Christian like himself had gotten into such a mess, but his depressed lethargy prevented it. Later at lunch, after refusing to eat, he shared the story himself. He'd had dinner with a family down the street and the host had "gone berserk" with the after-dinner vodka shots. Paul, not wanting to insult, had done shot after shot with him until two bottles, along with the two of them, were gone.

He staggered most of the way home before stopping to hurl in the yard beside the Pension, where he must have passed out. That's when a group of older students came upon him and tried to help. But Paul had flashed the knife at them too, and they wisely let him be. Soon after is when me and Trevor were summoned.

Paul thanked us for getting him up to the room, and Trevor and I looked at each other, wondering if he remembered the poking.

Paul was relating this story in the dining room amid the 30 students, and the buzz was clearly on. The students were all looking at him with a somewhat fearful deference, and the chatter wasn't quite as loud as normal. I sure would liked to have been a fly on the wall for Paul's classes that day.

But the thing was, Paul was humiliated and told us that he wanted to quit. It was two weeks to the end of camp at that point, and Trevor and me cajoled him to stay for a few reasons – the first being that if he left, we'd be royally screwed by having to teach his class load as well. The other reasons were that he should finish what he started, that the kids hadn't really seen him out there, and that everybody would miss him.

It was only later in the day, apparently after consulting the proper passage in his good book, that Paul decided to stay until the end of camp.

Me and Trevor were relieved but edgy because he apparently still had that knife somewhere.

Those two weeks passed quickly, and on the last day of camp, the teachers, students and counselors were all acting nostalgic and bittersweet that our time was drawing to a close. I myself didn't feel I'd miss Węgierska Górka, nor Paul and Trevor. But I would definitely miss Basia, one of the counselors I had grown quite fond of during the last two weeks of camp. She was smart and pretty, with long, twisty brown hair, very full lips, and seemed to enjoy my company as much as I hers.

Anyway, as the last activity of the summer, we decided upon a hike in the mountains – those students wishing to join were welcome to – and we got perhaps 15 of them to come with.

We set out from the Pension after breakfast in rather low spirits (not only because of the steady drizzle), but by the time we had walked through town and across the bridge over the Sowa River, we had warmed up and the mood had lightened.

We walked steadily uphill for three hours, taking breaks here and there, until we reached a high plateau. There, the path joined a cindered logging road and we wandered down it in the rain, sporadically picking blackberries from the bushes that abutted the high pine forest on each side. The pine trees protected us from the wind and their smell gave a cozy feeling.

Basia, myself, and two students of mine who were very pleasant, Marcin and Marush, had fallen further and further back as we picked berries and chatted, and the rest of the group had been out of sight for perhaps five minutes.

Suddenly, the road emerged from the forest and we found ourselves standing on the edge of a large mountain meadow that sloped downward to our right. Beyond the meadow, far away across the Sowa River Valley, were the opposing, gently-sloping mountains bathed in mist. The rain had been letting up, and as we came to the field the sun broke through the clouds and bathed our hillside in warm, glowing rays – the air literally turning golden.

As we looked out over the meadow, to our wonder a rainbow slowly formed across the valley. We were caught up in it a long time until someone noticed an absolute bumper crop of blackberries right under our noses. So we happily waded in and ate berries amid the natural spectacle that surrounded us. The berries were still wet from the purifying rain and were, fittingly, bittersweet.

As we foraged, I stood up and stepped back for a moment to look around. There was the aromatic fecundity of the pine forest, the meadow with its profusion of wildflowers, the rainbow, the misty mountains across the valley, and finally the three people whom I had grown so fond of. Taking all of this in, I found myself filled with a sudden, ardent immensity of emotion, and I stood there in joyous awe of the moment's beautiful simplicity. But at the same time I felt a terrible emptiness knowing that it would be over so soon.

I guess Basia had been watching me, because she walked over to me through the bushes and to my surprise and complete fulfillment, stepped into me for a hug. We embraced for a long moment and then she pulled back to look up at me. Her blue eyes were awash with serenity and we gazed at each other in kindness before slowly becoming aware of our students again. When we looked over they were smiling at us in complete understanding, so, still holding each other and now with our students' sanction, Basia and I stood cheek-to-cheek and watched them pick berries in front of the rainbow.

After a while, we slowly parted and smiled at each other, and not even 10 seconds later someone came into view and yelled at us to catch up to the group. We waved in answer, but dawdled our way up to them, loathe to relinquish our special group dynamic. The fleeting nature of reality, however, forced us to give in and we found ourselves back with the others all too soon.

Camp ended later that day, and as with most endings, this one was both joyful and sad. As the two buses were boarded, lots of addresses were traded and accompanying promises of future correspondence were made.

There were plenty of hugs and tears, but not for us teachers. Trevor, Paul and me gladly shook farewell, no promises of contact forthcoming. Basia and I hugged goodbye and promised to keep in touch. Finally, both coaches drove off with the students plastered against the windows and waving.

In my experience, the end of every summer camp involves two complex emotions: the first is relief upon leaving the relative inconveniences of shared bathrooms, communal dining, lack of privacy and a regimented schedule. The second emotion is sadness over the dissolution of that singular, unique character that any given camp comes to personify over the summer; this sadness is compounded by the loss of individual friendships.

But life trundles onward, as did the buses on their way through the town and eventually northward, out of the mountains.

From an educational point of view, Earnest later told me, the camps had been a success, and despite my relative inexperience I was offered further employment with the American School for the upcoming school year. Accommodations, a huge selling point, were provided in the contract, so I trained up to Katowice to check out the school again and talk to the teachers about their experiences.

A story that helped me make up my mind: a teacher, Matt, told me that while on a trip back to the U.S., he'd gone to the doctor for a routine check up. The doctor asked him why he'd started smoking, to which the non-smoking Matt replied, "Uh... I don't smoke, doc."

To which the doctor replied, "Well, your lungs are full of something."

To which Matt replied, "Well, I've been living in Poland for the last six months..."

"Any factories nearby?"

"Uh, sure. Katowice is a big industrial town."

The doctor gave him a knowing nod and advised him to move away for his health's sake.

So while Katowice may in fact be a very fine town, for me at the beginning stages of an extended European stay, it was about as alluring as Sheboygan, Wisconsin. In fact, being so close to Lake Michigan, Sheboygan offered a great deal more than its Polish counterpart.

But I wasn't about to live in Sheboygan, Poland, nor in Katowice, Wisconsin. I had my sights set a bit higher, and found, via the Internet, the names of a dozen private language schools that were looking for English instructors in Prague. One of them, Lingualux, even extended me a preliminary job offer over the phone, pending a personal interview the following week.

The six-passenger sleeper compartment I was assigned to was full of snoring drunks and their fetid exhalations when the train picked me up in Katowice. Backpacks were strewn about on the floor, making it a struggle to get my duffel bags in, but my sleeping berth was thankfully on the bottom of three levels, so I didn't have to climb over anyone to get to it. (Though I must confess to later having a strong desire to stomp on several snoring faces).

The air in the compartment was noxious and after I had situated myself, I stumbled over to open the window but found it fixed shut. Holding my breath, I lay down and propped the compartment door open with my arm to get some fresh air. I flirted with the idea of sleeping like that, but then my head would be just six inches away from some fictitious hand reaching around the corner to get me in my sleep. No, thank you.

Plus, Earnest had told me a story about a friend of his who'd been on a Polish overnight train. Sometime during the night, a group of bandits had managed to release the latter half of the train's cars from the engine's forward half. The half of the train that then rolled to a stop was gassed, knocking everyone out and thus enabling the gas-masked bandits to rifle through the passengers' valuables at will, in many cases taking whole suitcases with them. Earnest speculated that some of the women were raped as well.

I fell asleep worrying about just that and sometime later a loud banging on our door jolted me awake. I forced myself to play possum and watched through slitted eyes as a man with a gun opened the door and stepped into the compartment. I mentally freaked out, wondering what the hell to do as the rest of the compartment stirred awake. There *were* six of us after all. We might be able to-

And then the gunman asked to see our passports.

It was a border guard.

After the border posse had checked our papers and moved on, the fetid stench, the lack of cushioning on the "bed" and the anxiety of being in a foreign land with all of my important belongings reduced me to a fitful half-sleep. Worse, every time I did manage to drift off, I jolted awake to check that no one was rifling through my valuables or coming to thump me.

But of course there were no bandits, no gassings, no problems that weren't only in my head, and the train rolled safely into Prague's main railway station at 6 a.m. on a glorious late summer morning.

Alas, I didn't make it without a loss. I discovered an hour after disembarking that I'd forgotten my rose-colored sunglasses on the train. What I didn't know is that I'd arrived in a city that didn't require them.

❀

The following excerpt from Every Thing Counts (The Akashic Reader) has not been published prior to its inclusion here.

Preface

When I was in graduate school I attended a fascinating slide presentation given by a black-haired female alumnus who had been on a Space Shuttle mission. She delivered exuberant commentary and engrossing pictures of the earth and Shuttle lifestyle, and we in the audience rewarded her with a standing ovation.

In the lobby afterwards there was a heap of free NASA goodies, among which was a poster that portrayed the Milky Way galaxy as a wavy horizontal line. But the poster didn't contain just one line: It was a stack of 5 horizontal lines, each one of the Milky Way, each one in a different color and pattern. One couldn't tell, just by looking at them, that they were images of the same thing because they were all portrayed by sensors that detected various portions of the electro-magnetic spectrum: gamma rays, x-rays, ultraviolet radiation, and so on.

Each of these sensors refined their images of the galaxy in a drastically different manner, sometimes showing bulges where others showed narrows, sometimes showing brightness where others showed its absence.

I took the poster home and put in on my wall, and one day while staring at it instead of studying, it occurred to me that our 5 senses are pitifully limiting. Indeed, the fact that our galaxy appears so drastically different when viewed through various filters convinced me that we have about zero understanding of different dimensions, ESP, or even the spirit.

And why?

Because essentially, we humans are really only a set of filters, and we understand just as much of reality as those filters permit. If we wish to see beyond that, we need to somehow increase our perceptual abilities.

Act I
Golden Prague

I first met Magdeline at the Internet café nestled in the art nouveau Prague Municipal House. It was a relatively expensive Internet provider, but its central location and atmosphere of gentility it exuded were such that I didn't mind the price. There were crystal chandeliers, sumptuously padded wooden booths, and also an English-speaking staff – namely, Magdeline – who brought coffee, Pilsner Urquell, or cigarettes as required.

During my third visit in early September, Magdeline told me she was a senior at one of the city's art high schools, and that she lived with her parents quite close to the university where I'd be teaching English. As we spoke more and more, it also came out that she was 18 and had spent a year in Virginia as part of an exchange program.

Magdeline's American experience had enhanced her language skills to the point that, as many young Americans do, she peppered her English with well-placed variations of the word fuck. Sentences with *fucking, fuckhead, fuckwad, mother-fucker, rotten fuck, stupid fucker, shitfuck* – they all rolled smoothly off her tongue. She even used *fuckingly* in new and creative placements, and that she did this cursing in the middle of the highbrow Prague Municipal House struck me as a terribly interesting juxtaposition. I was attracted to her despite (or perhaps because of) her brazen youth.

Oh, I know – being 27 and interested in an 18 year-old girl makes me a weirdo, right? Well not exactly, because it was legal in the Czech Republic, at least it was then, to have relations with a girl of 15. (Magdeline herself is the one who told me this, and I later verified it with a Czech colleague.) In the eyes of society, then, I was Mr. By-the-book.

At any rate, on my fourth visit to the Internet joint, Mad, as she liked to be called, invited *me* out on a Friday night. She knew of a great party if I wanted to come along, and we could get to know each other better.

I gladly accepted and was early for our bus stop rendezvous. And my goodness, when I saw her walking towards me through the twilight, I had to catch my breath. She was a sexy little thing, dressed in a short mini-skirt, boots, and tight sweater. Moreover, she came on to me from the start, and her flirty brashness was at once titillating and – truthfully – unsettling.

On the bus ride into town, Mad told me we were meeting two English guys at the Metro station. At first I was disappointed I wouldn't be alone with her, but after thinking about it, I saw that it was probably better this way – maybe I wouldn't be so preoccupied with her legs. Or any other parts of her, for that matter.

At the Metro station Dejvice, Colin and Tim had already arrived, and after brief introductions we all boarded the Metro and began chatting. Right away I saw that Colin and Tim were great guys; funny, open, and most importantly interested in the world around them. Later at the party they were full of questions and jokes, and the night turned out *swimmingly* (a word I picked up from them). In fact, we got along so well that when Mad had to leave, I stayed instead of accompanying her home. I did walk her to the Metro stop, though.

"Will you stay out late," she asked as we walked.

"Just a couple more beers."

"Uh-huh. Well, when I get home I gonna…" she looked meaningfully at me, "I gonna touch myself."

I blinked.

"And I will fantasize about you helping me..."

"Uh...."

Mentally and physically, I took a deep breath.

"Well, I… I like helping people," I responded.

"Uh-huh... so maybe you help me sometime?" She moved close to me, rubbing against my chest, and kissed me on the neck.

She stood back and smiled at me again. Turning and walking towards the Metro, she shook her hips at me and then quickly turned to see if I was watching.

Of course I was watching.

We waved goodbye, and as I walked back to the party I could not stop grinning.

Colin, I discovered later that night, had a connection that he was willing to share, and next Sunday at noon, we rendezvoused with Priestly underneath The Horse at the top of Wenceslas Square. Priestly told me that he was from Sudan and was living in the Czech Republic illegally, hoping to one day gain asylum status. In the meantime, he'd been making money this way.

The three of us walked together down the square and turned right onto Na Příkope. We walked all the way up to the Powder Tower and then turned left onto Celetná ulice. On the right-hand side we found a small café and went inside. We sat down and had a drink and talked about life, and by the end of our meeting, Priestly had taken to calling me "my friend." He did this to Colin as well.

At the end of the meeting, there was a slippy exchange of the grass and the money, and I was given Priestly's phone number. It was implicit that I no longer needed Colin to come along.

The other Brit, Tim, was a funny, thoughtful kid, and we began to keep in touch almost daily.

Two weeks after we met, Tim began a Big Boy Job as a Marketing Director with a Czech firm, but on the fifth day he hit some sort of wall and resigned – just walked out at lunch and didn't go back. Further, he decided to move back to London. He'd had enough of Prague and needed a change. Or money. Or both.

An interesting thing about the people I was meeting: we all seemed to need constant variation, and to find it, we no longer thought in terms of cities or states, but in terms of countries, continents and hemispheres.

The world that our parents had inhabited – full of Iron Curtains, Cold Wars and well-entrenched prejudices – was gone.

In its place stood countries to be explored, customs to be discovered, languages to be learned. Never mind that going in, most of us had no in-depth knowledge of our adopted countries. It was the adventure, the wanderlust that courted us and placed us fully in the midst of the hardy expatriates – the Global Village Idiots – who gypsied our way across the globe, seeking *experiences*, short-term under-employment, and a type of fulfillment that could never be provided by the grist-mill of efficiency- and profit-seeking corporations.

It was a rainy autumn afternoon when Mad knocked on my door for the first time, and when I opened up I simply had to admire her a moment before letting her in. Spread apart was a long, black jacket, and underneath was a white sweater short enough to reveal a svelte, pierced stomach. She was also wearing a plaid miniskirt and over-the-knee white stockings. I simply couldn't believe how hot she was, and my sudden sexual energy convinced her to... well...

Afterwards, Mad lay on top of me under the covers.

"Mmm. We do this again?" she asked.

Twenty-seven or not, it seemed just a little quick for me to consider. "Uh… *now?*"

"No, no, I have to go home until 5 o'clock. I think another time…"

"Oh, PLEASE," I enthused. "You just tell me when."

"I come back tomorrow if you like…"

"Absolutely… say, 4 o'clock?"

"Yes, 4 o'clock. I will finish fucking school then. Tell me, you like me in this skirt? I can wear another…"

"Mad, it doesn't matter what you wear – I'll just take it off you!"

We laughed and kissed, then she threw off the covers and stood up, both of us shivering from the relative coldness of the room. I covered back up and propped up my head with a pillow. My eyes danced over her as she collected her clothes from around the room.

Sitting on a chair opposite the bed, she pulled on her stockings, then stood up and slid on her skirt. She found her shoes and slipped them on, and then as she was putting her shirt on, a hand-lettered sign on the wall caught her attention. She read it aloud: "Pride. Envy. Lust. Gluttony. Anger. Ava… avarice. Sloth. What the fuck is that?"

I considered telling her about my recent dream, but realized I didn't feel close enough to her, which was odd given what we'd just done. I gave her the stock version instead.

"Well, in Christianity, those are the seven deadly sins – the things that everybody has to avoid to live a good life."

"I don't fuckin' believe in God," she asserted as she buttoned her sweater.

"I can understand that – I myself was an atheist until a couple of days ago…"

I took a deep breath as I again considered telling her about it… and decided not to.

"Anyway, those 7 sins are pinned on the wall to remind me to try and be a better person."

"A better person? Isn't it too fucking late for that? I mean, you're almost *30!*"

"Uh… *no*, it's not too late to be a better person. It never is."

She looked back up at the wall and said, "Well, one word I do know is lust! I am full of it, and you will continue having problem with it when I am with you! You know this, yes?"

"Oh, I know it. I'm having problems right now."

Mad looked at the blanket and said, "I see it. Want me to suck your cock before I go?"

I winced at the harshness of the offer. But harsh or not, I still let her.

Much like Mad, I considered myself an atheist for quite a long time. Just one of the many drawbacks of, let's say, Christianity, is the postulate that humans are the only inhabitants of the universe. I mean, ok, perhaps God placed us here on Earth, but when you consider the sheer vastness of space and the number of stars that are out there, it becomes an exercise in buffoonery to really maintain that earth contains the only life in the whole of creation.

And even if you weren't convinced that NASA photographed something human-like on Mars, here are some numbers that might help: what we call the Milky Way Galaxy contains approximately 200 billion stars. That's 200,000,000,000 stars, which by any reckoning is a boatload. And what we call the Milky Way Galaxy is *only one of the billions* of galaxies scattered about the universe's rumpus room. Now, I'm no mathematician, and I still can't convert Fahrenheit to Celsius, but when we start to talk about this many stars, the church's claim that we're alone in the universe approaches delusional and I simply cannot accept it. Far from being the only life, I think we merely lack the sophistication to detect other civilizations.

But back to the religion thing – right before I met Mad, I came to see – rather, was *made* to see – that atheism is completely wrong.

And I know this next bit may be hard to swallow, but I can't stress enough that it's the truth: I was given a message in a dream – an unbelievably moving dream – that there is something out there higher than we can perceive – something that unmistakably plays a hand in the Big Scheme of things.

Which naturally begs the question: Why would a sexed-up fool like me be the one to receive such a message? My only answer, the one I arrived at after careful consideration, is this: Who better than a sexed-up fool to be shown The Way?

And anyway, even assuming that the dream *wasn't* a message from God, it had a big impact on me. At the very least, it pushed me into a phase of spirituality in which I realized that my soul was blessed, and no harm – aside from my own neglect – could come to it.

I had to giggle when I first put it into words, but the simple, pure truth is that I found God in Prague.

Or rather, God found me.

It took awhile amid the total traffic chaos, but I finally recognized Mad on the massive round-about of *Vítězné náměstí* (Victory Square) at 5 p.m. on Friday. She was on the far side of the bustle and from there we walked, holding hands, through progressively quieter parts of the De-jvice quarter. We were going to her cousin's birthday party, then Mad had to work at 8 that evening (in addition to her Internet café job, she was a part-time waitress at a disco).

During the walk, because I didn't want to do it in front of an audience at the party, I gave Mad the small gift I'd made the previous evening. It was a dream catcher, the sort that Native American Indians used, and I had collected the various components in the forest. There was no occasion for the gift – I had just always wanted to make one. Anyway, as I gave it to her, I saw the girlish light flash in her eyes before she kissed me.

We arrived at the party early, the only other people being the Birthday Girl cousin and Mad's older sister. The cousin was in her early 20's, black-haired, and spoke a bit of English. Mad's sister Simona was in her late 20's, had short red hair, and wore tight jeans and a slightly-cropped t-shirt that revealed a healthy midsection. She also spoke a bit of English.

Introductions were friendly and I was led to a cozy chair and brought a glass of whiskey on ice while Mad and Simona, on either side of me, tried to include me in their sisterly Czech conversation as much as possible. More people came in, and in less than an hour the party was going strong.

During one of the many periods when the girls were speaking Czech and I couldn't under-stand a word, I looked around the studio, taking in the party and my surroundings. We were in the lobby/bar of a fashionable fitness studio operated by a blonde Slovak man. I knew this because the week before I had walked by this very same fitness studio, and upon seeing that they gave massages, had gone in and made an appointment. It turned out to be a mistake, as the owner had a horrible Iron Grip philosophy when it came to massaging, and I walked out feeling terribly crooked of back. Because of that, and also because my Gaydar had gone through the roof there, I promised myself never to return. So it was with a feeling of smug confirmation that

I looked over Simona's partially-bared shoulder and saw a young, cross-dressed boy twirling around, wearing a skirt and a bleached-blonde wig.

Later, on my way up to the bar, the same boy approached me and said something in Czech.

"I'm sorry, I don't speak Czech," I replied.

"Oh, you're American," the boy said. He continued dancing, getting closer to me. "What I said was, 'You're really hot.' Are you a fairy?"

"Uh… no… But thanks for asking."

The boy's smile dimmed and he said, "Pity," before dancing away.

For who, I wondered, and continued up to the bar. I ordered three more whiskeys from the now-bartending cousin, and secretly hoped that Mad wouldn't want hers because of work.

When I arrived back in the sisters' midst carrying the drinks, my hope was confirmed. Mad was already thinking about leaving and didn't want hers, so it sat on the table untouched. The girls talked a moment more in Czech and then Mad got up to go to the toilet.

When she got up, Simona slid closer to me and asked, "So, you like sister?"

"Your sister? Oh, sure. And you?"

"Yes! He's my sister! But tell me – who is my English?"

"It's good – like your sister's English…"

She smiled and looked downward. "You do fun."

"No, really. We're talking, aren't we? That's good English for me."

She looked back up at me. "But I need a help. I need teacher too, like Mad. She said me I ask you for lesson…"

She looked at me expectantly, and I responded just a bit *too* quickly through the whiskey, "Oh, sure! I'll be your teacher."

"Fine! Tonight after Mad go – you stay by me."

I hesitated, already feeling vaguely guilty at being alone with her. "Uh… I'm sorry, but I promised Mad I would walk her to the Metro station."

"No problem. We tell her it." Simona sat back and smiled, apparently satisfied things had been worked out.

I took a drink and then Mad came back and sat on my right. Simona was on my left and they spoke over me in Czech – a second or two later, Mad asked me, in English – "So you'll stay with Simona tonight, yes? Perfect. She likes you."

At the mention of her name, I had looked over at Simona, but at Mad's last statement, I snapped my head back to her and said, "No … I'm going with you."

"No, stay with my sister – she will be lonely if you go."

"Mad, I don't want to stay. I'm more comfortable going with you."

"You don't like my sister?"

"Of course I do, but-"

"Then what's the fuckin' problem?"

"I just don't want to stay."

"But she will think you don't like her."

"Tell her I do like her, but I don't want to stay – I can teach her next week. In the daytime."

I sat back and the girls spoke in Czech again. I watched their non-verbal cues, trying to see how Simona was taking the news – she was clearly disappointed.

Mad turned to me. "She says it is a pity for her, but good that you like me."

She smiled, pecked me on the cheek, and asked if I was ready to go. We all stood and walked over to the cousin, wished her well, then Mad and I said goodbye to Simona.

"We have English, not forget," said Simona as we shook hands. "Last week, ok?"

"I will call you next week," I said, shaking her hand.

The sisters spoke in Czech and laughed, and then Mad and I walked out of the party and into the still-sunny streets.

After the door closed behind us, Mad led me around the corner and hungrily kissed me. She looked into my eyes. "You want to fuck my sister, don't you?"

"*What?*"

"You like her and want to fuck her."

"Uh, no... I like you."

She smiled when I said this and kissed me deeply again.

Czech girls... so refreshingly simple to deal with, I thought.

Then we walked, holding hands, to Hradčanska metro station. I was relieved I didn't have to be at the party anymore and that I had the whole evening – with a nice buzz, to boot – in front of me. But just as we got to the stairs that led to the underground station, Mad stopped and said, "Shit! I fuckin' forgot your gift! Someone will throw it away now!"

I looked at her for a second, then sighed and shook my head.

"They won't throw it out. I'll go get it."

"Will you? I'm so sorry... and I'll pick it up when I visit on Monday! Will you really go back?"

"Yeah. Don't worry about it."

She smiled, kissed me again and said, "I'm so sorry. I'll make up on it on Monday, ok?"

She started backing away.

"You'd better!"

"I promise I will! See you Monday!"

"See you Monday."

She turned and quickly walked away, and didn't look back as she hurried down the stairs. I watched her go, disgusted that I had to go back to the party, before I turned and walked up the street. It was only a five minute walk back, but it took me 15 heel-dragging minutes. It was early – not even 8 o'clock yet, which meant it would be difficult to extract myself from the party again.

I breathed deeply before I opened the front door. There were a lot more people there, and my entrance went unnoticed by everyone but Simona, who at once saw me from across the room. Our eyes met and we smiled.

I worked my way to where we had been sitting before, and Simona met me there.

"Mad forgot something," I said.

"I know."

"What do you mean, you know?"

"She said me."

"*What?* She told you she was leaving the gift here?"

"Yes. We plan. Now you mine for night."

"Simona, I-"

She put a finger to my lips and said, "Yes."

I sighed deeply and looked at her.

"Yes," she repeated, and arched her eyebrow.

I took off my jacket and sat down. The glass of whiskey Mad had left was still there among some empty glasses, and I picked it up and drank it in one go.

When I looked up at her, Simona smiled and went to get me another.

Two hours of whiskey, dancing and flirting later, Simona got up to use the toilet, and while she was gone, from out of the crowd the black-haired cousin materialized. She walked over to me and said, "What's your relationship with Simona?"

"Uh… I like her sister. I just met Simona tonight."

"Good," she said, and melted back into the party.

I sat there wondering about the question and then Simona came back and sat on a chair to my left. She looked at me provocatively, ensured that I was watching her, and then leaned over to get her drink. As she leaned, her loose neckline dropped low enough to expose her chest. I saw this out of my peripheral vision but struggled to maintain eye contact with her. I swallowed hard. After a moment Simona sat back with her glass in hand, smiling.

I looked at her and covered my mouth and cheek with my hand. I breathed deep, feeling the smoothness of my freshly-shaven face, then stood up. I indicated that I was going to the toilet, and walked back the darkened hallway. The music faded slightly as I went.

Opening the door to the toilet, the light was already on and I looked at myself lazily in the mirror against the far wall. Then my eyes shot open when I saw, behind my own reflection, that of Simona.

I whirled around and saw her sultry smile wane when she realized I hadn't intended to invite her in with me. She became terribly red and apologized all over herself as she backed out the door and scurried up the hallway.

I slapped myself on the forehead and shook my head. After I closed the door, I looked at my reflection. How did I get myself into these situations?

I found that I didn't have to masturbate any longer, which was the reason I'd gone to the bathroom in the first place, and when I returned to the party, Simona had apparently left.

Relieved but still feeling guilty, I finished my glass, picked up Mad's gift and slipped out the door.

Czech girls are so simple to deal with, I chided myself.

I was peeved at Mad for her little games. She'd pretty much lied to me about leaving the gift at the party, and overall she was a negative influence on me that night – I ended up drinking too much and getting to bed late. Plus, there was the whole scene with Simona, which still felt like a punch to the gut.

Nevertheless, when Monday rolled around, I planned on hiding my negative vibes because I wanted to… well…

The knock on the door came while I was still arranging things, so I yelled "Moment," and hustled about. I was thinking about the dust in the corner when I opened the door and found both Mad and Simona standing there.

Smooth me, I said, "Uh…" and looked between them.

Mad leaned over to give me a kiss. She looked very happy, and asked if they could come in.

"Uh. Sure. Of course."

I stood aside. Mad went first, followed by Simona. When they passed me up, both were smiling.

After they sat down, Mad on the bed, Simona on the reading chair, I offered them beers. Both accepted, so I went back to the fridge and opened three, wondering what was going on. I returned to the bedroom, we toasted, and then I couldn't wait any longer.

"So," I ventured, and sat on the bed.

"Elijah," Mad started, "we want to apologize…"

"Yes, we very sorry," nodded Simona.

I looked between them and said, "Oh, don't worry. It was my fault, too."

"Yes," laughed Simona, "you confuse me with toilet!"

"I am *so* sorry for that! Really. I didn't mean to–"

Mad stopped me and said, "It's all right, Elijah. We already spoke about it and it was just a confusion. But we wanted to apologize in person…" She looked at Simona, who nodded, "…and we want to apologize in a special way."

I looked at Mad and said, "It's ok. I accept your apology. Really."

I drank my beer and watched them over the bottle. The put their own beers down and moved cat-like towards me.

I swallowed all wrong and coughed, then asked, "What are you doing?"

"We want apologize," said Simona.

"You already did," I said, standing up and backing away.

Mad, still on the bed, grabbed my forearm with both hands and pulled me towards her.

Simona suddenly pulled her sweater over her head and threw it onto the chair. I gaped and strained at Mad's hold while Simona came over and took the beer from my hands. I watched her naked back and jeaned bottom as she walked over and put my beer between theirs.

Having both hands empty allowed me to pry my hand free from Mad's grip, and when Simona started back for me, I held both my hands up in front of me.

"Wait, I – "

Mad grabbed at my arm again, getting a hold and pulling me towards her. Seeing me off-balance, Simona pushed and hipped me until I fell onto the bed. I curled up fetal with both of them on top of me, laughing and saying they needed to apologize.

I stayed curled up, feeling Simona's breasts against my bare arm and kinda liking it, until they started tickling me.

Writhing around and giggling, I tried not to hurt anyone as I pushed them away, but holding back just got me further underneath. Finally they had me on my back, Mad straddling my chest and arms. Simona was sitting over my knees and pinning my hands.

I looked up at Mad and said, "Ok, really! Let me up and I won't have to hurt you."

She smiled and said something in Czech, and I felt Simona's hand begin to unfasten my jeans.

As Mad was pulling her shirt off, I looked up at her fullness and wondered if I should freak and muscle my way out, or just…

The face-to-face student placement interviews that took place in October were the beginning of the semester for me and my three English teaching colleagues at the Czech Agriculture University. They were actually an occasion for fun and socializing, but I was taking my job seriously and approached the interviewing process as such. For example, while none of my colleagues had even dressed smart casual, I showed up wearing a tie.

That's not to say my colleagues were somehow less engaged – they merely had varied approaches to things. Katherine – Kat – was from southern California, had studied art, and had the whitest smile in the city. She lived up the hallway from me, and on her second day in Prague had gone to Ikea to dress up her foreigner-ghetto room. She was the most naturally sociable of all of us.

Ryan was also from California, but further up the coast. He was the real Bohemian of the group: he and his girl had been traveling around the coastal cities of the world, surfing and taking work wherever they could find it before ending up in Prague.

Andrew – not Andy – was the lone Brit among us, and was the most depressed, depressing individual I'd ever met. A recent breakup and move-out, coupled with his talk about how crappy Prague was, convinced me to avoid him wherever possible.

The classroom we used for the interviews was very 1950s, outfitted with straight-backed wooden chairs, tables made of painted particle board, and a 30-grit green chalkboard on the front wall. We conducted the interviews at the rear of the classroom, two of us per table asking questions of the prospective students. A sample interview might include, "Where are you from? <present tense diagnosis>, Have you studied English before? <present perfect tense>, "What did you do last weekend?" <past tense>, What will you do next weekend? <future tense>, and so on.

I was paired up with Andrew and making the best of a bad situation; to my right were Kat and Ryan, having a ball. At the front of the room was the waiting area where between five and ten students stood at any given time.

We had been there for about two hours when she walked into the room.

Just a glance was enough for me to be impressed – she had long, chestnut hair, was wearing a stylish blue suit, and was beautiful in a wholesome, natural way.

I couldn't ignore her presence, couldn't concentrate on our interview, and luckily Andrew picked up the slack until it concluded and the student walked away. I dearly hoped it was the beautiful girl's turn, but instead another boy came to our table, bright-eyed and talkative. The lovely girl walked back to Kat and Ryan's table and I simply could not keep my eyes off of her.

As Andrew conducted our interview without me, I listened to and watched Kat and Ryan speak to my sparkling beauty.

"Elijah… *hellooo…*"

It was Andrew.

I turned and smiled sheepishly at him. "Hey, can you handle this one alone?"

"What? Uh…"

Both Andrew and the interviewee looked at me blankly.

"Thanks," I said, and scooted my chair over next to Kat. Andrew, abandoned yet again, returned to the interview. At Kat's table, my chair-skidding had taken everyone aback.

I took it in stride, gave them my Big Smile and said, "I thought you might need some help."

Ryan shook his head at me, Kat smiled, and the beautiful girl held out her hand and said, "Liliana."

Shaking hands with her was like licking a 9 volt battery. I actually stuttered my name.

"Uh… Elijah. Nice to meet you, Liliana."

Kat giggled at me and said, "Liliana is looking for a private teacher…"

"Oh, really," I almost sang.

"…and Ryan can't do it because he lives so far away. That leaves me or you, because we both live here on campus."

Genius me asked, "Do you live here on campus, Liliana?"

"Yes, I live in campus but I am away too often for normal classes, so I need private teacher." She smiled.

Ears ringing, blood pressure skyrocketing, I sat and gaped.

Kat nudged me on. "So… do you want to teach her?"

I spun on her quickly and blurted out, "I can't teach her!"

Ryan and Kat looked at me as if I'd deliberately poked myself in the eye, and when I looked back at Liliana, her smile had drooped slightly.

Kat ventured, "Are you sure?"

"Yeah… uh… I just don't have time for private students. I'm sorry Liliana, but Kat is a great teacher, you'll really like her."

Liliana smiled politely at us all, and made the necessary arrangements with Kat. Standing up, she shook all our hands and walked toward the front of the room. As she walked out, she turned back for a final goodbye and was away.

I sighed in relief; bells were still ringing somewhere in the distance.

Ryan leaned over and looked at me, "Are you a idiot, or what? She's a fox, dude! Why don't you wanna teach her?"

I swallowed hard and said, "Man, I'd just slobber at her the whole time. How could I concentrate on teaching?"

Ryan shook his head again. "Dude, you're a fuckin' *idiot*."

"Well," said Kat, "I think you were sweet."

A sweet idiot.

That's me all right.

This untitled excerpt of Every Thing Counts (The Akashic Reader) first appeared in Falling in Love Again (2005), an anthology published by Outrider Press.

When I wasn't examining it, I carried the ring in my pocket. I thought of it as a charm, a type of connection with my grandmother's spirit. It had been her ring, after all, and perhaps it would bring me some of her wisdom. Perhaps it would even see me through the turmoil of deciding between tying myself to a Central European lady or remaining Mr. Freeandeasy.

Both paths beckoned, and the situation really didn't need exacerbated by the re-appearance of one of Liliana's old boyfriends. But sometimes I guess these things happen for a reason.

The story: On Feb. 1st I told Liliana I was going into town to meet Josh. No problem, she said. She had a lot of work. So into town I went. After two beers and no Josh, I called my message service and he'd left one saying he couldn't make it. Great. So, being the in-love fool that I was, I hurried back to spend a quiet evening with baby. But when I knocked on her dorm room there was no answer.

Ok...

Since I didn't have to teach the next day, I headed over to the big campus bar to see if Karel was there. Maybe we'd play some pool.

I went in, got a beer, and looked around the large hall. There were perhaps 30 square tables in the middle of the room, the pool tables off to the right. It was sparsely peopled, and thus easy to pick out Liliana. She was sitting with a man I didn't recognize; her back was towards me, the man to her left. I could partially see his face.

Like an idiot, I skulked over to a nearby table and watched them. They were enjoying each other's company, and every now and again they'd explode into laughter.

I chugged at the beer and watched, my throat burning, constricting as they carried on. I was finished with the beer when Liliana stood and turned in my direction. She was carrying two glasses, and as she walked away from the table I noticed that the guy was watching her. She must have felt it too, because she spun around to bust him. He smiled. When she turned forward again, she looked... pretty happy.

The bile had never been so thick in my gut, and as Liliana came closer to my table and recognized me, she stopped short.

I stood up and nodded toward the bar. "I'll come with," I said.

When I got there, I turned and saw her trailing behind. I ordered three beers and she came to stand beside me, placing her empties on the bar. I watched the barman fill the first glass.

"I thought you were working tonight."

"Tomaš surprised me."

Second glass.

"You seem to be having a good time."

"He's just an old friend."

Third glass.

"*Just friends* don't watch your ass as you walk away."

Silence.

I paid for the beers before saying, "So enjoy yourself. I'm outta here."

"Wait. Come join us."

"Yeah, right."

As I walked around her she said, "Don't be like that."

My only comeback was too ferocious to voice, so I choked it down and walked out the door feeling a lot shittier than when I'd gone in.

Nothing can plunge me into blackness as quickly as the jealousy can, and I was neck deep in it, my breathing shallow and inadequate. I couldn't think past how happy they looked together.

It was too late to go back into the city and the pub was now out of the question, so I went for a long walk. In the middle of it, like a clever boy, I bought a pack of cigarettes at a vending machine and set about chain-smoking.

As I walked, I jumped to the conclusion that I had been given a perfect illustration of what to expect from marriage to Liliana.

I mean, hadn't I once been the other man in her life? Hadn't I caused her to end a seven-year relationship?

Once a two-timer, always a two-timer.

Can't trust her.

She's sleeping with him.

After walking to exhaustion, I returned to my room. A note was stuck between the door and frame. I snatched it down but didn't read it, and went inside to obsess instead.

After fitful sleep, I got up at 07:30 and read the note from Liliana. It was apologetic. She said she missed me and could I please come and get her – anytime – when I returned from wherever I was.

I crumpled it and threw it out. I wasn't ready yet. I knew she had to teach at 08:00 and that's when I wanted to slip off campus.

I was in the shower when I heard the knock on my door – it had to be her but I didn't have anything to say.

Plus – and I know this is wrong – I wanted her to feel bad as well.

St. Vitus' opened at 10:00, and I was in a pew shortly thereafter. I needed counsel, but bad. Just 12 hours before I had been ~~relatively~~ sure about asking Liliana to marry me. Now I wasn't even sure I trusted her.

Shaking my head and being pissed off, I unpacked the Bible from my backpack and all I could picture was Liliana flirty and happy with that dude the night before.

I obsessed for a long spell until remembering where I was, and that I was actually there to cut that shit out. I closed my eyes and began to breath deeply, berating my nasty self until I was able to drive it into the corner and back into its trunk. I shut the lid and tried to affix the latch, but again realized there isn't one. When I opened my eyes I looked up at the far end of the church's stained-glass windows and relaxed my shoulders, placing my hands in my lap.

My mind finally empty, I took the ring from my pocket.

It hadn't lost any of its beauty, but it had somehow lost a great deal of its allure.

Marriage to an unfaithful partner was the last thing I needed. It would drive me to a number of things I'm predisposed to anyways.

Did I *really* want to get involved with a woman who saw no problem in evenings out with old boyfriends?

Suddenly the entrance door burst open and an older red-haired lady exploded into the room. With my cup suspended in mid-air, I couldn't help but stare at her. Her cheeks were doing a Dizzy Gillespie thing as she fought for air.

I pressed the ring between my palms and closed my eyes.

I prayed for forgiveness.

I prayed for Liliana and I prayed for the strength to act with integrity – to dispel my doubts and fears and to replace them with courage. I prayed for the ability to minimize the negative and maximize the positive.

Courage.

Compassion.

Patience.

I asked for help in determining whether Liliana and I belonged together. I pressed the ring harder and asked that it be blessed with the wisdom of my grandmother and the caring and love a proper marriage should possess.

When I opened my eyes again, they struggled to adjust to the sun streaming through the stained glass, and I blinked until I could see properly.

I sat there, holding the ring in my hands and breathing calmly until my mind was again empty.

Then I repeated my prayers.

At length I opened my eyes and appreciated the beauty of the church's architecture before I packed and stood to bundle up. Donning my pack, I walked out, pausing only to anoint my forehead with the holy water. I left the church, went through the long, dark passage to the second courtyard, and then turned right toward the side exit of Prague Castle.

I felt a solemn lucidity as I walked out of the plain arched passage. There were very few people about as I exited past the cloaked castle guards and strolled across the high earthen bridge and past the gates of the closed summer garden. At the corner of the castle proper, on a whim I ducked into the touristy café there.

It was cozy inside. The seating area was small, perhaps five tables, and the walls were painted a warm orange. I ordered a cappuccino and sat down.

As I waited I took out the Bible, turned to the Book of James, and commenced to reading. By the time the coffee came I was halfway through. I put the book down and sipped at the coffee, which burnt my tongue.

Suddenly the entrance door burst open and an older red-haired lady exploded into the room. With my cup suspended in mid-air, I couldn't help but stare at her. She was wearing a long, reddish fur coat with a high protective collar, and the wind-burnt red of her cheeks and forehead gave evidence of the nasty weather. Her cheeks were doing a Dizzy Gillespie thing as she fought for air.

She grabbed the back of a chair and put her weight on it, breathing heavy. Looking at me as if I were an old friend, she started speaking in German and I understood nothing. I looked around to make sure she was speaking to me and when I looked back at her, she nodded theatrically.

I smiled at her, puzzled.

Behind her, a tall, grayed gentleman came in and closed the door. He was wearing a long navy blue trench coat and carrying an umbrella. He took off his cap and came over to the red lady, who continued her gesticulations.

The man smiled and asked if the table next to mine was free.

I said that it was and they took off their coats.

The woman spoke quickly and the man translated, "We just walked up the hill. She says I am trying to kill her."

I smiled, and when they started to discuss what to order, I placed my cup down and picked up where I had been reading. I got through two sentences before I realized the woman was speaking to me again.

I put the book in my lap and looked up at her. The man walked around the corner to order and she continued jabbering away at me.

As I was shaking my head and shrugging my shoulders at her, the man came back to the table. He asked if I spoke German.

"Not yet," I replied.

"Ha! That's a good answer!"

The man said something to his wife that made her stop yammering at me, and I gratefully took up the book and started to read.

They spoke in German for a moment and then the man said, "Excuse me…"

Sigh.

Why fight it? I closed the book, put it on the table and gave them my full attention.

"Yes?"

"I'm sorry to interrupt… but my wife doesn't speak English. Do you permit me to translate for her?"

"Of course."

The woman spoke for awhile, then the man asked me how to get to the castle's National Art Gallery. I gave him the directions and he translated for her. Then he asked me if I were a tourist. I told him I lived in Prague, and he seemed very pleased by this.

"When I was a young man," he said, "I also lived in Prague…"

The woman reached over, patted my forearm and rolled her eyes.

"… and I had the nicest Czech girl. The Czech girls are beautiful, aren't they?"

"They are."

"We were going to get married but I was in love with another girl, a German girl, and I went back to her."

"Really? Is this her?"

"Yes. This is her."

The lady spoke while looking at me, then gestured that her husband would translate.

"Well… she wants me to ask the name of your Czech girlfriend."

How did she know I had a girl?

I looked at her and said, "Liliana."

"*Wunderschön Name,*" she said.

The man asked to see a picture of Liliana, and I dug around for the snapshot we'd made in a photo booth.

He looked at it, nodding a long time before passing it over to his wife.

She nodded vigorously and said, "She is beautiful!"

I looked at the picture after she handed it back and nodded. "She is."

The man took off his glasses and leaned close to me.

"You must not lose her," he said.

I blinked at him.

"Pardon?"

"Do not lose her," he repeated.

I looked at his wife, who broke out her English again. "God is with you," she said.

I looked at the man for clarification, but the lady patted my arm to get my attention again.

"God is with you," she repeated.

I nodded dumbly. I probably should have been overjoyed and celebratory, but the whole thing was just too direct, too crazy strange for me to handle gracefully. I stood up and excused myself, saying it was time for me to go. They nodded at me, smiling indulgently.

As I bundled up, I offered my hand to the man. He shook it and smiled. "Remember," he said.

"I will."

I turned to the lady then, and as we shook she patted me on the cheek and gave me a little cherubic smirk.

I backed off and went around the corner to pay the waitress. On a whim, I paid for their drinks too, and walked out of the café amazed at how stupefying life can be.

On my way home after meeting the "Germans," I convinced myself that I had to forgive Liliana for her meeting with her friend the night before. But I also had to be sure that she had such things out of her system.

I went straight back to her room and knocked, halfway wanting *him* to answer the door so I could simply turn my back on what lay before me.

But no. She was there, alone.

Her puffy eyes turned *on* when she saw me and she hugged me so hard I stumbled backwards. It was a nice re-affirmation, and when she said, "I'm so sorry! I didn't sleep at all last night," I knew everything was going to be fine.

About the author

Together with his wife, Jim has lived in various European countries exploring the challenges and glories of the expatriate lifestyle.

Along the way Jim has worked as an actor, English teacher, summer camp counselor, editor and writer.

Further writings, including the novel titled Every Thing Counts, and the podcast titled It's Those Foreigners, can be explored at www.jimcurtiss.com.

www.ingramcontent.com/pod-product-compliance
Lightning Source LLC
Chambersburg PA
CBHW080822020726

47501CB00009B/2385